W9-AJO-770

IAN SAYER
JEREMY DRONFIELD

Hitler's Last Plot

The 139 VIP Hostages Selected for Death in the Final Days of World War II

Da Capo Press

Cover design by Kerry Rubenstein
Cover images: Front cover: US forces liberate the VIP hostages, Courtesy Imperial War Museum; Back cover: The original Müller execution order, Courtesy Walter Leschander Collection, Hoover Institution Archives.

Da Capo Press
Hachette Book Group
1290 Avenue of the Americas, New York, NY 10104
dacapopress.com
@DaCapoPress, @DaCapoPR

Printed in the United States of America

First Edition: April 2019

Published by Da Capo Press, an imprint of Perseus Books, LLC, a subsidiary of Hachette Book Group, Inc. The Da Capo Press name and logo is a trademark of the Hachette Book Group.

Print book interior design by Amy Quinn.

Library of Congress Cataloging-in-Publication Data
Names: Sayer, Ian, author. | Dronfield, Jeremy, author.
Title: Hitler's last plot: the 139 VIP hostages selected for death in the final days of World War II / Ian Sayer, Jeremy Dronfield.
Other titles: 139 VIP hostages selected for death in the final days of World War II | VIP hostages selected for death in the final days of World War II
Description: First edition. | New York, NY: Da Capo Press, [2019] | Includes bibliographical references and index.
Identifiers: LCCN 2018045430| ISBN 9780306921551 (hardcover) | ISBN 9780306921575 (ebook)
Subjects: LCSH: World War, 1939–1945—Germany. | Hostages—Germany—History—20th century. | Human shield—Germany—History—20th century. | Nationalsozialistische Deutsche Arbeiter-Partei. Schutzstaffel—History. | Political prisoners—Germany—History—20th century. | Prisoners of war—Germany—History—20th century.
Classification: LCC D755.7 .S26 2019 | DDC 940.53/43—dc23
LC record available at https://lccn.loc.gov/2018045430

ISBNs: 978-0-306-92155-1 (hardcover), 978-0-306-92157-5 (ebook)

LSC-C

10 9 8 7 6 5 4 3 2 1

This book is dedicated to the memory of Douglas Botting (1934–2018) and Squadron Leader Bertram "Jimmy" James (1915–2008).

Contents

Main map: Europe 1945 (pre-war borders). Inset: South Tyrol.

SS Rank Table

The equivalents of SS ranks in the US and British armies are approximate, and can vary from source to source, especially the noncommissioned ranks. The equivalents used in this book are as follows. (United Kingdom ranks are given in parentheses where different from US ranks.)

SS	US
SS-Oberstgruppenführer	General
SS-Obergruppenführer	Lieutenant General
SS-Gruppenführer	Major General
SS-Brigadeführer	Brigadier General (Brigadier)
SS-Standartenführer	Colonel
SS-Obersturmbannführer	Lieutenant Colonel
SS-Sturmbannführer	Major
SS-Hauptsturmführer	Captain
SS-Obersturmführer	First Lieutenant (Lieutenant)
SS-Untersturmführer	Second Lieutenant
SS-Sturmscharführer	Master Sergeant (Sergeant Major)
SS-Hauptscharführer	First Sergeant (Colour Sergeant)
SS-Oberscharführer	Staff Sergeant (Sergeant)
SS-Scharführer	Sergeant (no exact equivalent in UK)
SS-Unterscharführer	Corporal

Prologue

Thursday 3 May 1945: Borgo Valsugana, Italy

Forward position of 351st Infantry Regiment, US Army

From behind a bush at the leading edge of the Allied front line, a GI kept watch on the Brenta river valley, a picturesque vista of farms scattered along the wooded foothills of the mountains. Those hills were full of German paratroopers. Walking directly toward the GI's position from the enemy lines were several figures—half a dozen partisans carrying weapons, a better-dressed civilian who appeared to be unarmed, and a lean figure in a threadbare, blue-gray uniform. Every man awake in the American lines had watched these men appear from the German positions and pick their way down the slope into the valley. What it could mean was anybody's guess.

Officially, the war in Italy was over. But on the ground the situation wasn't so simple. The previous evening, the BBC and Allied forces radio had announced the end of hostilities; then came an official order from the commanding officer of the 88th Division: "Stop fighting and hold in place pending further orders."[1] But the men of the 351st were taking no chances; a battalion of paratroopers from the German 1st Fallschirmjäger Division were holding the far side of the valley—hardened, dedicated warriors who might not honor the cease-fire.

Only yesterday afternoon, before the official announcement, the colonel of the 1st Fallschirmjäger Regiment had come across under a white flag to talk terms. He'd offered a cessation of hostilities, but warned that his men had orders to fire if the Americans continued to advance. Ignoring the warning, elements of the 351st had carried on pushing toward Trento; within a few hundred yards they had met brutal resistance and took casualties.[2] Then came more white flags, more talks. After the official decree that evening, an uneasy truce had settled over the Brenta valley and the town of Borgo Valsugana. The atmosphere was tense. The men of the 351st had a healthy respect for the paratroopers; the unit opposite them had given them a bloody nose twice the previous year—in May 1944 at Monte Grande and in October at Vedriano. The Americans kept their heads down and their weapons at hand, and waited to see what would happen next.[3]

Leaning on his rifle, the GI watched the motley line of men approach. As they got closer, the man in the blue-gray uniform spotted the GI and halted.

"I'm a British officer," he called in a crisp English accent. "Can we come over?"

"Sure," said the GI. "You can all come over."[4]

They filed past him and were directed toward the company HQ, located in some nearby farm buildings.[5]

The English officer introduced himself to the company commanding officer as Wing Commander Harry Day of the Royal Air Force. He'd been a prisoner of war, and until a few days ago he had been one of a group of over 130 high-ranking military and civilian prisoners being held hostage by a fanatical SS detachment in the mountains of the South Tyrol. A seasoned escaper (the Great Escape from Stalag Luft III was just one of his adventures), Day had slipped away and, with help from partisans, had traversed over one hundred miles of German-infested territory looking for the Allied lines. His fellow hostages—including women and children—were still in deadly danger, held under threat of execution, a sentence that might be carried out at any moment. Day had escaped with one purpose: to summon help. Would the Americans be willing and able to send a lightning force to pluck the hostages from danger?

Wing Commander Day was taken immediately by jeep to the regimental HQ, then higher up the chain to the headquarters of the 85th Infantry Division and II Corps. At each stage, he told and retold the story of how the hostages had come to be in their present plight—an incredible story of concentration camps and Gestapo dungeons, families torn apart and SS execution squads. And he begged the American commanders to do something to rescue the hostages.

One month earlier . . .

One

The Corridor of Death

Tuesday 3 April 1945: Germany

If the Nazi eagle adorning the Reich Chancellery facade were to come to life and take flight, it would witness a scene of ruination: the gutted shell of the Chancellery itself—beneath which the Führer and his staff are lurking in their claustrophobic bunker—and, for miles around, the bomb-devastated streets of the German capital.

Flying now northwest from Berlin, away from the approaching Soviet forces, the eagle would pass over the Lehnitz forest and the blue waters of the Lehnitzsee. Between the lake and the outskirts of the town of Oranienburg, it would see a curiously shaped enclosure. A triangle, a third of a mile from end to end, like a vast arrowhead pointing northwest. It is surrounded by walls, electrified fences, and guard towers. Inside are barrack blocks arranged in an arc like the blades of a fan, and the "death strip" between the inner and outer perimeters. The eagle's acute vision would see the gallows between the barracks and the enclosure at the triangle's base containing the SS administration blocks and Gestapo offices. On the western edge, smaller enclosures sprout from the triangle: factories, the shooting range, the execution block, and the gas chambers.

This is Sachsenhausen concentration camp, one of the ultimate expressions of the system the Nazi eagle stands for, a machine for the production of human misery. Nearly forty thousand prisoners have been murdered here: Jews, political prisoners, and Russian prisoners of war.[1]

Joined to one edge of the triangle are two more enclosures: small and barely noticeable from the air beside the huge spread of the main camp. One is subdivided into four tiny sections, each with a single building, almost like suburban houses on their own small plots, but surrounded by guard towers and unusually high walls. The second enclosure contains a few small barrack buildings.

These are Sonderlager A and Sonderlager B—Sachsenhausen's "special enclosures." Here, and in similar facilities at Buchenwald and Dachau concentration camps, the Third Reich houses some of its most valuable prisoners: the presidents and prime ministers of conquered countries, anti-Nazi plotters, spies, enemy officers who have been habitual escapers from POW camps. The Germans call them *Prominenten*.* Some have been in captivity for years, some have only recently arrived. None will remain for long now. The Führer, raging in his Berlin bunker as the carcass of the Reich falls apart above him, has approved a bitter, vindictive plan for these prisoners. Heinrich Himmler and other senior figures believe that their lives might serve as bargaining chips with the Allies. Failing that, the prisoners will make suitable targets for revenge.[2]

The handsome, rather earnest face of Wing Commander Harry "Wings" Day looked up from the bleak barbed-wire enclosure of Sonderlager A at the predawn sky. Air activity was reduced somewhat these days. Bombs had fallen on neighboring Oranienburg, but the really big raids on Berlin were rare now, the main weight of the Allied air assault diverted elsewhere. A heavy daylight attack by hundreds of American bombers had hit the capital the previous week, but since then there had been just small night raids by the Royal Air Force: lightning strikes in fast twin-engine Mosquitos.[3]

Around Day, some of the other Prominenten were gathered under the eerie glow of electric lanterns held by their SS guards, who stood with

* Prominent ones, VIPs, celebrities

casual menace, machine pistols at the ready. The Prominenten of Sonderlager A were a curious bunch: an international collection of men in the ragged uniforms of the Royal Air Force, the Red Army, and other military outfits, including British, Italian, and Greek. Usually their patter ranged from Irish brogue to Italian braggadocio, but this morning they were quiet.

They'd been roused from their bunks at an ungodly hour and ordered to pack their things. Many suspected the worst, and the atmosphere of weary resignation was tinged with fear of impending slaughter. The Soviet prisoners especially were convinced that they were about to be shot. The Third Reich was in its death throes, and those who had served it slavishly over the years showed every intention of wanting to drag everyone else down with them.[4]

From the east, barely fifty miles away, the faint, insistent rumbling of Red Army guns was becoming ever more distinct. From the west and south, reports of the Allies' relentless advance were becoming more urgent by the day. And over the whole of Germany, endless streams of Allied bombers stoked the Reich's burning embers. In Sachsenhausen's overcrowded hospital, medical staff had been struggling around the clock to cope with the influx of civilian casualties from Oranienburg. Meanwhile, the wretched inmates of the main camp died from rampant disease, starvation, and maltreatment—or were shot in the "death pit" where thousands before them had perished. Their remains were piled up, awaiting cremation. The chimneys belched out a foul smoke, the stink of which was impossible to escape. The SS personnel were beginning to panic, and additional streams of black smoke had begun drifting across the administrative complex as records and other sensitive documents were hastily burned.

There were rumors of plans to liquidate the remaining witnesses to Sachsenhausen's darkest secrets.[5] As they waited to be told what was to be done with them, Wings Day and the other Prominenten wondered whether they would be next to vanish up the crematorium chimney.

Standing beside Day, Flight Lieutenant Bertram "Jimmy" James drew his greatcoat tighter—the same faithful, battered, blue RAF coat that had seen him through nearly five years of captivity (the last eleven months here in Sachsenhausen) and thirteen escape attempts. Over his shoulder was a haversack containing his few meager belongings. Still a couple of weeks short of his thirtieth birthday, James wore an expression of breezy good humor and untrammeled optimism, which rarely deserted him. During their captivity, he and Day had come close to being shot several times and had risked being buried under tons of soil in the many "tunnel jobs" they'd participated in at a variety of POW camps. They'd endured interrogation by the Gestapo and witnessed firsthand the depravities of the Nazi regime.

In contrast with Jimmy James's youth and zest for life, Day was forty-six, with a more sober, sardonic outlook and an urbane and deceptively languid manner. He'd been shot down and captured barely six weeks into the war and, as a senior officer, had been de facto commander of his fellow RAF prisoners for much of his time in captivity.[6] He was a cool hand in a crisis and a determined escaper. Like James, Day was a veteran—and one of the key organizers—of the legendary Great Escape of March 1944, when seventy-six men tunneled out of Stalag Luft III. Like almost all the other Great Escapers, James and Day had been recaptured, but unlike most they'd been spared execution. Along with two of the other survivors, they had been transferred to the special compound at Sachsenhausen. Again they had escaped, again they'd been recaptured, and again they had been spared execution and returned to Sonderlager A.

Compared with the bestial conditions in the main concentration camp, the two VIP compounds were enclaves of civility.[7] Besides the Great Escapers, Sonderlager A was home to a number of British, French, Polish, and Russian officers, their Italian orderlies, and four Irish soldiers. They included some of Joseph Stalin's senior commanders, three secret agents from Britain's Special Operations Executive (SOE), a celebrated British commando known for his daredevil bravery, and several RAF officers. They inhabited quite comfortable, spacious quarters in timber barrack buildings and had reasonable rations and rudimentary sanitation. Except for certain enmities (the Poles and Russians did not speak, such was the mutual loathing between their two countries), this disparate group of nationalities generally enjoyed each other's company—sharing meals, socializing, and engaging in animated discussions about the war and politics.[8]

They never saw inside the neighboring special compound. Sonderlager B was even more comfortable, consisting of four "villas" (actually large, six-room huts), each enclosed by its own high walls. The inmates were the real VIPs, at various times including former presidents and prime ministers of conquered countries. These prisoners were provided with amenities that were positively luxurious. They were even permitted radios, and the camp authorities turned a blind eye when they tuned their sets to the BBC, a crime severely punished in the rest of the Reich. They were allowed books and newspapers, and some had brought their own home furnishings, paintings, and other decorations.[9]

Nobody, inside or outside the camp, was supposed to know the VIPs were there. Some were registered under false names and ordered by the SS never to reveal their true identities to anyone—be it guards or fellow prisoners. They were victims of Adolf Hitler's 1941 *Nacht und Nebel** directive, which caused inconvenient opponents to disappear.[10] Full secrecy, however, was often impossible to police effectively, even by the all-powerful SS.

By the time the officers in Sonderlager A gathered in the dawn of 3 April, the last of the great statesmen had already left Sachsenhausen, plucked from their compounds without warning a few weeks earlier and taken to an undisclosed destination. The villas were now occupied by senior members of the Russian and Greek general staffs, including the famed Lieutenant General Aleksandros Papagos, formerly commander in chief of Greece's armed forces. Gaunt and hooknosed, Papagos had conducted a spirited defense against the Italian invasion in 1940 and 1941, and his fame had won him the accolade of a romantic portrait on the cover of *Time* magazine.[11] Although Wings Day had discovered Papagos's identity from his Greek orderlies, the SS determinedly kept up the pretense of secrecy, and every week a little pantomime took place when the generals were led though Sonderlager A to the showers in the main camp.[12] The British and

---

* Night and fog

other officers were locked in their huts under close guard, and only when the Greeks had completed their ablutions and returned to the privacy of their villas were the Sonderlager A prisoners allowed out again.[13]

Now the pretense had been dropped, and as the prisoners in Sonderlager A assembled in the cold dawn gloom, the elusive Greeks joined them. The haughty Papagos and his entourage stood disdainfully apart from their shabby neighbors, with their ragged old greatcoats and humble knapsacks. Standing beside their surprisingly large quantity of luggage, the Greeks seemed less concerned about being shot by the Germans than being robbed by their allies.[14]

As the sun rose—their curiosity and nervousness about what was going to be done with them rising with it—the British officers spotted a familiar friendly face coming toward them through the line of SS guards: Inspector Peter Mohr of the Berlin criminal police.[15]

Five months previously, Mohr had almost certainly saved some of the British officers from being executed. Five of them—including Wings Day and Jimmy James—had staged a remarkable escape. Using nothing more than their barrack cutlery, they had dug a 120-foot tunnel out of Sonderlager A, probably the only escape tunnel ever dug from a Nazi concentration camp.[16] The breakout caused enormous confusion and prompted a manhunt across the Reich, involving over a million police, home guard, Hitler Youth, and ordinary Germans. The escape had caught the SS high command completely by surprise and, in terms of inconvenience to the Third Reich, it surpassed the Great Escape in importance.[17] It prompted ill-disguised merriment inside Sachsenhausen, even among the starving inmates who could expect bloody retribution from their guards for displaying such insubordination.

The SS had reacted with cold fury. The British officers had been warned that if they ever escaped again they would not live to tell the tale. Consequently, when they were all recaptured and manacled in Sachsenhausen's punishment block, they expected the worst; Himmler himself had ordered that they be tortured before being disposed of.[18] It was Inspector Mohr who had stood in the way of this happening. He argued that if the prisoners had committed any misdemeanor, it came within his criminal jurisdiction rather than the Gestapo's. He insisted on a properly arraigned criminal tribunal to judge whether the escapers had committed any crime. After many hours of testimony from Wings Day, the tribunal had concluded that they had not broken any laws.

Ever since, the British officers had had a warm place in their hearts for the benign figure of Inspector Mohr.[19] As they stood waiting to learn their fate this April morning, it was reassuring to see his face.

Mohr spoke to Day and assured him that the prisoners were not going to be shot. Instead they were to travel by train to a location some distance south of Berlin. He refused to disclose their exact destination but did reveal that, along with a complement of twenty or so SS guards, the Prominenten would be traveling under his supervision.

Soon afterward, with the early light growing in the sky, the order came through: *prepare to move*. Knapsacks were shouldered, servants hefted the Greeks' luggage, and—guarded by an SS detachment led by a friendly SS corporal known as George—the prisoners were marched out of the camp. Outside the gates, they found two well-appointed buses waiting for them. Eager to get out of the morbid surroundings of Sachsenhausen, the men climbed aboard.[20]

They were taken to the main railway station in bomb-damaged Oranienburg, where a train with two carriages was waiting in a siding. Under Corporal George's genial supervision, the small party embarked and found seats. The whole business was proving to be remarkably polite and civilized, without the usual threats and bellows of impatience. Day noted that Mohr was keen to ensure that the prisoners were comfortable and happy.[21] As Wings settled into his surprisingly pleasant seat, however, he was determined not to be lulled into a false sense of security. He had learned through experience that some Germans were thoroughly duplicitous, perfectly capable of turning from civility to unrestrained savagery in an instant. The war was still on, and Day would remain on his guard.

As the train pulled away, the Prominenten were warned that Allied aircraft were in the habit of strafing railway traffic. Far from being concerned by this news, the British were delighted by it; as habitual escapers, they had no doubt that the ensuing panic and confusion would provide them with a suitable opportunity to slip away.

None of the prisoners had allowed the years of captivity to diminish his enthusiasm for troublemaking. Aside from Day and Jimmy James, the other Great Escapers aboard the train included Flight Lieutenant Sydney Dowse, a dashing blond Spitfire photoreconnaissance pilot, and Flight Lieutenant Raymond van Wymeersch, a flamboyant Hurricane pilot from Charles de Gaulle's Free French Air Forces. As the miles of German countryside clattered slowly by, Van Wymeersch itched for any opportunity to make mischief for his captors. His character showed in his face: tight-lipped, with narrow, intense eyes under a shock of dark curls. He was an irrepressible soul, who had gone to England after the fall of France and joined the RAF's No. 174 Squadron. Van Wymeersch had suffered terribly after the Great Escape, interrogated by the Gestapo and told that his parents—his mother lived in France and his father was in Buchenwald concentration camp—would be killed.[22] But his experiences hadn't defeated his spirit, and now, as the train traveled south, Van Wymeersch was full of optimism.

Lieutenant Colonel John Churchill was a British commando officer. Thirty-eight years old, hard faced, and aggressive, he was nicknamed Mad Jack and renowned for carrying a Scottish broadsword into action. He believed an officer was not properly dressed without his sword, and he had actually used his in hand-to-hand combat with the enemy. During the retreat to Dunkirk in 1940, Mad Jack Churchill had scored World War II's only kill of an enemy soldier with a longbow.[23] Captured in 1944, he had become one of the Prominenten by error, the Germans mistaking him for Randolph Churchill, the British prime minister's son. Whatever the circumstances, Mad Jack was not a man who took captivity lightly.

In contrast with his more hot-headed fellow prisoners, Wings Day was a calm, serious, even somber man, with the air of a commanding officer more than an adventurer. During his time in captivity he had cultivated an ambivalent attitude toward the Germans. He loathed those who served the Nazi regime willingly, but he drew a distinction between them and the officer class of the Wehrmacht, and particularly the Luftwaffe. He came from a military family and had served in both world wars—first in the Royal Navy then the Royal Air Force. Like many British and German officers—especially the airmen—he saw himself as a cut above the rest of humanity. Day always insisted that his men treat German officers with due military decorum, and he expected the Germans to reciprocate. Nonetheless, throughout his captivity his guiding principle had been to urge his men to fight the war from behind the wire. His approach to escape had always been strategic; even if there was little hope of reaching friendly territory, escapes caused trouble for the enemy, diverting men and resources from the war effort. Day sensed that this move from Sachsenhausen was the most critical in his five and a half years as a prisoner, and he watched and waited to see what would develop.

The journey was slow, interrupted by frequent stops.[24] The train trundled through Berlin's western outskirts, a wasteland of rubble, clattering over damaged tracks. The prisoners saw destruction and desolation like none they had ever witnessed before. Neighborhoods lay in ruins, some still smoldering. The roads, pocked with craters and littered with debris, were swarming with troops, tanks, and refugees fleeing the front lines. Old men and women walked with barefoot children in rags, carrying their remaining possessions stuffed in suitcases or piled on battered strollers and carts. Many had cattle, sheep, pigs, and chickens in tow. Some bore the homemade coffins of their recent dead. Women fought with one another over potatoes or coal they found lying on the road. Armageddon had arrived for Nazi Germany.[25]

Jimmy James "speculated on the outcome of this extraordinary train journey through the crumbling corridor which was all that was left of Hitler's mad dream."[26] Mohr and the SS escort—including Corporal George—behaved with punctilious correctness, but none of them would disclose the ultimate destination or why the prisoners were being taken there. A worrying rumor circulated that they were being taken to a mountain redoubt, possibly in Bavaria, where they would be kept as hostages—and, if necessary, executed.

One prisoner who took a dark view of their prospects was General Ivan Georgievich Bessonov, a garrulous Soviet officer who was friendly with the British. An anti-Communist who had collaborated enthusiastically with his Nazi captors (at one point forming a commando team of sympathetic Russian POWs to fight behind Soviet lines), Bessonov was deeply untrustworthy.[27] Wings Day, who had come to know him well, described him as "a man who would just as soon shoot you as kiss you."[28] Bessonov believed the rumor that they would be used as hostages. "Ja," he said, voicing the thought that nagged at them all, "then when the Allies will not meet their demands, they will shoot us."[29]

Whatever was in store, such important prisoners would certainly not be allowed to fall into the hands of the Allied armies. Instead they were being herded down an ever-narrowing strip of territory, compressed on both sides by the rapidly converging Allies, into the shrinking heart of the Third Reich. Day wondered what would happen when there was nowhere else to go. When further retreat became impossible, what then? What would their fate be at the end of the corridor of death?[30]

Two

Blood Guilt

Tuesday 3 April: Buchenwald concentration camp

The Sachsenhausen Prominenten were not the only high-ranking prisoners anxious about their fate. While they were being taken from their compound that morning, 170 miles to the southwest the inmates were waking in the cheerless environs of Buchenwald. Another group of Prominenten reluctantly greeted a new day of uncertainty.

Buchenwald was a sprawling complex, a small city of ninety thousand souls in torment, carved out of the beech forest from which it took its name, just outside the historic town of Weimar. Buchenwald was one of the Reich's oldest concentration camps, founded in the early years of the Nazi regime.[1] The main gate bore the slogan *Jedem das Seine*: literally "to each his own," although it could also be read as "everyone gets what he deserves." Above the gate was a second slogan reflecting the ethos expected of all Germans under Nazism: "My fatherland, right or wrong." An ancient seat of culture, genteel Weimar had been a beacon of the German Enlightenment and in 1919 the birthplace of the nation's first democratic constitution. The irony was not lost on the wretched inhabitants of the concentration camp, which had been built in the old ducal hunting forest on the summit of the Ettersberg, consuming the hill's woods and stone in the building. From the air it was like a patch of mange on the back of an animal.

The situation of the Prominenten was different here, their enclosure set well apart from the main camp. Buchenwald had been designed as part concentration camp, part SS training center, part playground for the Nazi elite—equipped with stables, hunting and falconry facilities, and even a zoo, in addition to the huge SS barracks, all built by prisoners in conditions of unspeakable cruelty. The main camp, in which the mass of prisoners lived, was enclosed by an electrified fence and watchtowers; outside this was the SS complex and an armaments factory and quarry in which the inmates labored, all enclosed by a ring of sentries. In the center of the SS area was the so-called Spruce Grove, Buchenwald's special compound, walled so that nobody could see in or out. Within it were the isolation barracks where most of the camp's many Prominenten were kept.[2]

By early April 1945, everyone in the camp had been listening for weeks to the rumble of distant artillery, imagining that liberation must come soon.[3] They feared that Himmler would order their liquidation at the last minute, and some had smuggled in weapons in anticipation of such a move. Meanwhile, the SS personnel, sensing their own approaching doom, were nervous about the huge mass of prisoners in their charge, while in Weimar the people were "as afraid of the camp as of the devil himself."[4]

Buchenwald's Prominenten now received the first definite indication that the end really was nigh. On the morning of 3 April 1945—at the same time as the order was given in Sachsenhausen—word came: be prepared to move within the next few hours. No further information was given.

One of the VIP prisoners—by far the most eminent in Buchenwald—had been given advance notice of the move. Léon Blum, former prime minister of France, had been in the camp since April 1943. To the Nazis, Blum "embodied what they hated most in the world, since I was a democratic socialist and a Jew."[5] He had also been a determined opponent of the puppet Vichy government. A few days away from his seventy-third birthday, Blum was in ill health. Given all these factors, it was a marvel he had survived this long. His face was thin, gaunt, and draped with his trademark walrus moustache, his bright, good-humored eyes gazing out at the world through round tortoiseshell spectacles.

Blum didn't live in the Spruce Grove with the other Prominenten; he had special private quarters in the SS falconry complex. This bizarre place comprised an aviary, a gazebo, and a large Teutonic hunting hall built with carved oak timbers and massive fireplaces, filled with trophies and furniture to match. It had been created for the personal use of Hermann Göring, in his capacity as Reich hunt master. Göring never even visited the place, but many local Germans did—for a fee of one mark they could come in and look around.[6]

In this remarkably insecure setting—no fences surrounded this part of the camp—Léon Blum lived with his young wife, Jeanne (or Janot, as she was known), occupying the falconer's house. "The severity of our isolation," Blum later wrote, "explains a fact which is incomprehensible at first; I mean our long-lasting ignorance of the unutterable horrors that took place only a few hundred metres from where we were." They were aware of a "strange smell that often came through the open windows in the evening and pursued us the whole night when there was a constant wind from the same direction: it was the smell of the crematorium ovens."[7]

Having been alerted in advance, he and Janot were already packed and ready to go on the morning of 3 April. A car drew up outside the house, an SS officer in the front seat. Blum, who was suffering a painfully debilitating bout of sciatica, could hardly stand and had to be carried to the waiting vehicle on a stretcher. Despite his undoubted moral courage, his experiences at the hands of the Nazis had sometimes reduced him to a state of abject anxiety. As he was propped awkwardly in the back seat next to Janot, the thought must have crossed his mind that his last hours could not be far away.

Blum had had a hard journey through life. As the first socialist and the first Jew to serve as prime minister of France, he'd been disliked by both Catholics and the anti-Semitic far right. There had been repeated efforts to assassinate him. Shortly after taking office, he was dragged from his car and almost beaten to death, but as a man of tremendous equanimity he never let his experience color his attitude toward political opponents. When the Germans occupied France in 1940, Blum made no effort to leave the country, despite the extreme danger he was in. Instead he moved to the unoccupied zone, where he became an ardent opponent of its puppet Vichy regime. He was put on trial for treason, but, as a skilled and wily politician, he used the trial to deliver a searing indictment of Vichy's politicians, which gained him worldwide respect and so embarrassed Vichy that Berlin stepped in and had the trial suspended. Subsequently, Blum had been arrested and interned in France before being transferred to Buchenwald.[8]

Janot, who had stood by him during his most difficult years, lived with him in Buchenwald voluntarily. Born Jeanne Levylier, she was a society beauty who boasted that she had fallen in love with the firebrand Blum when she was just sixteen years old. After his arrest, she had spent weeks cajoling the authorities to allow her to follow him. The couple were married shortly afterward, possibly the only case of Jews marrying in a Nazi concentration camp with the sanction of the regime. In Buchenwald, Janot enjoyed the same privileges as her husband, but as a voluntary prisoner she could come and go as she wished.

Like other imprisoned VIPs, Blum had been allowed books, French newspapers, and a radio. He and Janot even had an SS orderly to wait on them. Blum spent time in philosophical and political debate with some of his fellow prisoners. After the invasion of Normandy, the Blums had rejoiced as they followed the progress of the Allied armies on the BBC. These were intoxicating months. But Blum had sensed the approach of doom when in July 1944 the Gestapo came to take away his compatriot and fellow political prisoner Georges Mandel. After being returned to France, Mandel had been murdered by Vichy's pro-Nazi paramilitary force. The German ambassador in Paris wanted Blum dealt with in a similar fashion.[9]

Blum wondered at the Nazis' ability to intensify the terror even in their hour of defeat. He wrote of them, despairingly, "You are already conquerors in this sense; you have succeeded in communicating to the entire world your cruelty and hatred." He was amazed by their "sadistic ferocity" even when there was no hope of victory and their "exasperated rage," observing that "everywhere it takes on the face of Biblical extermination."[10]

These words must have been at the forefront of his thoughts as the SS car pulled away from the house, taking him and Janot along the forest road away from Buchenwald and toward their mystery destination.

Early that same morning, in the Spruce Grove enclosure, which stood in a wide-open space in the middle of the great arc of SS barracks, young Fey Pirzio-Biroli heard the depressing order: "Pack your bags! Bring only what you can hold on your laps!" She had dreaded hearing those words, particularly on a spring morning when liberation seemed so close.

Only twenty-five years old, Fey was one of a select category of Prominenten known as *Sippenhäftlingen*—kin prisoners, Germans whose only crime was to be related to people who had opposed the Nazi regime. Most were the families of officers who had taken part in Claus von Stauffenberg's plot of July 1944, in which a bomb had been detonated in Hitler's operations room, nearly killing him. The associated coup attempt in Berlin had come perilously close to succeeding, giving Hitler and his loyal followers the fright of their lives and leading to a terrifying campaign of torture and vengeance against the plotters.

The campaign extended to rounding up the conspirators' families. These entirely blameless individuals had fallen foul of the ancient German custom of *Sippenhaft*, which dated back to the era of witch burning and had been reinvented by Heinrich Himmler as a quasi-legal method of instilling terror and enacting vengeance.

Fey's father was Ulrich von Hassell, a distinguished lawyer and former ambassador to Benito Mussolini's Italy who had become disillusioned with the Nazi regime and had joined the Stauffenberg conspiracy. In the aftermath, Hassell had been found guilty of treason by the People's Court, presided over by notorious Nazi judge Roland Freisler, and hanged. Fey was married to a young Italian nobleman, Detalmo Pirzio-Biroli, currently fighting in the Italian resistance. Dazzlingly pretty, with a coy tilt of the head and a bright, dimpled smile, Fey could pass for a teenager, but eight months in the hands of the SS had left her jaded beyond her years.

The news of Ulrich von Hassell's execution had been broadcast on the radio, but Fey had not been listening. She only learned of her father's fate when an SS officer turned up at her Italian villa. Surprised that she hadn't heard, he told her abruptly, "Your father has been arrested and executed. He has been hanged!" Shaken to the core, she wondered what her own fate would be, immediately fearing for her little boys, Corrado and Roberto, aged four and three, who watched in terrified silence as Fey was arrested.[11] They were to be taken away separately. With a forced calmness, Fey put the boys' coats on. Corrado gave way to wild panic, trying to escape from the SS nurses. Fey was compelled to stand frozen, listening to his wails growing fainter and fainter as he and Roberto were pulled down the stairs away from her. They would be sent to a children's home, the arresting officer told her. "I felt sure this was a lie," Fey later recorded. "Only lies and more lies!"[12]

The separation was conducted under a Nazi law allowing the SS to assume custody of children related to political "criminals" and to "reeducate" them to be *führertreu*, faithful to the Führer. Fey was beside herself with grief.

As Fey endured her subsequent cheerless odyssey through the dark heart of the Third Reich, she found herself among dozens of kin prisoners who also had the unfortunate burden of being linked to members of the Stauffenberg plot. Among them were several members of the extended Stauffenberg and Goerdeler clans, relatives of Claus von Stauffenberg, the ringleader, and Carl Goerdeler, who would have governed Germany as chancellor if the coup had succeeded. During late 1944 and early 1945, Fey had been moved between various prisons and camps, where she witnessed the increasing depredations of the Nazi regime. All that time, she suffered the agony of not knowing what had happened to her sons. Nightmares about their fate kept her awake every night.

Arriving at Buchenwald, she had been taken to the Spruce Grove and placed in a barrack surrounded by a high wall, painted red and topped with barbed wire. The ground inside was scorched and pitted from a bomb that had hit the enclosure during an American raid on the factory attached to the camp. This was the isolation barrack, a hidden compound within a hidden compound, which she shared with several dozen other Prominenten, some of them fellow kin prisoners. Their companionship at least brought her a little relief from her anguish.

Despite her isolation, Fey had witnessed more of Buchenwald's horrors than Léon and Janot Blum had. Overcome by curiosity, she had feigned a toothache in order to be taken to the dentist in the main camp. What she saw as she was escorted past the endless barrack blocks confirmed her worst fears. At one point, a truck drove past piled high with dead bodies. Nobody showed the slightest surprise or interest. On the way back, she and her escort had to stand aside as a work detail from the factory marched by; dressed in their striped uniforms, they were like walking corpses. Any who moved too slowly were beaten with rifle butts. The column was led by the prisoner orchestra playing martial music. It was one of the most sadistic things Fey had ever seen.[13]

She didn't have long to contemplate this hell. After being told to get ready to move on the morning of Tuesday 3 April she and the other Prominenten began packing their bags—most of them ignoring the SS's injunction to bring only what they could hold on their laps. During her captivity, each new move had been heralded by a similar shouted injunction: to carry no more than was absolutely necessary and be ready to go within an hour or so. Each time Fey had carried as much as she could squeeze into her battered old suitcase, and each time the expected evacuation had happened days later rather than hours. Therefore, she prepared for this latest move without any great sense of urgency. She and her fellow prisoners really didn't want to go anywhere. Those with military knowledge had assured her that the Allies could not be much more than fifteen miles away. Rumor had it that Würzburg, only 93 miles to the west, had fallen, and American tanks were already supposed to be at the nearby city of Bamberg.[14]

It was nightfall before any sign of departure materialized, and it was not a reassuring sight. An SS squad marched into the Spruce Grove and led the Prominenten out through the gate. Outside, three gray army buses were waiting. Out of one of them stepped a tall, thin man wearing the uniform of the dreaded security and intelligence arm of the SS, the Sicherheitsdienst (SD). He was about forty-five, a "cold blue-eyed type with high cheekbones," and dislikeable on sight.[15]

His name was Friedrich Bader, and he was a thoroughly nasty piece of work. He had joined the army at the age of fifteen and served in World War I, later serving as a noncommissioned officer in the Iron Division, a Weimar paramilitary unit fighting the Red Army in the Baltic region. After a period as a police officer, in 1932 he joined the Nazi Party, transferring to the Gestapo in Weimar in 1934. He then joined the SS and, in 1940, was commissioned in the SD. Since November 1941, he'd been involved in the expulsion of non-German residents of Alsace-Lorraine, and during the whole of his service he had been employed on counterintelligence duties.[16] On this first encounter, however, none of the Prominenten knew anything about SS-Untersturmführer Friedrich Bader, nor about the part he would play in their ultimate fate. One of Fey's fellow prisoners, sprightly twenty-six-year-old cabaret singer and actress Isa Vermehren, thought he looked a "real perfect specimen of his kind." Although middle aged, Bader was "slim with long, straight legs, narrow hips and broad shoulders, and a tanned face, with a big chin, two sharp lines around the straight mouth, his leathery skin taut over his hollow cheeks and cheekbones that were a little too wide." His dark eyebrows were "like two thick beams above his little, quick and dark eyes. . . . It was not a pretty expression. One could sense that the stubbornness that lay within him could turn out to be deadly."[17]

As soon as he descended from the bus, Bader began yelling at the prisoners, ordering them to gather their belongings and embark at once, warning them that anybody or anything that could not be squeezed on to the three vehicles would be left behind.

Until now, the women prisoners had been guarded by female SS personnel, but they were nowhere to be seen. Instead, the male guards began violently pushing the prisoners on to the buses. Eventually they were all squeezed inside in a variety of uncomfortable positions around their baggage. Dusk had fallen by the time the engines started and they began to move.

As her bus pulled slowly onto the so-called Blood Road, the main thoroughfare connecting Buchenwald to the Weimar road, Fey saw thousands of prisoners laboring in their work details, all wearing expressions of dull resignation. Fey reflected that the kin prisoners, too, had adopted an air of weary hopelessness. They would have felt even more hopeless had they known the full nature of their cold-eyed SS lieutenant. They would find out soon enough.

Long after the three buses had rumbled away down the Blood Road, yet another group of Prominenten were still waiting to depart. Near the falconry complex was a pleasant road running through the forest, along which were several large, very fine villas occupied by the camp commandant and his senior officers. Following the air raid that had damaged the Spruce Grove barracks, one of the officers' houses had been remodeled as a prison, its large basement divided into twelve cells, in which seventeen Prominenten were housed.

Captain Sigismund Payne Best, who had spied for Britain's Secret Intelligence Service (SIS)* until his capture in 1939, had been prepared to leave for two days, advance notice having been given on 1 April by an SS corporal called Sippach, one of the guards in charge of the cellar prisoners. Sitting alone in his tiny cell, waiting for the final order to move, Payne Best could hear distant gunfire; the American front line had reached the Werra river sixty miles to the west.

He had been in some uncomfortable quarters during more than five years of captivity, but this was the worst and coldest of them all—a little subterranean box with a tiny window at ceiling height and water running down the walls.[18] Throughout his imprisonment, Payne Best always managed to keep his appearance impeccable, maintaining his clothes in

* Also known as MI6

good repair, a routine that lately included brushing off the incipient mildew caused by the damp. He affected a monocle, and whenever he went outdoors he was never without his immaculately kept fedora and a neat collar and tie. He always held a cigarette clasped between his long, elegant fingers and spoke with the well-modulated drawl of the expensively educated English upper class. Physically, however, he wasn't in good shape; he was approaching sixty years old and had lost weight since his capture, his figure growing lean and his features gaunt, and he'd become prone to ill health.

Payne Best had been captured in November 1939, implicated by the Nazis in a failed assassination attempt against Hitler. He had been in the Netherlands at the time, where SIS conducted intelligence operations under the cover of the passport control office (PCO) of the British Embassy—a standard practice for intelligence agencies. Payne Best had run the Netherlands branch of Z section, a duplicate network established by SIS as a shadow in case the primary network was blown. Unfortunately for him, both the Hague embassy's PCO and Payne Best's network had been penetrated by the German SD. On 9 November 1939, he and his immediate superior, Major Richard Stevens, accompanied by a Dutch intelligence officer named Dirk Klop, arrived in the town of Venlo, a sleepy place on the German border. They had been briefed by their London office for secret talks with a dissident German general representing the Wehrmacht resistance. Britain had declared war on Germany two months earlier, but hostilities had not yet started in earnest. Prime Minister Neville Chamberlain's government hoped that they never would and was anxious to explore any avenues that might avert full-scale conflict.

Stevens, a forty-six-year-old former Indian Army officer, was not greatly au fait with either Germany or intelligence tradecraft. He therefore saw the vastly more experienced Payne Best as a godsend. Payne Best was less impressed. The cloak-and-dagger aspect of the discussions caused him to confide later, to an SIS friend, that the preparations he was required to make had all the ingredients of a Whitehall farce.[19] When he and Stevens arrived at the liaison point, a nondescript café near the border post, they were ambushed by a carload of armed SD agents in disguise, led by the wily Walter Schellenberg, head of SD-Ausland, the SS's overseas intelligence department. There was a brief gun battle, in which Klop was shot, and Payne Best and Stevens were seized and spirited across the border into Germany. It was a double coup for the SD, because Stevens was carrying in his pocket a full list of British agents in the Netherlands.

The two Englishmen were taken to the SS headquarters in Berlin and interrogated at length. Payne Best was interviewed personally by Reinhard Heydrich, who was head of the Reich Main Security Office (Reichssicherheitshauptamt, or RSHA) and one of Hitler's most feared henchmen.[20] The Nazis had a very special use for their new captives. The plot to ensnare them had been hatched over many weeks, but fate had intervened when, on 8 November, a bomb went off in a Munich beer cellar, nearly killing Hitler. The Bürgerbräukeller assassination attempt was the work of a lone bomber—a German tradesman named Georg Elser—but some within the German security services were convinced that the British must have been behind it. Even if they weren't, who better to pin the blame on than the two secret agents? Their alleged involvement helped provide a pretext for the German invasion of the Low Countries a few months later.

Payne Best and Stevens were transferred to Sachsenhausen concentration camp. At first this was an unpleasant experience for Payne Best, who was shackled to the walls in the cellblock. Amid the omnipresent smell of effluent from the toilets next door, he could often hear the sounds of torture or murder.[21] His situation improved over months and then years. He was allowed out into a garden where he grew flowers and vegetables; he was granted double SS rations and allowed to buy wine and spirits from the SS canteen out of his British pay. The SS even arranged for a wardrobe to be installed in his cell and filled it with his tailored suits. With his monocle in his eye and wearing his best tweeds, Payne Best became an incongruous sight in the dismal precincts of Sachsenhausen.

Stevens was kept apart from Payne Best, and they were not permitted to communicate in any way. It was the authorities' intention to hold a show trial when the war was won. The Reich would prove that the British secret services were behind the Bürgerbräukeller bomb outrage. Eventually, Stevens had been transferred from Sachsenhausen to Dachau concentration camp, near Munich. Payne Best, after five years in Sachsenhausen and a brief return to Berlin, had been transferred to Buchenwald in February 1945 along with two other Sachsenhausen prisoners: the Russian Vassily Vassilyevich Kokorin, who had been captured while fighting with a special unit behind German lines and was said to be the nephew of Soviet diplomat and foreign minister Vyacheslav Molotov, and Squadron Leader Hugh Falconer, a thirty-four-year-old Special Operations Executive agent who had been captured in Tunis in January 1943.

With the care and cunning of a spy, Payne Best had managed to meet all his fellow prisoners in the Buchenwald cellar, despite their being kept separate. Besides Kokorin and Falconer, this select group included German officers and public figures who had in one way or another betrayed the Reich, plus one Nazi war criminal. A fluent German speaker and skilled manipulator, Payne Best had siphoned information from them and had made himself de facto leader of the cellar group.

Around ten o'clock in the evening, after waiting most of the day for the order to depart, there was a burst of activity outside Payne Best's cell. The door was flung open, and he was ordered out. Gathering up his rather large quantity of luggage—including a suitcase, a typewriter, and three big boxes—he emerged to find the others, mostly similarly encumbered, being herded out. They were led up the steps into the open air, where darkness had fallen on the beech forest.

Waiting for them was their transport—an emerald-green prison van, the type known as a *Grüne Minna*.* Designed to carry eight prisoners, it was about the size of a standard delivery van. This example was a most peculiar version, with a motor fueled by a wood-burning generator. Germany's oil shortage throughout the war had forced some remarkable improvised solutions, and this was one of them.[22] A large part of the space in the rear compartment was taken up by wood for the generator. Into

* Green Minna (equivalent to "Black Maria")

this compartment the seventeen prisoners plus luggage were expected to fit.

Payne Best would be damned sooner than leave anything behind (he'd been furious earlier when led to believe that the prisoners would leave on foot and that he'd have to abandon some of his precious belongings).[23] One way or another, everyone and everything was crammed in—so tightly that nobody could move a muscle. The rear door was slammed and locked.

At that moment, the air-raid sirens began to howl across the camp. The prisoners, trapped in the tight, stifling van, listened helplessly as their guards ran for cover. Time ticked by, and they strained their ears, listening for the drone of bombers, waiting for the crash of explosions.

The silence dragged on until, at last, the all clear sounded. It had been a false alarm. The prisoners heard the guards returning, and the vehicle shifted and the doors slammed as the driver and guards got in. The engine thundered to life and they began to move. The Grüne Minna could not have gone more than a hundred yards when it jolted to a halt and sat idling. Almost immediately, the prisoners began to smell exhaust fumes. The engine continued to run, and the fumes grew thicker, the smell choking. At least one prisoner, Sigmund Rascher, took fright. A small man with a ginger moustache, Rascher was a former SS doctor who had helped design gas chambers for the death camps and had conducted horrific human experiments on prisoners.[24] His career had come to an end amid allegations of financial fraud and falsifying scientific results.

"My God," said Rascher as the van filled with fumes. "This is a death van, we are being gassed!"[25] If anyone should know, it would be him; as one of the technical architects of the Final Solution, Rascher was aware of such vehicles being used in early experiments in mass killing.

Payne Best, keeping a level head, drew Rascher's attention to a glimmer of moonlight coming through a ventilator in the sidewall of the van. "Do they have such things in gas chambers?" he asked.

Rascher had to admit that they didn't. "We are probably all right," he said.

Whether by design or not, the fumes were increasing dangerously, becoming suffocating. Eventually, the Grüne Minna lurched and drove on. Air flowed in through the ventilator, and gradually the fumes diminished. The Prominenten were not going to die after all.

At least, not yet.

Three

Alpine Fortress

While the Prominenten were being evacuated from Sachsenhausen and Buchenwald, in Berlin Adolf Hitler seethed in his gloomy bunker beneath the Chancellery garden. Armageddon was looming for his thousand-year Reich, but he continued issuing increasingly hysterical commands, often to armies that had long disappeared in the fog of defeat.

Some of his more fanatical followers had succumbed to the same delusional paranoia, incubated by their enclosed existence. But Hitler's less loyal officers were quietly planning their own salvation. The treachery surrounding the Führer was never more abundant than among the ranks of his Praetorian Guard, the omnipotent SS, who now feared for their own future and began formulating schemes—often mutually conflicting—that would have dire consequences for the VIP prisoners caught in the middle.

The most perfidious schemer was Heinrich Himmler, head of the SS and chief overseer of the Holocaust, who was convinced that he could replace Hitler as Führer and negotiate peace terms that would see a renewed Germany joining America and Britain in a war against the Soviet Union. He had been making secret overtures to the Allies through neutral intermediaries since March 1944, first letting Franklin Roosevelt and Winston Churchill know that he was prepared to oust Hitler. The proposition was treated with contempt by both leaders.[1] Once defeat started to look inevitable, Himmler began secretly releasing batches of inmates from his concentration camps, an initiative that opened him up to suspicion from his subordinates and infuriated Hitler when he found out about it.[2] Himmler hoped in vain that these token gestures would improve his image in Washington and London.

Himmler's two most senior deputies had slightly more realistic, albeit divergent, plans. For some weeks SS-Obergruppenführer Ernst Kaltenbrunner in Berlin and his counterpart and rival in Italy, SS-Obergruppenführer Karl Wolff, had been engaged in a struggle over how to conclude the war to Germany's best advantage. A factor in both their schemes was the defense of the Nazi heartlands of Austria and Bavaria. The mountainous Alpine Tyrol region, spanning the Austrian-Italian border, was seen as a potential site for a last-ditch *Alpenfestung*, or Alpine Fortress—a formidable network of heavily fortified mountain bases.

Kaltenbrunner and Wolff had once been friends, but their rivalry had brought them to a state of open hostility. As chief of the hydra-headed RSHA, Kaltenbrunner—a scar-faced giant whose presence intimidated even Himmler—was one of the most powerful men in the Third Reich. The RSHA embraced the Gestapo, the Kripo (criminal police), and the SD, which together represented a network of absolute totalitarian control in the Nazi state.

Karl Wolff, unlike Kaltenbrunner, was an engaging, pleasant-looking man of easy charm, whose charismatic personality appealed to almost everyone, including Himmler and Hitler (much to Kaltenbrunner's irritation). A former public relations man, Wolff was a smooth operator and somehow contrived to appear aloof from the barbarity of Nazism. Formerly third in command of the SS, he had been Himmler's eyes and ears at Führer headquarters. But he had fallen out of favor, and by April 1945 Wolff was the plenipotentiary for German armed forces in Italy, holding the grandiloquent title of Höchster SS- und Polizeiführer (supreme SS and police leader) for the region.

Kaltenbrunner and Wolff held broadly equal positions in the SS hierarchy but were unequal in influence. Kaltenbrunner's headquarters were on Prinz Albrecht Strasse in Berlin—just around the corner from Hitler's Chancellery and not far from Himmler's headquarters in the resort town of Hohenlychen. Kaltenbrunner spent virtually every afternoon with

Hitler in the bunker, and he exploited these advantages to undermine his rival isolated in Italy.

By April 1945, most of Italy had fallen to Allied forces, leaving only the plains of Lombardy and Veneto and the mountainous South Tyrol as a last buffer protecting the Nazi heartlands of Bavaria and Austria. It was Kaltenbrunner's firm view that both could withstand the coming onslaught from the Allies in Italy, but only if German forces there held firm. He was one of the diehards who believed that a successful last stand could be fought in the natural defenses of an Alpine Fortress.

On 15 March, Kaltenbrunner discussed the matter with his subordinate, SS-Sturmbannführer Wilhelm Höttl, head of the SD in Italy and Hungary. Kaltenbrunner believed in the feasibility of the Alpine Fortress. The man chosen to help with the defense was the legendary SS commando leader Otto Skorzeny, one of Hitler's favorites, who had helped lead the 1943 airborne raid to free Mussolini from his mountaintop prison.[3] Kaltenbrunner hoped to use Skorzeny's resources, his notoriety, and the threat of continued Nazi resistance in the Alpine Fortress to cajole the Allies into making peace. Skorzeny, like Himmler, was one of those Nazis who believed that the Allies would join with a reformed Germany under new leadership in an anti-Bolshevik alliance.

However, Wolff—in whose domain the Alpine Fortress would partly lie—had no illusions about the proposed last stand, nor about the outcome of the war. In this he found himself increasingly at one with Himmler. Wolff knew that Germany was defeated, with no possibility of a heroic last stand. Italy was as good as lost, and it would be better to swiftly withdraw German forces with a view to extracting favorable peace terms from the Allies. Wolff was quite prepared to surrender himself and all his forces to bring about an end to hostilities.[4]

Since early March, Wolff had been making clandestine advances to the enemy via the American intelligence chief Allen Dulles in neutral Switzerland. Dulles was President Roosevelt's personal emissary in Bern and head of the Office of Strategic Services (OSS), forerunner of the Central Intelligence Agency. Wolff had twice been smuggled over the border for top-secret talks with Dulles.[5] Wolff would later portray his mission as selfless, his only concern being to bring an end to the bloodshed. In fact, his grand strategy was motivated by self-preservation and a desire to secure himself a good position in postwar Germany.[6]

Wolff had persuaded Luftwaffe Field Marshal Albert Kesselring, the supreme commander of German armed forces in Italy, of the wisdom of this course of action. Kesselring had given his tacit, if somewhat vague, endorsement to Wolff's secret talks. This arrangement was put in jeopardy in March, when Kesselring was transferred to the western front, but his replacement, Colonel General Heinrich von Vietinghoff, gave tentative signs of coming around to Wolff's view that Italy was not worth fighting for. Wolff and Vietinghoff, together with other senior German officers, formed a conspiracy to make peace with the Allies in Italy.

They acted with the utmost discretion in order to prevent word of their perfidy from reaching Berlin and the ears of the Führer. But the conspiracy proved vulnerable to Ernst Kaltenbrunner's vast network of Gestapo and SD spies, and Wolff's deadly rival was soon made aware of his seditious machinations. Kaltenbrunner was incandescent with rage, not least because his own tentative attempts to appeal to the Allies in Switzerland had been firmly rebuffed. Dulles had discounted Kaltenbrunner's advances because he could not promise, as Wolff did, to withdraw huge numbers of SS and Wehrmacht troops from the fight.[7] Thus Kaltenbrunner and the more fanatical elements in the Berlin regime pinned their hopes on the Alpine Fortress.

In reality, the chances of Germany creating such a defensive network—a colossal project for any nation, let alone one in its death throes—were slim to nonexistent. But it was a powerful propaganda weapon nonetheless. The mere possibility of major defenses in the Alpine region—with its vast mountain ranges, narrow valleys, and winding roads—would force the Allies to alter their strategy significantly in the last weeks of the war.

The idea of such a redoubt had first been proposed by Himmler as early as May 1944. It was not until September of that year, however, that the army had commissioned an engineering team to produce a feasibility study.[8] Time passed, and no concrete plans were developed for construction or manning. At first, neither Washington nor London took reports about its existence seriously. However, in September 1944 two developments awakened new interest in the mythical *Alpenfestung*.

A confidential US intelligence dispatch to Washington reported the existence of tremendous fortifications in the Alps, incorporating underground factories, weapons and munitions depots, secret airfields, and more. It speculated that, in the event of a military collapse in the spring of 1945, the Germans might hold out for a further six to eight months in such a setting. No US commander would want to sustain the high casualties inevitable in an assault on such formidable defenses.[9] However, if this last bastion was not attacked, the Nazis could hold out for two years—a situation that might encourage widespread guerrilla activity throughout Germany.

Following this worrying assessment, the OSS Research and Analysis Branch studied southern Germany and its potential as a redoubt. They took into account the fanaticism of the SS, noting that Bavaria had been the birthplace of National Socialism, and that many of its leaders, not least Hitler, displayed an almost mystical attraction to the mountains.

In truth, all these worrying details, which caused such a stir among American military planners, were part of a disinformation operation by the SD. Many of the details about the Alpine Fortress had been planted by Hans Gontard, head of the SD office in the Austrian town of Bregenz. When he intercepted the OSS report, Gontard could only marvel at the gullibility of the Americans. He showed a copy to the all-powerful Nazi Gauleiter* for the region of Tyrol-Vorarlberg, Franz Hofer, who immediately moved to exploit the Allies' fears. In his view, those fears were proof that the Alpine Fortress would be effective and should be made real. In November, Hofer sent a memo to Martin Bormann, head of the Nazi Party Chancellery and private secretary to Hitler, suggesting that the project be

* Nazi Party leader of a region within German-occupied territory

initiated. Hofer proposed diverting huge quantities of machinery, munitions, equipment, and personnel. In addition, he suggested drafting thirty thousand Allied prisoners of war to act as human shields.[10]

The memo was ignored for several months, but then Joseph Goebbels seized upon it, perceiving the propaganda value of the *Alpenfestung* and deciding to exploit the "redoubt hysteria" among the Americans. In December 1944, he convened a secret meeting of journalists, with the purpose of encouraging Allied fears about the "National Redoubt." This would be achieved simply by forbidding any mention of it in German newspapers or publications. Word of the ban would reach Allied intelligence and confirm their belief that the redoubt was real.

Following Goebbels's initiative, Bormann presented Hofer's memo to the Führer. Hitler gave orders to begin construction of defense fortifications at once, as a way to frighten the Allies into making political concessions.[11] With Hitler himself having blessed the idea, competing elements in the Nazi regime now adopted the proposal in various ways to suit their own ideas of how to exploit the enemy's concerns to their own advantage.[12]

In January, Goebbels set up a propaganda section devoted to concocting stories about the redoubt. The results were spectacularly successful. First *Collier's* magazine ran a story about a German operation, codenamed Werewolf, involving gangs of guerrillas trained to launch raids from an impregnable fortress around Berchtesgaden.[13] Shortly afterward, a Zurich newspaper reported that a massive redoubt was being constructed in the Obersalzberg area.[14] Then, on 11 February 1945, the *New York Times* published a story entitled "'Last Fortress' of the Nazis." It depicted a fortified zone 280 miles long and one hundred miles wide, stretching from the western extreme of Switzerland to central Austria—a "formidable barrier" incorporating the "gigantic chain" of mountains, infested with concrete pillboxes and other fortifications buried in the rocks.[15]

The article added a new wrinkle. Invoking the specter of "a monstrous blackmail," it claimed that the Nazis had another devious ploy up their sleeves. "Since D-Day," it stated, "all the main political hostages from Allied countries have been moved by the Gestapo from various parts of the Reich into this Alps quadrangle." Among others, it named the former French prime minister, Léon Blum, as one of the many potential hostages.[16]

In fact, at that time Blum was still confined in the falconer's house at Buchenwald, hundreds of miles north of the Alps. Neither was there any Alpine Fortress outside the imaginations of fanatical Nazis like Kaltenbrunner and Hitler. But, however unwittingly, the *New York Times* had accurately prophesied the Nazi high command's ultimate strategy.

Two months after the article appeared, in the early days of April, Hitler gave the order to round up all the VIP hostages of the Reich and send them south.[17]

Four

Journey South

Wednesday 4 April: Southern Germany

Leaving Buchenwald and the town of Weimar behind, the Grüne Minna had driven on through the night and the following morning, its wood-fueled gas engine laboring unevenly and its leaky exhaust rumbling. It couldn't manage more than six miles per hour and had to stop every hour to be stoked with wood or have its flue cleared.

Sigismund Payne Best, crammed in among his fellow prisoners, was concerned that, despite the air coming in through the ventilator, the interior remained thick with the smell of fumes. Some of the prisoners felt ill, and a few of the less robust were becoming light-headed. With their arms pinned to their sides, their legs clamped in a press of luggage, and the sharp corners of cases and boxes digging into them, the prisoners' journey had gone beyond discomfort and become painful.[1]

Three people succumbed to the fumes and passed out. One was Friedrich von Rabenau, a craggy-faced and deeply religious former general who had been implicated in Stauffenberg's July 1944 plot but never formally charged. The two others were women. Heidel Nowakowski was a pretty young German whose origins were mysterious but who was suspected by her fellow prisoners of being a spy for the Gestapo.[2] The other was Margot Heberlein, the fiery and domineering wife of diplomat Dr. Erich Heberlein, another of Stauffenberg's fellow conspirators in the July plot. The two had been imprisoned together, sharing a tiny cell in the Buchenwald basement. In the confined space of the van, the prisoners tried to make the unconscious comfortable, holding out their arms to support them so that they could lie flat.

Eventually a faint dawn light began to seep through the ventilator, and Payne Best could make out the faces of his companions. There was the mass murderer Dr. Sigmund Rascher's genial countenance; he was quite open about his crimes, and none of the other prisoners held them against him. Death and suffering had been such an intrinsic part of their surroundings for so long that they seemed little more than facts of life.

In contrast to Rascher, one could hardly find a more different soul than the Lutheran pastor Dietrich Bonhoeffer, an anti-Nazi Christian dissident and close friend of Rabenau. Bonhoeffer was a founding member of the Confessing Church, a breakaway Protestant sect, which had formed in opposition to Hitler's move to create a single pro-Nazi Protestant Reich Church. Another man whom Payne Best especially liked was the most illustrious of all the cellar Prominenten: General Alexander von Falkenhausen, the former military commander of occupied Belgium, who had been indirectly implicated in the July plot. Falkenhausen was never seen outdoors without his cape, with its vivid scarlet lining, and his *pour le mérite*, Germany's highest military honor of World War I, on a red silk ribbon around his neck.

As the hours passed, the exhausted inmates, who hadn't slept at all, began to need the toilet. As their need became ever more urgent, one by one they began to complain. "I can't wait any longer." "They'll have to stop—I have to get out." The complaints grew louder and more desperate, and the prisoners started banging on the sides of the van. Eventually the vehicle shuddered to a stop and the rear door was flung open by one of the SS guards.

"What's all this?" he demanded.

The situation was explained: there were ladies among the prisoners, the gentlemen pointed out delicately, and they must all be allowed out to see to their needs privately. Death and suffering might be part of life, but these prisoners hadn't yet reached the point where civilized toilet requirements could be disregarded.

Less delicately, the guard shouted to his two comrades that the prisoners needed to piss. The SS men argued over whether to allow it. In the end, the doors were opened.

Payne Best, extricating himself from the crush of limbs and luggage, followed the others out of the vehicle. They were in a flat landscape of open fields with no hedges or trees nearby. While one of the guards led Mrs. Heberlein and Miss Nowakowski across a field to a distant copse, the men peed by the side of the road, while the other two guards covered them with their machine pistols.

Fresh air and daylight lifted the spirits of the prisoners. They also had a little more room in the Grüne Minna now that much of the wood had been used up, and under the practical-minded direction of SOE agent Hugh Falconer, the luggage was stowed much more efficiently.

After some bread and sausage provided by the guards, the Prominenten felt much happier and began to take an interest in their destination, noting the landscape through which they were passing. One claimed to recognize a village, indicating that they were entering Bavaria—about 125 miles south of Buchenwald. Some of them had spent years in captivity in various prisons and camps and had picked up a fair knowledge of the SS network; based on location, they reckoned their probable destination must be Flossenbürg concentration camp.

Their hearts sank and hopes faded. Flossenbürg, located near the former Czech border, not far from Nuremberg and Bayreuth, was infamous among those who knew of such things as a place where unwanted prisoners were sent for execution.

Passing through rolling hills and woods, the Grüne Minna eventually reached the small town of Weiden, a pretty place of bright, gable-ended houses fronting cobblestone streets and a market square. Its attractiveness was deceptive; those in the know were aware that Weiden was the nearest town to Flossenbürg. The vehicle pulled up in front of the Gestapo headquarters and the SS guards went inside, leaving the prisoners locked in the van.[3] When they came back, one of them—who was friendlier to the prisoners than his comrades—opened the hatch and explained: "You'll have to go on farther. They can't take you here—it's too full."[4] The hatch slammed shut, and the engine coughed into life again.

Rascher—who had grown quite gloomy—now cheered up considerably. From his extensive professional knowledge of concentration camp practices, he guessed that they were safe, at least for the time being. If the intent was to kill the Prominenten, he reasoned, they would not have been turned away: "Flossenbürg is never so crowded that it cannot accommodate a few more corpses." Despite the thirty-six-year-old Rascher's evil history, Payne Best couldn't help feeling affection for the young doctor. "He was a queer fellow," he acknowledged, "possibly the queerest character which has ever come my way."[5]

As it turned out, Rascher's optimism was short-lived.

Shortly after leaving Weiden, the Grüne Minna caught up with several vehicles pulled over at the side of the road—three gray buses and a car. The buses were filled with civilians and had SS guards standing by. The car contained Léon and Janot Blum; the bus held Fey Pirzio-Biroli, Isa Vermehren, and the other Spruce Grove inmates.

They had traveled in considerably greater comfort, but it had been a long night. The buses had driven without pause from Buchenwald. By the time they passed through Weiden, most of the passengers had been in desperate need of a toilet break. The buses had pulled over, but nobody was allowed to get off. The sergeant in charge of Fey's bus answered the prisoners' pleas angrily: "You'd better be careful; we could treat you differently if we wanted to!"[6]

A furious female voice came from the back of the bus. Maria von Hammerstein was the widow of General Kurt von Hammerstein-Equord, who had been one of the most brilliant soldiers of his generation and an ardent anti-Nazi. Maria's force of will and moral courage matched those of her late husband. "If you do not let me off this bus this very minute, I will make a lake right here on the spot! That will not be pleasant for anybody!"

The guards ignored her, so she left her seat, forced her way through the mountains of luggage filling the aisle, and physically shoved the SS sergeant barring the door. Embarrassed and confused, he gave in and opened it. The prisoners were allowed out one at a time, accompanied by heavily armed guards, to answer the call of nature.

Fey felt encouraged by the incident and sensed that her fellow kin prisoners were also growing "more determined and impertinent with our captors." At the same time, she was acutely aware of the need to be careful; the SS men were ill-tempered and aggressive, and if they were pushed too far they would start slaughtering the prisoners out of spite.[7]

The buses hadn't been parked by the roadside for long when the car carrying the Blums arrived, followed almost immediately by the Grüne Minna. Both vehicles pulled over behind the buses. For the first time, all the Prominenten from Buchenwald were together in one place.

But not for long. The Grüne Minna had scarcely pulled to a stop when a large black Mercedes screeched to a halt behind it. Out stepped two men in the uniform of the SS security police.[8] They spoke briefly to the three guards in charge of the Grüne Minna. Payne Best and the others could see this going on through the small windows in the rear doors. Suddenly the door was pulled open and one of the police officers leaned in. "Müller, Gehre, Liedig," he barked at three of the German prisoners. "Get your things and come with us."[9]

Shocked by the suddenness of the summons, the three men began to disembark. Payne Best watched with dismay; although the three were very different men, they shared an admirable courage in resisting Hitler and withstanding the punishment and abuse they had suffered. Dr. Josef Müller was a man who hated Nazism with every sinew of his being and was said to be Hitler's bitterest political opponent within Germany. Nicknamed "the Ox" for his powerful build, Müller had been an influential politician and lawyer, unrelentingly outspoken in his criticism of an ideology he despised. He had infuriated the Nazi Party by defending many opponents of the regime. Müller had been arrested in 1943 and thrown in the dungeons of the Gestapo in Berlin, where he was frequently beaten. Only his strong constitution helped him withstand months of mental abuse and physical torture.[10] His ordeal had made him mistrustful of his fellow man, and he adopted a somewhat hostile attitude toward strangers, suspecting everyone of being an informer for the Nazi authorities. Nonetheless, he and Payne Best had become good friends during their time in the Buchenwald cellar.

Captain Ludwig Gehre, the second man called out of the Grüne Minna, had been Müller's cellmate, but not his friend; Müller had never lost his suspicion of him. Gehre was typical of the anti-Hitler plotters who surrounded Admiral Wilhelm Canaris, head of the Abwehr. He had been involved in one of the earliest serious attempts to kill Hitler with a package of high explosives concealed in the Führer's plane. Gehre had managed to stay one jump ahead of the Gestapo until November 1944; knowing it was the end of the road, he shot his wife and attempted to commit suicide, succeeding only in blowing out his right eye.

The third of the unfortunate trio was Commander Franz Liedig, a forty-five-year-old former lawyer and friend of Admiral Canaris. Tall, clean-shaven, and well-built, Liedig had served in the navy during World War I. His fall had come during the investigation of the July 1944 plot, when the Gestapo stumbled over the plans for an earlier aborted attempt on Hitler's life, in which Liedig was to have been one of the assassins.

As the three men descended from the Grüne Minna, their bags were extracted from the general confusion of luggage and they bade their farewells. There was no ceremony; the three men gave a simple "see you later," although everyone somehow sensed that they were unlikely ever to meet again in this world. The men were led away and put in the Mercedes, which turned and sped back toward Weiden.

The Grüne Minna, the three buses, and the Blums' car set off again. Inside the van, the good cheer that had sprung up at learning that they were not going to be murdered at Flossenbürg had been extinguished. Some of them pretended to be in high spirits, but the underlying mood was bleak.

Inside Fey Pirzio-Biroli's bus, the atmosphere was tense. SS-Untersturmführer Bader had expected to deliver his prisoners to Flossenbürg but had been rebuffed, and he now had only the vaguest orders to follow: head south until he found somewhere suitable to accommodate them.[11] He hadn't been given money or supplies to last beyond the journey to Flossenbürg and didn't know what to do; his temper was fraying badly, and his men were nervous and irritable. One of the Stauffenbergs suggested, half-jokingly, that he knew some people locally who would be more than happy to put them up. Bader and his men were furious, while Fey and the others laughed behind their hands.

The three guards in the Grüne Minna were completely different. Mere lackeys with no real responsibility, they seemed to feel almost liberated by the lack of firm direction from above. They acted as if they were sharing the prisoners' plight—all of them in a mess together. Whenever the van made its regular stops to fuel and clear the wood burner, the guards opened the rear doors and let the prisoners out. At one stop, they found themselves outside a farmhouse, and Heidel Nowakowski and Margot Heberlein were allowed inside to freshen up while the men washed at the pump in the farmyard. The farmer's wife brought out milk and rye bread, which the hungry prisoners devoured with gratitude.

Back in the van, with more space after the departure of the three unfortunates and the window wide open to the balmy spring air, the prisoners began to regain their spirits somewhat.

It was dusk when the convoy entered Regensburg, a picturesque Bavarian town on the banks of the Danube, hardly touched by the war. Bader hoped to find a haven here for the prisoners but was rebuffed at every turn; the vehicles drove from one large government building to another. "If we can't get you in here," one of the guards said to Payne Best, "I don't know what we'll do."[12] In their irritable state, some of the guards on the buses might well turn violent if they were inconvenienced any further.

At last, after several hours of driving around Regensburg, Bader gained permission to lodge the Prominenten in the city's state prison. The three buses and the car were first to arrive, the slow Grüne Minna having been left behind. They had journeyed over 180 miles since the previous evening, and the prisoners, stiff and exhausted, disembarked in miserable drizzle. Fey looked up at the hideous bulk of the prison with gloom and foreboding.[13] The bus guards, having reached the last of their patience, began shoving and prodding the prisoners at gunpoint. Fey and the others hefted their luggage and climbed the steps to the entrance.

Inside, they were herded up iron staircases and along corridors to a cellblock, where they were allotted just a handful of tiny, filthy cells to accommodate dozens of people. As the cell doors slammed, Fey heard one of the prisoners shouting furiously at the warders. Major Dietrich Schatz, a Wehrmacht officer and loyal Nazi who'd had the misfortune of being related to one of the July plotters, was deeply indignant about his arrest; to be confined in a prison cell was more than he could bear. "You have no right to lock us up like criminals!" he yelled through the narrow window. "We are not ordinary prisoners!"

Bader's second in command was affected by Schatz's outburst, as were some of his men.[14] Schatz had a point. After some discussion, the prison governor was consulted, but he was obdurate: Cell doors must be kept locked at all times. No, he could not make exceptions, no matter how important the prisoners believed themselves to be. The prisoners remained in their cramped, unclean boxes with the steel doors firmly locked.

Shortly after the buses had unloaded, the car carrying Léon and Janot Blum pulled up outside the prison. The long journey had been unbearable for the former statesman. Already in poor health, Blum been driven to the edge of physical and mental collapse, and the sight of the grim, formidable building was a dreadful shock. Carried up a flight of stairs and placed in a cell alone, Blum was overcome by anxiety, believing he was being separated from Janot. He was relieved when she joined him shortly afterward.[15]

Later that evening, the Grüne Minna finally reached the prison and began to unload. A couple of prison warders who were hanging around the entrance set about harrying and bullying the prisoners, but one of the SS men—in a much better mood than those guarding the buses—intervened.

"These are very important people," he said. "You should treat them with respect."[16]

"Oh! Some more aristocrats," said one of the warders disdainfully. "Well, put them with the other lot on the second floor."

Inside, loaded with luggage, they ascended the stairs and were greeted by a pleasant, elderly warder who allowed them to attend to their own accommodations. Unfortunately, the place was so overcrowded that he could only give three cells for the fourteen of them.

While Heidel Nowakowski and Margot Heberlein shared one cell, the men squeezed themselves into the other two. Payne Best shared with the men he felt most in tune with, including Hugh Falconer and Alexander von Falkenhausen. The others were Vassily Kokorin, the Red Army lieutenant who was Molotov's nephew, and Colonel Horst von Petersdorff, a highly decorated German who had involved himself in the July plot. Petersdorff was only alive because the Gestapo had failed to find any hard evidence of his involvement. The five men were provided with three straw mattresses and told that there was no food because the kitchens were closed.

After the day they'd had, this was the final straw. They protested loudly, arguing with the warders and starting up a chant of "We want food!" which quickly spread to the kin prisoners in their cells.

The warders—who weren't used to such spirited inmates—relented and brought ersatz coffee (made from acorns), a hunk of bread, and a bowl of soup for each person, which Payne Best thought "quite passable."[17]

It was a dismal night for the Prominenten. Despite many of them having spent years in concentration camps and Gestapo prisons, this seemed somehow worse; being crammed in dirty cells like common prisoners undermined the self-respect that had helped keep them going through the darkest times. For those like Fey who had become used to living in a barrack community, the cells felt horribly confined. But for those like Payne Best who had spent long periods shackled and tortured, Regensburg prison was little more than another stop on their odyssey.

❖

Thursday 5 April: Regensburg prison

As the blackness of the night gave way to morning light, the Prominenten were relieved to hear the clanking of keys in locks and the cell doors grinding open. The governor had had a change of heart and decided that the VIP prisoners should be allowed out of their cells to mingle and exercise in the corridors.

It was the second day since leaving Buchenwald, and for the first time the various groups of Prominenten—British secret agents, foreign statesmen, dissident German officers, anti-Nazi activists, and the kinfolk of conspirators—met one another.

Regarding himself as the senior figure, despite being a mere captain among German officers who outranked him by several grades, Sigismund Payne Best made it his business to get to know everyone. As a ladies' man who'd spent years in isolation or in exclusively male company, he was especially drawn to the attractive young German women, Fey Pirzio-Biroli and Isa Vermehren. He thought Fey looked too young to be married and was surprised to learn the story of her husband and two children.[18] Isa Vermehren, a blonde with boyish features and a chirpy manner, had incurred the wrath of the Nazis as a teenager in 1933, expelled from school for refusing to give the Hitler salute out of sympathy for a Jewish school friend. As an adult, Isa had sung and played the accordion in Berlin's cabarets, a subversive role that brought the scrutiny of the Gestapo. Despite that, she had avoided arrest and even performed for Wehrmacht troops. Her fall had come in January 1944, when her brother Erich, German military attaché in Turkey, defected to the British; Isa and her other brother, Michael, were arrested under the *Sippenhaft* law.[19]

She and Fey were impressed by the Englishman, who was more than old enough to be their father. Fey took an immediately liking to the "tall, gaunt man with a monocle and protruding front teeth."[20] Like Fey, Isa noted his prominent teeth; they were the handiwork of an SS dentist at Sachsenhausen, whom Payne Best suspected of deliberately modeling them to protrude. Isa thought they looked like "big false horse's teeth," and they were frequently displayed when Payne Best gave "an obliging smile," indicating the "trustworthy discretion which engenders deepest confidence."[21]

While the Prominenten milled about, the prison warders fretted over what to do about the breach of discipline. Payne Best overheard them prompting each other to start locking the prisoners up again, and from time to time a warder would call out, "Everyone back in their cell!" Each time, the order was greeted with laughter and cheering from the Prominenten.

Visiting the cellblock lavatories, Payne Best managed to look out of the window, which gave a view onto the neighboring railway marshaling yard. Here were the first signs he had seen of war damage in Regensburg. "I have never seen such a mess in my life," he recalled. The tracks had been torn up, forming a tangled mess, and burned-out and smashed carriages and locomotives lay on their sides.

The warders managed to get a few prisoners back in their cells by putting food inside, waiting for them to go and get it, and then slamming the doors on them. But just as they were making headway, the air-raid sirens began to howl. Immediately all the prisoners on the block were shepherded down to the cellars, where, in Payne Best's words, "the fun started again."[22] Adding to the jollity, the warning was a false alarm, and although hundreds of American bombers were heard passing overhead, no bombs fell; their targets were at Ingolstadt, Nuremberg, and Bayreuth, to the west and north.[23]

Reveling in their defiance of Nazi authority and enjoying what felt like a taste of freedom, the Prominenten failed to realize that it was all an illusion. They were by no means free, and very far from safe.

Five

Flossenbürg Concentration Camp

Tuesday 3 April: South of Berlin

Wing Commander Harry "Wings" Day watched the German countryside flowing slowly by the carriage window. It was mid-morning and the train had been traveling for several hours, leaving Sachsenhausen and the bomb-ravaged suburbs of Berlin far behind. As far as could be judged, the prisoners were heading southwest, in the general direction of Saxony and Bavaria: the heartland of Nazi Germany—or what remained of it, pinched between the ever-advancing Allied fronts. The train passed town after town ruined by Allied bombing and airfields where Luftwaffe fighters stood parked and useless for want of fuel.[1]

Day and the other Great Escapers—flight lieutenants Jimmy James, Sydney Dowse, and Raymond van Wymeersch—were keeping a constant watch for potential escape opportunities. So far there had been none. The train kept moving, and Inspector Peter Mohr and the SS guards were vigilant.

The prisoners regarded the journey and their prospects of survival with varying degrees of anticipation, jadedness, and dread. General Ivan Georgievich Bessonov, the ruthless, untrustworthy Russian, was convinced that their ultimate destiny was to be shot in retribution for Germany's impending defeat. Colonel John "Mad Jack" Churchill, the belligerent, sword-wielding commando leader, considered escape. Unlike Day and the other Great Escapers, Mad Jack wasn't a team player or a systematic planner; if any opportunity presented itself, he was ready to seize it in the moment.

Taking a more jaded view was thirty-six-year-old Captain Peter Churchill. No relation to Mad Jack, Peter Churchill was a gentle-looking, bespectacled member of the English upper class, with the air of a scholar rather than what he actually was: an agent with the Special Operations Executive specializing in sabotage. Having parachuted several times into occupied France, he had coordinated SOE's Spindle spy network, at the same time developing a romantic relationship with his French courier, Odette Sansom. Unfortunately, Spindle had been penetrated by the Abwehr, and both Churchill and Sansom had been arrested and tortured. Although sentenced to death, Churchill had avoided execution by allowing his captors to believe he was related to Winston Churchill and therefore a highly valuable catch.[2] In fact, neither he nor Mad Jack were related to the prime minister, but the magic of the name was like a talisman. Accordingly, he had been sent to the Sonderlager at Sachsenhausen as one of the Prominenten.

Sometime before noon the train pulled into the main station at Dresden, some 140 miles south of Sachsenhausen. The destruction of Berlin had shocked many of the prisoners, but the spectacle they now saw was even more appalling. The ancient baroque capital of Saxony had been laid to ruin by Allied firebombing raids less than two months earlier. It was a ghostly wasteland. The hollow shells of whole streets and districts of buildings loomed precariously over roads choked with rubble and debris. Desperate people traveled through and away from the ruins, crowding with their belongings onto the roofs of the handful of jam-packed trains still running.[3] Jimmy James was dismayed by what his fellow RAF men had done to this place and to the tens of thousands of civilians killed—"one of the most beautiful medieval cities in Europe destroyed," he thought, "to no purpose."[4]

Wings Day contemplated the desolate scene with a heavy heart. It gave him no satisfaction to see such wanton devastation wrought upon the enemy. He loathed the Nazis, and had spent five and a half years fighting them from behind the wire, but he had a degree of sympathy for the ordinary German people who had been caught in the whirlwind of hate and annihilation. His thinking on this subject, however, was contradictory. Day thought, for example, that his commandant at Stalag Luft III had been a "perfect gentleman," despite the fact that the wealthy and aristocratic colonel, while behaving decently to his American and British prisoners, had allowed their Soviet "*Untermenschen*" counterparts to die in the elements or starve to death.

Day's quixotic attitude toward the Germans had surfaced in Sachsenhausen when Sydney Dowse pranked the SS by reversing the long row of skull-and-crossbones signs lining the warning wire around Sonderlager A. The SS commandant had been apoplectic and gave Day—as senior British officer—a severe dressing-down. Day agreed with the commandant that Dowse's stunt had been a juvenile display of insubordination and promptly reprimanded him for insulting a symbol held dear by the SS.[5] However, Day also objected to the tone taken by the commandant and determined that escape was the only way to exact revenge. Day told his men, "I feel very strongly that we as RAF are being insulted, defamed or what have you by these SS types." For the honor of the RAF (and, rather weirdly, the Luftwaffe), he felt it was necessary to defy the SS; therefore, "let's see if we can make a break."[6] The break was made, leading to the escapees being rounded up and their lives saved by Inspector Mohr.

For five and a half years, Wings Day had been under intense strain. Not only had he been the senior British officer in charge of running the affairs of thousands of RAF prisoners, but he was also something of a father figure to many of the young men. He had had a nervous breakdown early in his captivity and had been nursed back to health by Luftwaffe medical orderlies. Throughout his imprisonment, the Luftwaffe's civilized attitude toward its RAF captives had undeniably been a reassuring and comforting factor against an unsettling backdrop of increasing Nazi barbarity. Naturally, it hadn't stopped him from causing the Luftwaffe huge trouble by escaping from its camps.

During his years of confinement, Day had derived a great deal of moral sustenance from the close friendships he had formed within a tight circle of like-minded officers, among whom the irrepressible Jimmy James was the foremost.

The train left Dresden behind, heading west. It carried them through Chemnitz and Zwickau as dusk grew and night fell, and finally pulled into a siding at Plauen, near the border between Saxony and Bavaria. There it stood motionless in the dark, the carriages firmly locked. The Prominenten dozed in their compartments. Suddenly, they were jolted awake by the rising howl of air-raid sirens. Boots thundered along the corridor and doors were flung open as the guards dashed for shelter. The prisoners were left locked in, knowing that the exits were covered from a distance by machine guns.[7] They could do nothing but listen as bombs thumped in the distance, hoping this section of the railway wasn't one of RAF Bomber Command's targets tonight, praying for the noise to die away and the all clear to sound. Fortunately, the raid was light and brief—a precision strike by a single squadron of RAF Mosquitos—and no bombs came near the train.[8]

The next morning, the journey continued, chugging on slowly southwest into Bavaria. Speculation about the ultimate destination was unrelenting, but Inspector Peter Mohr and his assistant, Corporal George, still refused to disclose it. In the afternoon the train pulled to a halt at the small town of Weiden, not long after the Prominenten from Buchenwald had been turned away. Here, the Sachsenhausen group was ordered to disembark. Unlike the Buchenwald prisoners, none of them knew anything about this area, and they had no idea what to expect. Also unlike the Buchenwalders, they were not turned away; after leaving the train that had carried them from Oranienburg, they were transferred to a small narrow-gauge local railway.

Crossing the river bridge, the train took them east out of town, puffing slowly along a steep valley lined with forest. The track meandered, climbing higher through a landscape of rolling hills, woodland, and picturesque Bavarian farmland. At last Mohr revealed that they were nearly at their destination, though he still wouldn't identify it. The climb grew steeper, the surrounding hills rose higher, and the farmland gave way to forest.

After about twelve miles, with evening approaching, the landscape leveled off into a bowl, over a mile across, surrounded by higher hills. The railway went past several factories where the workers were gaunt men and women in striped uniforms, and the Prominenten guessed they were approaching a concentration camp.[9] In the center of the bowl nestled a tiny village overlooked by the ruin of a medieval castle perched on a lone hill. The village was Flossenbürg, and just beyond it, laid out in a huge grid across a rising slope topped by a stone quarry, was the concentration camp. This was the place whose very name had caused Dr. Sigmund Rascher to quail, the place where unwanted prisoners were sent for final disposal. The Prominenten knew nothing of Flossenbürg, but the sight of it cast their spirits down. Peter Churchill, for one, felt a greater foreboding than any he had experienced when approaching Sachsenhausen.[10]

Flossenbürg concentration camp had been built in 1938, initially to accommodate "asocial" prisoners: the "workshy," social misfits, drunks, addicts, and so on. Since then it had swollen in size and purpose. The inmates, overseen by more than four thousand SS guards, labored in the quarry and the Messerschmitt aircraft works; they were routinely beaten, starved, tortured, and murdered. Flossenbürg was not a death camp—there were no gas chambers—but its death toll was enormous. The newly arrived Prominenten would have felt even more gloomy if they had known what Dr. Rascher knew—that since 1941 this place had been a regular venue for extrajudicial executions. Most of the victims had been Poles and Russian prisoners of war; however, only the previous week, thirteen Allied POWs had been hanged, all of them SOE agents.[11]

The Prominenten were divided into groups. While the Greeks and Russians were sent to accommodations somewhere outside the camp perimeter, the British—as renowned escapers and therefore a security risk—were marched in through the gate.

Flossenbürg's entrance was quite plain; there was no large gatehouse, just a high iron gate between stone pillars set within the tall electrified fence. On the left-hand pillar was engraved the common Nazi slogan *Arbeit macht frei.* As soon as they were within and the gates had clanged shut, the SS guards began (as Peter Churchill expressed it) "screaming their hymn of hate."[12] Taking over from Corporal George's men, the Flossenbürg guards berated the new arrivals, driving them like cattle along the street toward the camp infirmary.

Meanwhile, Inspector Mohr, having said goodbye, went to the camp administration block; his mission would not be complete until he had formally handed the prisoners over to the authorities here. He found the commandant, SS-Obersturmbannführer Max Koegel, in his office.[13]

Koegel was a brutal-looking man, with a balding head shaped like a blunt-tipped bullet, a thick neck, and a mouth like a stab wound. A dedicated anti-Semite, Koegel had begun his career as a guard at Dachau in 1933, rising to be commandant of Ravensbrück concentration camp and the infamous death camp of Majdanek (the "other Auschwitz") before his transfer to Flossenbürg.[14] He greeted Mohr and glanced over the paperwork. "When can I shoot this lot?" he asked casually.[15]

"They are not to be executed, Herr Commandant," said Mohr. "They are to remain in your custody until further orders."

Koegel was incredulous. "What? But the camp is overcrowded; they aren't dying quickly enough to keep up with the overflow. Special executions can't be carried out fast enough!"

Mohr explained that his orders came directly from Berlin, implying that they were from the Führer himself. The prisoners were of great importance and were to be held for the purpose of bargaining with the Allies. They should not only be spared but should receive the best treatment, so far as that was possible in a concentration camp. If any of them were found to have been liquidated or even harmed, it would bode ill for any peace negotiations—and for Koegel's life.

Even faced with this direct threat, Koegel struggled to understand the concept of keeping prisoners alive. It would take until the following day, when Mohr took him to see the regional SS commander in Nuremberg, for Koegel to finally accept his orders. Immediately after his initial interview with Mohr, the commandant stormed off to the infirmary to take a look at these "greatly important" prisoners for himself.

They had been herded into an empty ward, and as they wandered around the room, taking stock, Koegel burst in, in such a furious temper that he knocked down a medical orderly standing in his way. He glared around at the prisoners with naked hatred.

"You will stay confined in this room," he said. "If you misbehave you will be punished. Do not even think about trying to escape. It is impossible; the camp is entirely surrounded by minefields. If you are caught so much as attempting to escape, you will be shot."[16]

Wings Day, who spoke good German, asked him, "What is the name of this place?" At no point had Mohr revealed it.

Commandant Koegel seemed about to react violently to this impertinence, but restrained himself and scowled. "*That* you will find out soon enough."

With that, he turned on his heel and marched out of the room.

Compared with their counterparts from Buchenwald, who at that moment were settling in at Regensburg state prison, the Sachsenhausen group had arrived at an exceedingly bleak destination.

⁂

The commandant was correct: it wasn't long before Wing Commander Day and his men discovered the name of this place. Although they had never heard of it before, it would leave an indelible impression on their minds.

Conditions in Flossenbürg were typically harsh. During their time in Sachsenhausen, Day and the others had been insulated from much of the day-to-day brutality of camp life. Here, the hospital in which they were confined occupied a raised position on the side of a slope, with the camp spread out beneath it. From here, they witnessed the emaciated prisoners being kicked and beaten as they marched to and from their daily toil in the quarry. The task of breaking granite twelve hours a day drove many of them to their deaths through a combination of starvation, exhaustion, and deliberate murder. The hospital also happened to stand between the cellblock and the crematorium, and it was common to see a macabre traffic between the two.[17]

After only a few days, Jimmy James concluded that nothing he had ever seen bore comparison to the vision of hell that he witnessed at Flossenbürg. The Prominenten often encountered the inmates in the hospital washroom, with "grey yellow skin stretched around shaven heads, sunken cheeks and glazed tortured eyes in hollow sockets, sores covering matchstick limbs."[18]

But it was another side of Flossenbürg that gave it its singular reputation. It was commonly known that if the Gestapo was unhappy with a not-guilty verdict handed down by Berlin's notorious People's Court, it would quietly dispatch the acquitted defendant to Flossenbürg to be killed.[19] The same was sometimes done with Allied prisoners, such as the thirteen SOE agents murdered in late March. The ritual and method of execution at Flossenbürg was sadistic. The condemned were incarcerated in the cellblock—a long, low building with a courtyard—often in abominable conditions, sometimes without food, and usually in complete darkness. When they were finally hanged, it was invariably a long, slow process, often employing the specially prepared thin rope referred to as "piano wire." There were so many executions at Flossenbürg in the last months of the war that the crematorium did not have the capacity to cope, and the SS had begun stacking corpses in huge piles, drenching them with gasoline, and setting them alight.

In this environment, with only Mohr's orders standing between them and the foul temper of Commandant Max Koegel, the Prominenten were in an extremely precarious situation.

Six
The Condemned

Thursday 5 April: Berlin

On the second day since the Prominenten's evacuation, while one group woke in Flossenbürg concentration camp and another in Regensburg prison, hundreds of miles away in the German capital, events were stirring that would have a profound—and lethal—effect for some of them.

A critical milestone was about to be reached in the ongoing investigation into the July 1944 plot. The attempt on Hitler's life at his East Prussian headquarters, coordinated with an attempted coup in Berlin, was still the subject of a massive Gestapo and SD manhunt in which thousands of people had been arrested. Many had been cruelly tortured in the Gestapo dungeons on Prinz Albrecht Strasse, some had been executed, and others awaited their fate with grim apprehension. Their families were among the kin prisoners currently being transported through southern Germany.

In overall command of the investigation was SS-Obergruppenführer Ernst Kaltenbrunner, head of the Reich Main Security Office, or RSHA. On this April day, he descended into the bunker beneath the Chancellery garden to attend the Führer's regular midday conference. When the meeting was over, Kaltenbrunner took the opportunity to hand Hitler a sheaf of papers he had brought with him. The hatchet-faced Austrian experienced a moment of triumph as Hitler read through the damning documents, holding them up close before his failing eyes.[1]

They were copies of selected pages from the diaries of Admiral Wilhelm Canaris, the former head of Germany's military intelligence agency, the Abwehr. They proved that Canaris was closely involved with the central conspirators of the bomb plot. Kaltenbrunner helpfully directed the Führer to certain highlighted passages. When Hitler read them, he flew into a rage, as Kaltenbrunner surely knew he would. From that moment onward, Canaris's days were numbered. Within hours, the order had gone out to liquidate the admiral and his circle of Abwehr associates.[2]

Besides the two leading members of the group—Canaris and his deputy Hans Oster—the names on the list included the judge advocate of the army Karl Sack and lawyer Theodor Strünck, both of whom had been active in the resistance. Also on the list was army officer Captain Ludwig Gehre, who until two days ago had been a prisoner in the Buchenwald cellar; he was one of the three men removed from the Grüne Minna on the road out of Weiden. Another of the Canaris circle—and perhaps the best known—was the theologian Dietrich Bonhoeffer; he had also been in the Grüne Minna and was now in Regensburg prison with the other Prominenten.[3]

A second list of names was issued that same afternoon, with a slightly more ambiguous instruction as to how they were to be dealt with. Along with the liquidation order from Hitler, this second list was dispatched by one of Kaltenbrunner's most odious functionaries, Heinrich Müller, chief of the Gestapo and a critical actor in the suppression of all kinds of resistance to the Nazi regime. The Müller Order was addressed to Eduard Weiter, commandant of Dachau concentration camp. It stated that on the orders of Heinrich Himmler and "after obtaining the decision of the highest authority" (meaning Hitler), the high-value prisoners named in the list were to be gathered and brought immediately to Dachau.

This list included generals Franz Halder, Georg Thomas, and Alexander von Falkenhausen; Colonel Bogislaw von Bonin; the banker Hjalmar Schacht; Soviet officer Vassily Kokorin; enemy agent Sigismund Payne Best; and former Austrian chancellor Kurt von Schuschnigg. The order was phrased in the politest terms: "As I know that you only dispose of very limited space in the cellblock, I beg you after examination to put these prisoners together."[4]

There was a subsidiary command contained within the order concerning a prisoner currently held in Dachau. Code-named "Eller," this was none other than Georg Elser, the man responsible for the attempted assassination of Hitler in the Munich Bürgerbräukeller in 1939 (the very same incident the Nazis wrongly suspected Payne Best of being implicated in). Elser had been held in captivity for years, with the intent of staging a show trial after the war had been won. With that now out of the question, it had been decided—"at the highest level"—to bring his ordeal to a conclusion. On the occasion of the next Allied air raid on Munich or in the neighborhood of Dachau, "it shall be pretended that 'Eller' suffered fatal injuries." Commandant Weiter was thus requested, "when such an occasion arises, to liquidate 'Eller' as discreetly as possible. Please take steps that only very few people, who must be specially pledged to silence, hear about this. . . . After noting the contents and carrying out the orders contained in it kindly destroy this letter."[5]

The two orders—the liquidation order for Canaris and his associates, and the Müller Order for gathering certain key Prominenten at Dachau and executing Elser—were dispatched that day. Both were carried by hand rather than entrusted to the mail system or wireless network, either of which might be subject to enemy interception.

The man tasked with bringing about the execution of the Canaris group set out from Berlin the following day. A prosecutor at the SS police court in Munich, SS-Standartenführer Walter Huppenkothen was a cold and distant sociopath who had risen through the ranks of the RSHA under the twin patronage of the late Reinhard Heydrich and SD-Ausland chief Walter Schellenberg. Like both his mentors, Huppenkothen had insatiable ambition: he was once described as "a typical ice-cold functionalist who unquestioningly performed any task assigned to him by the Führer's dictatorial regime."[6] In the wake of the July plot, Huppenkothen had gone about his task of interrogating and prosecuting the traitors linked to the conspiracy, not least those in Canaris's Abwehr circle, with single-minded ruthlessness.

In the hours after Kaltenbrunner's meeting with Hitler in the Berlin bunker, Huppenkothen received his orders. The next day, Friday 6 April, he set off from Berlin, heading initially to Sachsenhausen, where his first unknowing victim awaited him.

Hans von Dohnányi, the son of a Hungarian composer, had attended the same school as Pastor Dietrich Bonhoeffer, with whom he became friends. He was a supporter of the Nazis, gaining a passing acquaintance with Goebbels, Himmler, and even Hitler himself. Shocked, however, by the Night of the Long Knives in 1934, Dohnányi became an opponent of the regime. Recruited to the Abwehr, he was given the task of completing a detailed record of the crimes against humanity that were being committed under Hitler's rule. It was he who had enlisted his old friend and now brother-in-law Dietrich Bonhoeffer to the anti-Nazi resistance. His downfall came when, under the guise of espionage work for the Abwehr, he smuggled Jews out of Germany to Switzerland. Unfortunately for him, the Gestapo found out and pounced.

Dohnányi had suffered horrible torture in the cellars of Prinz Albrecht Strasse. His torment at the hands of Huppenkothen and his henchmen was so unspeakable that, in the hope of gaining at least a temporary reprieve, he had swallowed some diphtheria bacilli that his wife had sent him. The disease affected his heart and rendered him partially paralyzed, incapable of standing up or controlling his bowels. Dohnányi had been transferred to Sachsenhausen for medical treatment. But if he thought this act of humanity would save him from his tormentor, he was to be disappointed.

When Huppenkothen arrived at Sachsenhausen on 6 April, a makeshift court had already been arranged. Huppenkothen fulfilled his customary role as prosecutor. The proceedings did not last long. After the officials took their seats, SS guards brought in the defendant, who was so ill he had to be carried on a stretcher, semiconscious and probably barely aware of what was going on. When the unpleasant charade was over, Dohnányi was found guilty and sentenced to hang.[7]

Huppenkothen didn't wait around to witness the execution. Leaving Sachsenhausen that night, he headed back to Berlin. Shortly before midnight, he reported to Heinrich Müller and was told to make ready to travel down to Flossenbürg concentration camp the next day. He would be accompanied by SS-Obersturmführer Wilhelm Gogalla, who would be carrying the secret Müller Order.

Of the ten Prominenten slated for Dachau in the order, one—Colonel Bogislaw von Bonin—was currently in Berlin, held in the Gestapo headquarters. A handsome thirty-seven-year-old, Bonin held several bravery awards, including the highly prized German Cross in Gold. He was in custody for disobeying a direct order from Hitler. As head of the operations branch of the German Army High Command, Bonin had given permission in January for German forces to withdraw from Warsaw in the face of overwhelming Soviet opposition. Warsaw fell to the Russians the next day. Defying Hitler's "fight to the last man" directive, Bonin had saved tens of thousands of lives at the risk of his own. His arrest by the Gestapo had been at Hitler's order. Classed as an honor prisoner, Bonin was still entitled to be treated with the dignity of his rank; he still wore his Wehrmacht uniform and even retained his sidearm, concealing it under his clothing.

Now Bonin was to be sent south to Flossenbürg to be corralled with the other listed Prominenten. It had been decided that an additional four Prominenten currently being held at the Gestapo's Berlin headquarters should also be sent with him.

Their guardian and bearer of the Müller Order, Wilhelm Gogalla, was provided with a Grüne Minna—fortunately for him and his prisoners, a regular gasoline-engine version. Gogalla was looking forward to the trip, which would remove him from the miserable bombed-out remains of Berlin. He was also looking forward to being reunited with one of his favorite prisoners: Sigismund Payne Best, whose name was on Müller's list.

Gogalla had first encountered the British agent during his interrogation in Berlin in 1939 and again shortly before his recent transfer to Buchenwald. Gogalla had served in the notorious Einsatzgruppen death squads that had slaughtered their way through Poland in late 1939, but Payne Best—who seemed to have a soft spot for some of the most horrific Nazi war criminals—had always found him a friendly, helpful jailer and referred to him as his "stout warder friend."[8] Whether that good regard would survive their impending reunion remained to be seen.

Huppenkothen and Gogalla rendezvoused at three o'clock in the morning on Saturday 7 April on a deserted autobahn leading out of Berlin. Huppenkothen was in his own car with his pregnant wife Erika.[9] Leaving her, he climbed into the passenger seat of the Grüne Minna, with its five prisoners in the rear.

Bearing between them orders for the execution of several men and the roundup of many more, Gogalla and Huppenkothen drove out of Berlin and headed south in the direction of Flossenbürg, over 250 miles away. They were fortunate to be escaping the Reich capital; within little over a week, it would be encircled by the advancing Red Army. There would be no going back.

Seven
Bavarian Interlude

Thursday 5 April: Regensburg

In his cold, dirty cell on the second floor of Regensburg state prison, Sigismund Payne Best woke from an afternoon doze. The thin straw mattress beneath him was hard and uncomfortable, and he was cramped from keeping to his portion alongside Hugh Falconer, Alexander von Falkenhausen, Vassily Kokorin, and Horst von Petersdorff.

Nobody had slept much. All the Prominenten had spent the morning mingling and socializing, and the air-raid alarm had forced them to spend much of the day in the basement. Their exhilaration at the impromptu party had tired them, and most had dozed through the afternoon.

SS-Untersturmführer Friedrich Bader had been in a vile mood throughout the prisoners' short acquaintance with him—leaving Buchenwald, through the journey, and particularly during their convivial gathering, he had ground his teeth in irritation. At five o'clock in the afternoon, with the Prominenten wilting and in need of another night's sleep, he came strutting down the cellblock with two of his SS men at his heels. "All prisoners—prepare for immediate departure!" he bellowed. As he marched along the block repeating the order, he seemed to take pleasure in disturbing the prisoners—a petty, arrogant revenge for their contentment during the day.

Once again, Payne Best gathered his boxes, suitcase, and typewriter, and joined the other encumbered prisoners as they descended the stairs.

Outside, the transports that had brought them from Buchenwald were waiting. While the kin prisoners boarded the buses and the Blums were ushered into their car, Payne Best and his comrades climbed into the familiar, clunking Grüne Minna. The vehicles started up and pulled away, heading southeast out of Regensburg.[1]

Again, nobody had any real idea where they were going, and Bader wasn't telling. Even his SS men were in the dark. Aboard her bus, Fey Pirzio-Biroli heard a rumor—supposedly from one of the guards—that they were to be taken to Dachau "to await further decisions." However, there was a counter rumor that Bader had been told the camp was full.[2]

Heading apparently aimlessly along the south bank of the Danube, the convoy moved slowly, especially the doddering Grüne Minna. The van had barely left Regensburg behind when it suddenly lurched violently and came to an abrupt halt. The guards, desperate, asked the prisoners for help. Hugh Falconer, who besides being an SOE saboteur had a background in engineering, got out to see what he could do. He found right away that the steering was broken beyond any hope of a roadside fix.

They were alone, the other vehicles having driven on, oblivious—Bader apparently unconcerned about keeping his convoy together. The guards flagged down a passing cyclist and instructed him to go to the Regensburg police and ask them to send a replacement vehicle. The man agreed and rode off.

The prisoners sat in the back of the van as the night darkened. Payne Best, looking through the small window, saw an eerie landscape scarred by bombing. They were near a major railway line that had been hit heavily; the field beside the road was churned up with craters, and the blackened, rusty shells of burned-out cars lay by the roadside. It was cold and soon began to rain. Payne Best could sense that the SS guards were spooked by their lonely situation.

Dawn came, but there was no sign of a replacement van. The guards, who still felt a degree of solidarity in misery with their charges, let the prisoners out to stretch their legs and ease their aching backs. They were all hungry and thirsty, but had no supplies. Payne Best felt a longing for tobacco, but nobody had any. The road was completely deserted, with no passing traffic at all. At last, after several hours, a lone motorcycle came along, heading toward Regensburg. The guards flagged it down. Taking no chances this time, they commandeered the motorbike, and one of them rode back into town.

When the guard returned, he reported that a replacement van had been sent out during the night, but the driver had turned back, claiming he couldn't find the broken-down Grüne Minna. The guard had straightened things out, giving exact details of where they were stuck.

Toward noon, the replacement vehicle arrived. The Prominenten could hardly believe their eyes. Instead of another rattletrap Grüne Minna, it was a spanking fine touring coach. Less pleasantly, some communication had evidently been exchanged at high levels, because riding in the bus were ten SD troopers armed with machine pistols. They were to be the prisoners' escort from now on.

Despite this worrying development, Payne Best, Falconer, and the other eleven Prominenten hauled their luggage aboard the bus and settled delightedly into the commodious, softly upholstered seats. As they pulled away, Payne Best looked back to see their three former guards standing forlornly beside the crippled Grüne Minna. He felt a little sad to be parting from them.[3]

The miserably uncomfortable journey now became quite pleasant. "It was a delightful drive," Payne Best recalled, "through lovely rolling country past quiet farmhouses and fields with every now and again a stretch of dark pines."[4] Even with the new bus, it was a slow journey. The SD men apparently had orders to take the prisoners east, but the way was barred by the Danube, and the bridge at Straubing had been destroyed. The bus followed the river, finding bridge after bridge in ruins, eventually crossing via a makeshift pontoon bridge and heading through winding country lanes into the high forested country of the Bayerischer Wald.[5]

The SD men appeared to take a very relaxed view of their mission, but unlike the former guards they didn't harbor any sense of fellowship with the Prominenten. They stopped at a farmhouse and were given a hatful of eggs, which they refused to share with the hungry prisoners, and gallantly gave a lift to a group of village girls, who were puzzled by the odd assortment of passengers on board. The SD men explained that they were a movie crew on their way to shoot a propaganda film.

❖

Fey drowsed in her seat as the bus wound its slow, soporific way along lanes climbing through rolling hills patched with farm fields and thick pine forest. After unwittingly leaving the Grüne Minna behind, the rest of the convoy had driven on through the night, going slowly, stopping periodically to refuel and for the prisoners to obey nature. By morning the damp chill had warmed away, and the air coming in through the bus windows smelled of pine resin and hemlock.[6]

During the morning the convoy reached the small town of Schönberg, a charming place of white stucco houses with bright terra-cotta roofs spread along a shoulder of land between two wooded hills, hemmed in by pines and dominated by the needle spire of a church. The convoy stopped and the prisoners were ordered out. This place, apparently, was to be their new home.

Fey stepped down from the bus and, carrying her luggage, walked with the others up the street to their accommodations in the village school. Word of the new arrivals spread rapidly, and villagers came out of their houses to gaze at the supposed VIPs. They certainly didn't look like important people; they seemed miserable and half-starved. Some of the villagers came forward offering fresh eggs and fruit, which the prisoners gratefully accepted. Bader's men didn't attempt to prevent this act of charity; they had been eating well ever since leaving Buchenwald, living off the money that was meant to go toward feeding the prisoners. Thus far all they had given the Prominenten to eat were occasional loaves of bread and rancid cheese.[7]

The kin prisoners were allotted several classrooms on the ground floor of the schoolhouse. Fey found herself sharing with about fifteen other people. They included members of the Stauffenberg clan, as well as the family of Caesar von Hofacker, a Luftwaffe colonel who had been involved in the July plot and executed. Also sharing the room were Fritz Thyssen and his wife, Amélie, who were not kin prisoners. Thyssen was an elderly industrialist who had been an enthusiastic Nazi in the early days but had turned against the party because of its brutal treatment of Jews. Meanwhile, Léon and Janot Blum, as the most prominent of the Prominenten, were given comfortable rooms to themselves on the upper floor, formerly the schoolmaster's apartment.

Other than in the apartment, there were no washing facilities in the school. The SS guards provided Fey's classroom with a basin of water placed in the center of the room. What worried the occupants most was not so much the rudimentary bathing facilities but how to maintain privacy and decency in a room packed with both men and women. It was agreed that when the women were washing the men would retire to the corridor, and vice versa. In practice, things wouldn't work out quite so neatly. In the meantime, despite their privations, the prisoners were quite content, continuing the community spirit they had built up in Regensburg prison. The school was at least a lot cleaner and more pleasant.

Settling in cheerfully, chatting and arranging their spots to sleep, most of these Prominenten still had not grasped just how dangerous a situation they were in.

❧

In the early afternoon, the magnificent coach carrying the twelve former passengers of the abandoned Grüne Minna rolled into Schönberg. Sigismund Payne Best, Hugh Falconer, Dietrich Bonhoeffer, General Falkenhausen, and Erich and Margot Heberlein, Dr. Rascher, Heidel Nowakowski, and the rest all disembarked under the attentive eyes of their SD guards.

Loaded down with luggage, the procession marched to the school, where they were led upstairs to a large room. To Payne Best's eyes, it resembled a hospital ward, "a bright, cheerful room" with a dozen beds with thick feather mattresses and colorful quilts.[8] There were windows all around, filling the room with light; Payne Best looked out and was rewarded with a beautiful view of the forested mountain landscape.

As a mixed-sex group, they too faced the issue of privacy. Erich and Margot Heberlein and Heidel Nowakowski took the beds at one end of the room, and the housekeeper was persuaded to provide a screen, behind which Margot and Heidel could undress.

Payne Best, who had paid little attention to young Heidel thus far, began to take stock of her and didn't much like what he saw. Given his fondness for enemy officers—even the mass murderer Rascher—and his soft spot for women, this was remarkable. He found her impossible to gauge, and that made him uncomfortable. She was young, blonde, and handsome—he felt she "might have posed as a model for a youthful Germania," the embodiment of Germany.[9] Heidel claimed to have worked for some unspecified Allied intelligence service, and her vagueness about this aroused Payne Best's professional suspicions. Having been captured, she said, she had been subjected to dental torture at Ravensbrück, then forced to live in the camp brothel. Payne Best noted that she had acquired "much of the language and manners" of the bordello. She flirted incessantly and compulsively, believing herself irresistible. Margot Heberlein tried to befriend her "and shield her from trouble," without much success.[10] When the singer and kin prisoner Isa Vermehren got to know Heidel later, she thought her an "indefinable and most unpleasant young lady" who was generally believed to be either a spy for the Gestapo or, if she had worked for the Allies, a Nazi double agent.[11]

Once they were settled in, the famished prisoners asked their guards for food. The guards shrugged and summoned SS-Untersturmführer Bader.

Payne Best hadn't encountered Bader during the stay at Regensburg, and now they spoke for the first time. The Englishman's immediate impression, like Fey's, was that Bader was "a hard-bitten thug." He learned subsequently that the SS lieutenant had formerly been employed in a Gestapo execution unit that had traveled from one concentration camp to another, "like a pest officer engaged in the extermination of rats." The more perceptive Prominenten were acutely conscious that the choice of Bader as their chief jailer "did not presage anything particularly good."[12]

Bader told Payne Best that the village mayor had refused to supply food; it was a small place and already overwhelmed by 1,300 refugees. As far as the mayor was concerned, since the Prominenten were in the Gestapo's care, it was the Gestapo's responsibility to feed them. Bader had commandeered a motorcycle and was sending to Passau for supplies. In the meantime, the prisoners simply had to starve or make do with whatever they could scavenge.

The school housekeeper, taking pity on them, supplied a few boiled potatoes and some coffee, and Dr. Rascher had some scraps of bread he had brought with him from Buchenwald. In spite of everything, the general mood among the Prominenten was light, their spirits raised by simply being out and about in the world after long confinement, the sense of comradeship in adversity, and the knowledge of the Nazis' impending defeat. Payne Best described the mood as "nervous, excited," and the laughter "almost hysterical."

That evening, looking forward to their first night's comfortable rest in a very long time, the prisoners were in an excitable mood. In the dormitory the fun began as the screen was put up for the men and women to undress in isolation. Heidel managed to knock it down at the moment when Margot Heberlein's dress "had reached an abbreviated stage" and Heidel herself was virtually naked. At the same time, General Falkenhausen was discreetly covering his own nakedness with a kimono, unaware that it had a tear at the back from hem to collar, exposing the general's rear areas to everyone's view.

The night began blissfully, each person sinking into their soft, warm feather bed. But their rest was interrupted when the beds began collapsing violently. First to go was the bed of Dr. Horst Hoepner (brother of an executed July plotter). There was a noise like gunfire, and when the light was switched on he was found sitting in the wreckage of his bed as if in a pit. The next to go—with the same violent noise—was Payne Best's.

Investigation revealed that, due to a nationwide timber shortage, some of the wooden planks of the beds had been replaced with venetian blind slats.

Downstairs in the classrooms, the kin prisoners had to be content with makeshift straw-stuffed mattresses on the floor, but at least they were spared nocturnal collapses. For the women, however, there were more disturbing nighttime intrusions.

The arrangement whereby the men went out into the corridor while the women undressed had worked, up to a point. When the time came, the industrialist Fritz Thyssen, an elderly fellow with a large nose and hooded, watchful eyes like a lizard's, was still shaving. Pleading his age and infirmity, he begged to be allowed to stay in the room and finish his ablutions, solemnly swearing to keep his back turned. Taking pity on him, the women agreed. They were in the middle of undressing when Fey noticed that the old man's shaving mirror was angled so that he had a full view of the room. She and the other women, laughing but also affronted, called him a dirty old man, and he didn't deny it. "I've seen many women in the costume of Eve," he said. "You should allow an old man such small pleasures."[13] Even more distastefully, that and every following evening he would prowl among the women's beds, attempting in his old-fashioned way to flirt with them.

In this environment, which was becoming ever more like a school field trip, it was easy to forget the peril they were in. Three days after their arrival, the Prominenten were given a stark reminder.

Sunday 8 April: Schönberg

On this day, Pastor Dietrich Bonhoeffer held a small service for the Prominenten in the dormitory. Bespectacled with thinning blond hair and a round, pleasant face, Bonhoeffer was only thirty-nine but had a stature beyond his years as an important source of Christian and ecclesiastical resistance to the Nazi movement. Having made Bonhoeffer's acquaintance in the Buchenwald cellar and on the journey here, Payne Best considered the pastor "one of the very few men that I have ever met to whom his God was real and ever close to him."[14]

This Sunday morning was one that would live vividly in Payne Best's memory. Bonhoeffer spoke to his tiny congregation of eleven souls in a way that "reached the hearts of all, finding just the right words to express the spirit of our imprisonment and the thoughts and resolutions which it had brought."[15] Payne Best felt that "we were all lighthearted and gay; our adventures had knitted a strong bond of comradeship between all of us, and there was a complete absence of jealousy, impatience, or fear."[16]

In the classroom downstairs, Fey Pirzio-Biroli was sitting on her mattress when there came the sound of a car pulling up outside the building. She heard car doors slamming and the barking of orders. Then several pairs of heavy boots went thundering up the stairs.[17]

In the dormitory, Pastor Bonhoeffer was coming to the end of his concluding prayer when the door burst open and two men in civilian clothes entered. They had an unpleasant look about them, and it was instantly obvious that they were Gestapo. Quickly surveying the congregation, their eyes settled on the pastor. "Prisoner Bonhoeffer," said one of them. "Get ready to come with us."[18]

The phrase "come with us" from the Gestapo signified only two things: torture or death.

The gentle Bonhoeffer seemed to understand this. He didn't panic or even show fear; calmly he gave his farewells to his fellow prisoners. Last of all he took Payne Best's hand and drew him aside. "This is the end," he said. "But for me it is the beginning of life."[19] He gave Payne Best a letter, begging him to pass it on to his old friend the Reverend George Bell, bishop of Chichester, who had long been an ally of the German Confessing Church in its stand against Nazism.

The Gestapo officers pushed Bonhoeffer out of the room. Fey heard their steps coming back down the stairs, and she hurried to the window, where she saw the pastor bundled into the back of a large black car.

None of the Prominenten ever saw him again.

Eight
Death of the Damned

Saturday 7 April: Flossenbürg

A Grüne Minna prison van, engine whining in low gear, made its way up the winding road from the village of Floss, through the gap in the surrounding hills, and into the saucer-like depression in which sat Flossenbürg—the tiny, pleasant village with its ruined castle—and the dark blight of the concentration camp beyond.

Evening was drawing in, and the van's shuttered headlights cast a thin glow on the road ahead. Behind the wheel, SS-Obersturmführer Wilhelm Gogalla was road weary, having driven virtually nonstop from Berlin, a distance of over 250 miles. Beside him sat SS prosecutor Standartenführer Walter Huppenkothen. It had been a perilous journey, with Allied aircraft prowling the skies, routinely strafing roads and railways.

In Gogalla's briefcase was Heinrich Müller's order to transfer certain VIP prisoners to Dachau. In the back of the van were five prisoners, one of whom, Colonel Bogislaw von Bonin, was cited in the order. Other people named in the instructions included General Alexander von Falkenhausen, Lieutenant Vassily Kokorin, and Captain Sigismund Payne Best—all currently sojourning at Schönberg. Several others were being held here at Flossenbürg.

At least one of the men in the back of the Grüne Minna knew of Flossenbürg's gruesome reputation. Thirty-six-year-old Fabian von Schlabrendorff, a member of the resistance against Hitler, was one of those unfortunates. He was an unlikely subversive. An elegant lawyer and one-time lieutenant in the army reserves, he came from a wealthy and distinguished conservative clan. He'd been among those Germans who had worked to undermine Hitler's regime before the war began. After it started, Schlabrendorff's activities in the resistance became more urgent, as did those of his fellow conspirators: Abwehr chief Wilhelm Canaris and his deputy Hans Oster, as well as certain Wehrmacht generals, politicians, and diplomats, such as Carl Goerdeler, Ulrich von Hassell (father of Fey Pirzio-Biroli), and Dr. Josef Müller.

In 1943 Schlabrendorff had been part of a failed conspiracy to put a bomb on board Hitler's plane. He was eventually arrested in the wake of the July 1944 plot and taken to the Gestapo dungeons, where he was subjected to the most brutal torture.[1] First, there were finger screws that forced pinpoints into the fingers. When this method proved ineffective, Schlabrendorff was strapped face down on a frame. His head was covered with a blanket and cylinders studded with nails were placed around his bare legs. The tubes were then tightened, piercing his legs from ankle to thigh. Finally, Schlabrendorff was tied in a bent position and beaten with clubs, making him crash to the ground on his face.[2]

He was subsequently informed that, on the strength of a report by the Gestapo, the Reich court of honor had expelled him from the armed forces. He was charged with high treason. Schlabrendorff got his day in court, in which he gave detailed descriptions of the torture he had suffered. He argued that Frederick the Great had abolished torture in Prussia two hundred years before, and that it was unjust that he should have been subjected to it in modern times. Surprisingly, his pleas were given due consideration, and he was acquitted and released.

As far as the Gestapo was concerned, the verdict was unacceptable.[3] In the early hours of Saturday 7 April, Schlabrendorff had been roused from his cell and handed over to Wilhelm Gogalla for transport to Flossenbürg. He shared the long, exceedingly uncomfortable journey with Colonel Bogislaw von Bonin, two Slovakian secret agents, and a mysterious Swede named Carl Edquist, who at twenty-nine was the youngest member of the group. An enigmatic character, Edquist was a neurotic but dangerous "Walter Mitty" who variously claimed to have been an officer in the SS and a double agent.

Gogalla steered the unwieldy vehicle along the final approach to the camp. The main gate opened, and the Grüne Minna rumbled through. It came to a halt and the rear doors swung open. Bonin climbed down—an incongruous prisoner in his immaculately kept Wehrmacht uniform, including riding boots, wide-legged breeches, and sidearm tucked discreetly out of sight. He was followed by the bespectacled, slender figure of Schlabrendorff and the three other men. Ordering Bonin, Edquist, and the Slovakians back into the vehicle and shutting them in, the SS guards marched Schlabrendorff to the camp's cellblock, where he was locked in a cell.

As he sat and contemplated his situation, Schlabrendorff believed he could hear the voices of British prisoners. From the cheerful chatter and singing occasionally echoing along the corridor, they had clearly not been subjected to the same treatment as him. He would never find out who those English voices belonged to.[4]

Schlabrendorff didn't know it yet, but the long concrete building was also home to some of the main Abwehr conspirators and their circle, including Wilhelm Canaris and Hans Oster, as well as Ludwig Gehre, Franz Liedig, and Josef Müller—the three who had been removed from Payne Best's Grüne Minna outside Weiden. Dietrich Bonhoeffer should have been there, too, but the Gestapo agents had neglected to extract him from the vehicle along with Gehre, Liedig, and Müller. That error would soon be rectified: two Gestapo officers had been dispatched to hunt down the Buchenwald Prominenten and seize the missing pastor.

❧

Sunday 8 April: Berlin

In the ruined garden of the Reich Chancellery, two senior figures met and talked. SS-Obergruppenführer Ernst Kaltenbrunner and his subordinate SS-Gruppenführer Johann Rattenhuber each happened to be taking a breath of fresh air amid the bomb craters and debris surrounding the emergency exit from the Führer bunker. They hadn't intended to meet, yet their casual encounter was to have profound consequences for one of the prisoners being held in the Flossenbürg cellblock.

While Kaltenbrunner was head of the RSHA and oversaw a sprawling security apparatus, Rattenhuber, as chief of the Reich Security Service, was responsible for the Führer's personal security. Though he was one of Hitler's most trusted officials, Rattenhuber had testified in favor of Dr. Josef Müller, the anti-Nazi politician and lawyer, at his trial. That decision, he believed, had suddenly become relevant again.

As the two men took a few moments' respite from the clammy atmosphere of the catacomb below, their conversation turned to the impending close of the war. In Rattenhuber's opinion, there was no doubt about how it would end. All that senior Nazis such as themselves could do was make the best of a bad lot. Kaltenbrunner agreed, and Rattenhuber said, "If there is anyone who can help you it is Dr Müller with his connections with the Vatican—if he is still alive."[5]

Reflecting on this remark later, Kaltenbrunner recognized its wisdom. *If he is still alive*—there was the key. When he returned to his headquarters on Prinz Albrecht Strasse, Kaltenbrunner immediately dispatched an order to put Josef Müller's execution on hold.[6]

Sunday 8 April: Flossenbürg

A few hours after being snatched from his morning service at the school in Schönberg, Pastor Dietrich Bonhoeffer was being driven in a Gestapo car through the gates of Flossenbürg concentration camp. Having been delivered to the camp authorities, he was locked up in the cellblock. Accepting that his fate was sealed, there was nothing Bonhoeffer could do but pray for his immortal soul.

At about the same time, another person arrived at Flossenbürg—on a bicycle, a humble means of transport belying his position. SS-Sturmbannführer Dr. Otto Thorbeck was a judge based at Nuremberg. He had been ordered to travel to Flossenbürg to preside in the trials of Canaris and his alleged fellow conspirators. They were not to be accorded the full measure of due process—summary trials would be the order of the day. Walter Huppenkothen, who had arrived the previous day with Gogalla, would be the prosecuting counsel. As Thorbeck cycled into the camp, Huppenkothen met him, and the two shared a leisurely lunch in the officers' mess.[7]

At four o'clock that afternoon, the first of the trials began. Thorbeck, experienced in the procedures of Nazi justice, had a clear idea of how they would proceed. He was aware that with Huppenkothen in the prosecutor's chair conspiracy trials never took longer than three hours—usually far less. Defendants were not allowed lawyers and were kept in ignorance of the charges against them. The procedure was quite simple: Huppenkothen would shout the accusations at the defendant, who was permitted a brief period to respond. Inevitably the death sentence would be imposed.

This day's defendants were Wilhelm Canaris, Dietrich Bonhoeffer, Ludwig Gehre, Hans Oster, Karl Sack, and Theodor Strünck. One by one they were dragged before the court, one by one they were charged with treason, and one by one they were convicted and sentenced to death. The executions were to be carried out the following morning.

No record was kept of the order in which the men were tried, but Canaris was among the last, returning to the cellblock at around ten that night. He passed a final message to the prisoner in the neighboring cell, Captain Hans Mathiesen Lunding of the Danish general staff. During their incarceration, Canaris and Lunding had communicated in Morse code, tapping out messages on the pipes. When Canaris returned to his cell that night, he tapped out, "My time is up." The tapping continued: "Was not a traitor. Did my duty as a German. If you survive remember me to my wife."[8]

In the early hours of the next morning, Lunding was awoken by a commotion outside the cellblock: shouting, hammering, and the incessant barking of dogs. Putting his eye to a crack in the door, he saw the yard outside flooded with dazzling arc lights. It was around six o'clock when Lunding heard a harsh voice inside the building bark, "Get undressed!"

In the bath cubicle near the guardroom along the cellblock corridor, the condemned men were forced to strip. Dietrich Bonhoeffer, naked, knelt and prayed. From his cell, Lunding heard more shouted orders and saw the naked men filing out into the yard. He saw a pale body with gray hair go by and assumed it was Canaris. More orders rang out, but they were barely intelligible over the wild barking of guard dogs.

As they had been tried one by one, the condemned were marched to the gallows one by one. Each man climbed a low platform like a library step, the noose of thin cord was placed around his neck, and the platform was pulled away.[9]

It was a wretched end for six brave souls who had defied Hitler, and a chilling warning to any who were still on the Third Reich's list of enemies.

Monday 9 April: Flossenbürg

In the infirmary, Wings Day was gazing out of the window. From the building's raised position, he had almost a panorama of the camp and the surrounding landscape. The ruin of the castle on its steep hill stood out starkly. In recent years it had overlooked atrocities the likes of which its medieval builders—living in an age when horror was commonplace—could never have conceived.

It was now the fifth day since Day and the others had arrived, and they still didn't know what would be done with them. Five days in limbo:

observing the routine horrors outside their living quarters and mingling in the washroom with the half-dead skeletons in their striped uniforms.

A movement caught Day's eye, and he let out an exclamation of disgust. Jimmy James, Peter Churchill, and the others jumped up and hurried to the window. A group of prisoners—part of the Sonderkommando that was forced to do the grisly work of dealing with the dead—were passing by carrying three blanket-covered stretchers to the crematorium. There was fresh blood on the blankets and smears of flesh and brain.[10]

The Englishmen believed they knew who those corpses belonged to. Although that morning's summary murders had been conducted in absolute secrecy, like all overpopulated prison and concentration camps, Flossenbürg had an active rumor mill and information network. Day and his men were aware that at least three very well-known men had been executed: Canaris, Bonhoeffer, and Oster. Uncertain of the method used to kill them, they assumed that the bloodied blankets shrouded their bodies.[11]

With six inmates of the cellblock now dead, several cells had been freed up, and so later that afternoon Day's group was transferred from the hospital. As the prisoners were marched the short distance to the cellblock, the crematorium chimney was spewing a pall of foul-smelling smoke across the camp. The redoubtable old commando Mad Jack Churchill jabbed at the ground with his boot as they marched. "Solid rock," he muttered glumly. His fellow prisoners understood what he meant—there would be no possibility of tunneling out of here.[12]

They were assigned the executed men's cells, two men in each. Day found himself at the end of the block with Jack Churchill. The electrified perimeter fence ran past the cell window, and through it Day could see the stone quarry, in which slave-driven prisoners had labored and died every day for the past seven years.

As VIPs who weren't seen as a particular risk, Day and his men were allowed to wander freely about the cellblock corridor. Outside was the walled-in exercise yard, to which they had access for a short period each day. They quickly familiarized themselves with their surroundings, and when the guards weren't looking they knocked on the locked cell doors and introduced themselves to the inmates.[13] Most were severely depressed, knowing full well that they would be executed sooner or later. "Keep your chin up," Peter Churchill told them. "The Allies will be here in a matter of days."

"It had better be soon," most of them replied gloomily, describing the sights they had seen through the food slots of their doors. "Only yesterday they took out four men and a woman and hanged them in the shed outside," said one. "All were naked, all young and the girl was beautiful and walked like a queen."[14] The shed at the end of the exercise yard was where most cellblock executions took place; those who were not hanged were shot in the back of the neck—the SS's preferred method for efficiently dispatching their victims. Hanging was used only when they wished to make the victim suffer and tended to be reserved for the most despised enemies of the Nazi state.

Some of the inmates were cheered by the news of the Allied advance. "This means that things are going badly for these swine," said one man, who described how three days earlier an SS officer had opened the food slot of his neighbor's cell and shot him. It had taken several bullets to kill him. "I can still hear the echo of those shots and the screams of my poor companion."[15]

At each cell, Peter Churchill maintained a cheerful manner, addressing the inmates in their native language. At one, he opened the slot and inquired, "Are you one of the senior officers they're supposed to be hanging?"

"I think so," said the prisoner, rather taken aback. "My name is Josef Müller. I am the Chief Justice of Bavaria. Yesterday they took me to the hanging shed and I refused to be executed without a court-martial."

"It will soon be over," said Churchill. "The Americans are on their way."

"I hope the Americans come soon because I am sure they will shoot me," Müller said. "They took me twice to the execution shed and both times I said I refused to be executed without a proper trial." Müller was entirely unaware that his life had been saved not by his own legal standing but by the intervention of Ernst Kaltenbrunner.

"I don't believe you'll be killed," said Churchill. "Your friends are already dead. They've just been cremated behind the cellblock."[16]

Müller was stunned by the news. Later that day, he learned that the corpses of poor Bonhoeffer, Gehre, and the others had been stacked on a pyre and incinerated. He smelled the burning and saw specks of ash and what he took to be human skin in the air, some drifting in through the bars of his window. "I couldn't bear it. I was so grieved and shaken I wept."[17]

Talking to the other prisoners, Wings Day was able to build up a picture of the recent history of the cellblock—how inmates were regularly taken from their cells during lockup and marched to the washroom, where they were forced to strip naked before being taken to the execution shed. He learned about the methods of killing—how the victims' camp uniforms were removed to be reused by other prisoners, and how those who were shot were made to kneel in front of a blood-stained canvas stretcher, so that when the bullet shattered their spine and ended their life, they would fall onto the stretcher and thus be easier to carry away to the crematorium.[18]

He also learned the identities of some of the recent victims, including details of the hangings of the Canaris conspirators and about the thirteen SOE agents—two British, the others mostly French and Belgian—who had been murdered the week before. Jimmy James heard that they had gone to their deaths defiantly singing their respective national anthems.[19]

The SS officer in charge of the cellblock was making a grave error in allowing such freedom of movement to a tightly knit band of seasoned prison-camp inmates who had the cunning of hardened escapers, command of several languages, and in some cases special training in intelligence and subterfuge. Besides gathering information on their fellow prisoners, Day and his friends spoke to the women who were forced to work in the camp brothel. While some of the prisoners engaged the guards in conversation, Sydney Dowse—noted for his charm—sneaked into the washroom, which overlooked the garden where the women were allowed to relax. Chatting with them, he was able to learn a lot about the running of the camp.[20]

If they were here long enough, even if tunneling was impossible, the Great Escapers would almost certainly be able to achieve some kind of mischief. It was a dangerous game: there was no Inspector Mohr here to intervene, and the commandant was itching to have them shot.

❧

Even the cunning of the Great Escapers failed to unearth one of Flossenbürg's most closely guarded secrets.

As at Buchenwald and Sachsenhausen, the SS rigidly enforced a code of secrecy around the identities of the highest-profile prisoners. The people in the cellblock had no idea that there were several special inmates secreted in various parts of the Flossenbürg complex.

Among them was Dr. Hjalmar Schacht, formerly the president of the Reichsbank and Hitler's minister of economics, who had been active in the anti-Nazi resistance for many years. General Georg Thomas, who had been one of Germany's top armaments and ordnance experts, was another of Flossenbürg's secret Prominenten. Another was Colonel General Franz Halder, former chief of the army general staff and an anti-Hitler plotter. Halder's wife, Gertrud, voluntarily shared his imprisonment. These four had, until a few days ago, occupied cells in the block but were now being prepared for transfer.

The most famous resident of Flossenbürg in April 1945—his presence kept a strict secret by the SS—was Kurt von Schuschnigg, former chancellor of Austria.

As leader of Austria's fascist Fatherland Front party, Schuschnigg had been chancellor in 1938, when Hitler first began making aggressive moves to incorporate the land of his birth into the Nazi Reich. Schuschnigg resisted Hitler's threats for many months, acquiring an international standing as a champion of freedom despite his own government's repressive policies against socialists and trade unions. Just forty years old, dapper, bespectacled, sleek, and fair-haired, with a fashionable pencil moustache, Schuschnigg was very media friendly, and his portrait had graced the cover of *Time* magazine. But when Hitler threatened invasion in March 1938,

Schuschnigg was finally forced to capitulate. German troops marched triumphantly into Vienna, and Schuschnigg was arrested that very night by the SS.

Initially kept under house arrest, Schuschnigg had been transferred to solitary confinement in Vienna's Hotel Metropole, which had become the Gestapo's headquarters. Schuschnigg was ritually humiliated, made to clean toilets and perform other menial tasks. He was later imprisoned at a succession of places where his treatment improved. Like Janot Blum and Gertrud Halder, Schuschnigg's wife, Vera, had followed her husband into captivity. During this time, she gave birth to their daughter, Maria Dolores Elisabeth, known to everyone as Sissy.

In 1942 the Schuschniggs were transferred to Sachsenhausen, where they lived in one of the villas in Sonderlager B. Their life there was relatively comfortable. The villa was furnished with their own pictures and china and Schuschnigg's books. They were even allowed a wireless set on which they listened to BBC news. They enjoyed the same generous rations and healthcare that SS personnel were entitled to. Schuschnigg was paid a monthly allowance by the Reich, which he used to send his son to a private school in Munich. He had even managed to keep his revolver, though the SS guards were unlikely to have been pleased had they discovered it. Because she had joined her husband voluntarily, Vera von Schuschnigg was permitted to come and go from the camp as she pleased.[21]

Then, in February 1945, the Schuschniggs had been transferred to Flossenbürg. This camp had no special facilities for VIP prisoners; instead they were given rooms in an accommodation block. There was thus no easy way of keeping them insulated from the camp's daily barbarity. Commandant Max Koegel advised the couple when they first arrived that it was no place for a child. "When the wind blows you cannot escape the constant smell of corpses," he told them. On his advice, they had tried to send Sissy to stay with friends in the Austrian Tyrol, but the proposal had been turned down by the RSHA in Berlin. The Schuschniggs tried to shield Sissy from the horrific truth of Flossenbürg, but it was impossible. They knew when something awful was going to happen because the guards took particular care to shut them in at night. The family would sit and listen for the inevitable screams.[22]

Sissy celebrated her fourth birthday in this hell on earth. Once, when a kindly guard brought her a doll, the little girl asked if they could go back to Sachsenhausen. "It was nicer there," she said.[23]

The Prominenten at Flossenbürg were supposed to be kept in the dark about the other VIP prisoners in their midst, but it was impossible to keep their identities entirely secret. The Schuschniggs' former neighbors from Sachsenhausen, Prince Albrecht of Bavaria and his children, were now housed in a building almost opposite. And they learned through the grapevine that there were Danish, English, and French Prominenten in the camp. However, there was one prisoner whose identity the SS rigorously concealed. He lived a few doors away from the Schuschniggs in the same building, and every time he was taken out for exercise his guards erected a portable wooden screen around him.

These precautions only served to arouse the curiosity of the other prisoners, particularly the Schuschniggs. One day, a friendly guard told Schuschnigg that the mystery man wanted to talk to him urgently, and a clandestine meeting was arranged. The guard who oversaw the Schuschniggs' apartments was dosed with a sedative slipped into his coffee. While he was asleep, the secret prisoner was ushered into the Schuschniggs' presence. They recognized him immediately as Prince Philipp von Hessen, formerly a close confidant of Göring, Hitler, and Mussolini.[24]

The forty-three-year-old Prince Philipp, nephew of Kaiser Wilhelm II, son-in-law of the king of Italy, and great grandson of Queen Victoria, was head of one of the oldest, highest-ranking, and richest families in Germany, ruling over vast tracts of land. He had been an enthusiastic Nazi, one of the first and most prominent supporters of the National Socialist regime among the German aristocracy. The Hessens had lost little time in hoisting the swastika above the fairy-tale towers of their family seat at Schloss Friedrichshof when Hitler came to power in 1933. Prince Philipp joined the *Sturmabteilung*, the notorious Brownshirts, and became an intimate of Hitler's. The Führer was godfather to one of Philipp's sons, and Göring used the prince as an art dealer. Philipp became deeply complicit in at least two Nazi programs that came under the umbrella of war crimes, namely the plundering of art and the euthanasia of handicapped children. He also played a walk-on role in the Nazi subjugation of Austria and Czechoslovakia. Hitler's chief architect Albert Speer wrote of him, "He was one of the few followers whom Hitler had always treated with deference and respect."[25]

Prince Philipp's fall from grace began with the deterioration of the relationship between Italy and Germany. Hitler was suspicious of the Italian royal family and became convinced that Philipp was leaking sensitive information to them. In April 1943, he was put under house arrest, available for Hitler to use as a pawn in negotiations with the Italians. When Mussolini was removed from power in July and a new Italian government under Marshal Pietro Badoglio was formed, Prince Philipp's fate was sealed.[26] In early September, he was sent to Flossenbürg.

He was given two rooms with a washbasin and window; he was allowed to have three suitcases of clothes, and his precious toiletries were delivered to him. Like other Prominenten, he was fed generous SS rations rather than the meager scraps given to normal prisoners. His SS guards even constructed a wooden enclosure outside his cell where he could sit and take the sun. This facility also allowed him to witness the hangings that took place on the gallows a few paces away and to see the carts laden with corpses that passed by on the way to the crematorium every day.[27]

Deprived of all communication with his family, he was desperate to make contact with the outside world. On learning that the Schuschniggs were being held in Flossenbürg, he plotted to meet them. He particularly wanted to be reassured that his beloved wife Mafalda was safe. Unfortunately, the Schuschniggs were in exactly the same situation of ignorance and couldn't help. Perhaps that was just as well, for Mafalda's fate had not been as fortunate as Philipp's. Arrested by SD agents working with the Gestapo, she had been taken to Buchenwald, where she was placed in the isolation barracks in the Spruce Grove under the name Frau von Weber.[28] In August 1944 during the Allied air raid that hit the Spruce Grove, nearly four hundred prisoners were killed; Mafalda was one of them.[29]

Neither the Schuschniggs nor Prince Philipp were destined to suffer Flossenbürg for much longer. During the afternoon of Sunday 8 April, while the camp SS were beginning the trials of the Canaris conspirators in the cellblock, the Schuschniggs were ordered to get ready to leave.[30]

Carrying their belongings, and with a drowsy Sissy cradled in Vera's arms, husband and wife were led out onto the cold camp street. They were taken to SS-Obersturmführer Gogalla's Grüne Minna and ordered to get in.

They found the rear of the vehicle already occupied by several people. One wore the uniform of a Wehrmacht colonel: Bogislaw von Bonin, who had been confined in the vehicle since arriving at the camp the previous day, along with his companions since Berlin, the two Slovakian agents and Carl Edquist. Four others had been rounded up from Flossenbürg's cellblock: Colonel General Franz Halder and his wife Gertrud, General Georg Thomas, and Dr. Hjalmar Schacht. Schuschnigg knew Schacht's face well—he had been economics minister and chief banker in Germany when Schuschnigg had governed Austria. How the mighty had fallen, that they should meet in a squalid prison van in the precincts of this place of wretchedness and degradation.

They were kept waiting in the stuffy, claustrophobic space as hour followed hour, and the vehicle remained parked.[31] At last, in the early hours of the morning, the engine started and they began to move.

Gogalla drove the Grüne Minna out of the gates of Flossenbürg, through the village, and down the steep roads. He was destined for Schönberg, one hundred miles to the south. He had been briefed that some of the VIP prisoners he had been ordered to round up were currently accommodated there.

At 5:37 that afternoon, SS prosecutor Walter Huppenkothen sent his situation report from Flossenbürg to SS-Gruppenführer Richard Glücks, inspector of concentration camps.

The message, encrypted by the camp's Enigma machine, was picked up by the Bletchley Park code-breaking facility in England. It carried the priority code "Kr," urgent. Enigma messages were limited to no more than 250 letters, and the communiqué had to be split up into four parts. Decrypted and translated at Bletchley, it read:

> Secret.
>
> SS-Gruppenführer Glücks. Private. Please inform SS-Gruppenführer Müller as quickly as possible by phone, telex or through messenger of the following.
>
> 1. Mission carried out as ordered. Confirmation not necessary.
>
> 2. Gogalla is since 9 April at 4 am on the onward journey. Takes with him 3 Buchenwald prisoners.
>
> 3. 55 Buchenwald family and special prisoners together with further 12 cell prisoners are at Schönberg . . . with an escort commando from Weimar Gestapo under the command of SS-Untersturmführer Bader. Accommodation insufficient. Emergency hospital, former school. Further orders requested to Gestapo leader Regensburg.
>
> 4. Will be at PA 2 tomorrow morning. In case there are no further orders there intend immediate continuation of the journey to Berlin.
>
> 5. Radio messages or other orders for me have so far not arrived here.[32]

Despite the opacity of its allusions ("mission carried out as ordered"), the message gave the Allies the briefest of glimpses into the situation of the VIP prisoners in the hands of the SS. Whether it would motivate the Allies to do anything to help remained to be seen.

It was pitch black when the Grüne Minna left Flossenbürg, but the distinguished passengers in the back sensed a chink of light in the darkness.

They noticed that the attitude of their SS guards seemed to have altered; their strutting arrogance had gone. To Hjalmar Schacht's eye, their manner was uneasy, indicating that "the military situation must have deteriorated to an extraordinary degree. The foreign armies must have advanced considerably."[33]

Other groups of Prominenten had noticed this change in their guards too. In some SS men, it made them more malleable, less authoritarian, and more inclined to see themselves as fellow sufferers. But in others, it could turn them reckless and violent.

Nine

Murder at the Crematorium

Monday 9 April: Schönberg

Peering at his thin, craggy face in the mirror, Sigismund Payne Best stroked his razor along his bony jawline. Behind him, the other men who hadn't yet shaved were lined up waiting their turn at the dormitory basin. This orderly queue had become the men's morning ritual.

The previous day had been gloomy following the departure of Pastor Bonhoeffer. They didn't know what had happened to him, but instinct and experience told them that he was fated to die. That same evening, however, their SS captors had finally come through with food supplies, providing a veritable feast for supper—sausage accompanied by generous helpings of bread and potatoes. Such bounty after so many days of starvation couldn't help but lift their spirits. They grew cheerful and talkative once more, forgetting the morning's sadness for a while.[1]

With typical attention to detail, Payne Best meticulously shaved away the last of his bristles, cleaned up, and put away his razor, making way for the next man in line. At that moment, the door opened and SS-Untersturmführer Bader entered, bringing with him his perpetual aura of hostility and irritability. His cold eyes scanned the male prisoners. "Payne Best," he said, "von Falkenhausen, Kokorin. Get ready to leave at once."[2]

It was an exact replay of yesterday morning: the same clipped delivery, the same form of address, and precisely the same curt, chilling instruction.

The three men—the English secret agent, the German general, the Russian lieutenant—believed they could guess their fate.

Bader allowed them time to gather their belongings, the other prisoners helping. Margot Heberlein had been taking care of the prisoners' laundry and was distraught that some of it wasn't ready. The normally formidable woman apologized profusely to the three men. "I will keep it for you," she said, "and give it to you when we next meet." Payne Best could see in her eyes that she knew perfectly well that they were unlikely to ever meet again.[3] As Payne Best left the room, Erich Heberlein slipped a small pouch of tobacco into his hand, the last of his supply. Fey Pirzio-Biroli, watching through the classroom window as the three men were taken outside—Payne Best, tall and thin in his fedora and monocle, Falkenhausen in his scarlet-lined cloak with the *pour le mérite* at his throat, the youthful Vassily Kokorin in a motley assortment of uniform and civilian clothes—was also sure they were going to their deaths.[4]

Two of Bader's SS guards helped carry the men's luggage downstairs. Outside they found a Grüne Minna waiting for them. Standing beside it, Payne Best recognized his old jailer from the Berlin Gestapo HQ, SS-Obersturmführer Wilhelm Gogalla.

They had last met in Berlin a few months earlier, when Payne Best returned to the Gestapo dungeons prior to his transfer to Buchenwald. He had complained to Gogalla about his cold, lightless cell in the basement of the bomb-damaged building, and Gogalla had replied, "Don't blame us; it is your people who have done the damage. There are thousands of Berliners who have to live in cellars under the wreckage of their homes, who would be glad to be as well housed as you."[5]

Seeing his old prisoner again, Gogalla broke into a smile and greeted him warmly. "You know, Herr Best, I told you when you were with us in Berlin that you were to be moved to somewhere where you would be comfortable. Now I am taking you to Dachau. There will be no more solitary confinement, and you will stay there until your armies reach you."[6]

Payne Best scrutinized Gogalla's face. His experience of the man suggested that whatever crimes against humanity he had committed as a Gestapo jailer—not to mention his time in the Einsatzgruppen killing squads—Gogalla had at least been truthful to him. Or so he believed.

In a slightly more optimistic frame of mind, Payne Best climbed up into the Grüne Minna and immediately found himself looking into the bespectacled and rather harrowed face of the former chancellor of Austria. Beside him sat his wife—a handsome, Teutonic, blonde woman with strong, almost masculine features and sharply slanted eyes. She looked tired and drawn. On her lap was a little girl with blonde hair cut in a severe bob, wearing a rough greatcoat and boots, both far too large for her. There were several others in the van, including three senior German officers in uniform.

Climbing awkwardly over legs and piled luggage, Payne Best found himself a seat in the far corner. Falkenhausen sat opposite him. There wasn't a seat left for young Kokorin, who had to sit on a stack of luggage.

Kurt von Schuschnigg regarded the newcomers with interest. The thin fellow with the monocle introduced himself to the aloof and rather stiff Hjalmar Schacht, who was sitting next to him. "My name is Best," he said, speaking good German with an English accent.[7] "Schacht," replied the banker tersely. Schacht and Falkenhausen greeted each other warmly—clearly old friends. Then, taking it upon himself to play the host, Schacht introduced everyone: former chancellor Schuschnigg, generals Franz Halder and Georg Thomas, and Colonel Bogislaw von Bonin.

As soon as the introductions were done, Payne Best took out Heberlein's little packet of tobacco and began rolling a rather spartan cigarette. He lit it, took a drag, relishing the smoke in his lungs, then passed it to Falkenhausen, who took a drag and passed it on to Kokorin.

Watching the cigarette passed among the three men, Vera von Schuschnigg burst out laughing. She reached into her bag and took out a red leather cigarette case, flipping it open to reveal a plentiful supply. She passed it around, and each man gratefully took one.

It was an auspicious start to the journey. Payne Best would grow very fond of Vera von Schuschnigg in the days to come—the "Camp Angel" as she would become known. He could never adequately express his gratitude to "this beautiful, charming, and brave woman" who suffered hardships voluntarily with unfailing good humor.[8]

Under no circumstances could anyone look upon a journey to Dachau as a pleasant thing, but to the ten people in the Grüne Minna, who had endured months or even years of terror, imprisonment, and in some cases torture, and who expected every day to face execution, the knowledge that they were safe at least for the time being was enough to live on.

Payne Best conversed with Schacht, discussing politics and economics and the future of Europe once Nazism was defeated. They also compared notes on their experiences in the Gestapo HQ in Berlin and in the camps. Schacht struck Payne Best as emotionless—any enthusiasm he showed when talking about economics was "purely intellectual and cold"—but the more he got to know him, the more he came to believe that this was a shield against the world, and that inside Schacht was "shy and sensitive."[9]

As the vehicle rolled along, the prisoners who'd come from Flossenbürg began to give in to fatigue; they had been traveling in this uncomfortable way since four in the morning. A few, including Bonin, had been in the vehicle since leaving Berlin in the early hours of the previous morning. Little Sissy was at the end of her tether, tearful and irritable, demanding to know when they would reach their destination. "Is it a nice prison we're going to Mummy?" she asked over and over, begging to know why they couldn't go back to their nice house at Sachsenhausen. The poor child had never known anything but concentration camps. Eventually, having worn herself out with pestering, she fell asleep on her mother's lap. Rocked by the erratic motion of the van, Vera managed to doze.[10]

To Payne Best, the journey seemed quite brisk after the one from Buchenwald; this Grüne Minna was much faster than the wood-fueled contraption, without the requirement to stop continually for maintenance. Even so, the journey dragged on hour after hour. Despite his initial good cheer—which had come partly from a desire not to believe that they were going to their deaths—Payne Best didn't altogether trust Gogalla's word, and his optimism didn't survive the journey: "One could never quiet trust anything these people said."[11]

It was late evening when they finally reached their destination. It was, as Gogalla had promised, Dachau. He had at least been truthful about that.

Dachau was the oldest concentration camp in the Reich. Founded in 1933, less than two months after Hitler took power in Germany, it had been the very first of its kind. Located on the edge of the little medieval town of Dachau just outside Munich, Himmler's "model camp" had been established initially in the shell of an abandoned munitions factory left over from the previous war.[12] Its first prisoners had been political opponents of the Nazis—mostly democratic socialists.

Situated between the town and the farmlands beside the winding river Amper, during its early years the camp had grown rapidly and was now a sprawling SS complex of military barracks, housing, and other facilities. It had little of the grandiose design of Sachsenhausen or Buchenwald; the concentration camp itself was a simple rectangular enclosure on the east of the SS complex, surrounded by an electrified fence and watchtowers. It contained two long rows of barrack blocks on either side of a central street lined with tall fir trees (the SS liked to decorate their centers of murder with trees and immaculately kept grass borders). The roll-call square was at one end, along with the usual administrative and punishment blocks.[13]

Dachau had been infamous as a place of brutality and murder from the very start, its name known around the world and serving as a byword in Germany for state terror. By 1945, around thirty-nine thousand men and women had been murdered there.[14] Now, with the enemy front line growing closer by the day, morale among the SS was deteriorating. But the executions and torment went on apace.

At around nine o'clock in the evening of 9 April, SS-Untersturmführer Wilhelm Gogalla's prison van approached the Dachau gatehouse, a simple two-story white stucco building topped by a wooden watchtower. The archway was closed by a large steel gate with a smaller wicket set in the middle, in which the familiar slogan *Arbeit macht frei* was worked in wrought iron.

The gate swung open and the Grüne Minna drove through, then came to a halt. The prisoners inside heard voices, the clang of the gate closing, and then the rear doors opened. They disembarked, stiff, aching, and exhausted, and were herded inside the gatehouse building, where they found themselves in a large hallway that was unheated and freezing. There they were left, hungry and cold, with no furniture to sit on, for what seemed like hours.[15]

While the Prominenten waited, Gogalla was occupied with finishing the mission that had brought him from Berlin. He went off to report to the camp commandant, SS-Obersturmbannführer Eduard Weiter, and deliver the secret communiqué from Gestapo chief Heinrich Müller. Once Weiter had received the Müller Order—along with the accompanying VIP prisoners—Gogalla's mission would be complete.

He found the commandant in his office. Aged fifty-five, Weiter was an inscrutable little man, rather portly, who was ideally suited to the anonymous role he was required to play. A onetime book salesman, Weiter had been a pencil pusher in the army high command and the Bavarian police before joining the Nazi Party. He claimed to hold no particular political beliefs; he was a faceless bureaucrat. As commandant of Dachau, Weiter was rarely seen around the camp.

Taking Müller's letter from Gogalla, he read it through. The first part was simple enough. On Himmler's orders and with the "decision of the highest authority," the ten named prisoners were to be admitted immediately to Dachau and placed together in the cellblock. Some of them were referred to by code names. Kurt von Schuschnigg was "Oyster" and was to be registered at Dachau under that pseudonym; his wife, as a voluntary prisoner, was to be "allowed the same freedom as she has hitherto enjoyed." The order also directed that Halder, Thomas, Schacht, Schuschnigg, and Falkenhausen be well treated. Special mention was made of Bonin, who was "now in a kind of honourable detention. He is still a Colonel on the Active List and will presumably retain this status. I beg you therefore to treat him particularly well."[16]

The order's second key point was that the prisoner code-named "Eller"—Georg Elser, the man who had tried to assassinate Hitler in Munich in 1939—was to be put to death at the earliest opportunity, with his demise passed off as the result of Allied bombing.

This was vexing for the commandant; there had been an air raid on nearby Munich earlier that day.[17] Weiter thought it over. Room in the cellblock was at a premium, and he now had a van load of new prisoners to accommodate. He decided to expedite his orders without waiting for an alibi to appear overhead in the form of enemy planes. Within minutes of Gogalla's arrival, Weiter had set in motion Dachau's machinery of death.

The first indication that something was afoot came when the sergeant in charge of the crematorium, SS-Oberscharführer Theodor Bongartz, roused his staff in their quarters. Bongartz also alerted Emil Mahl, known as "the hangman of Dachau," and two "green triangle" prisoners (criminals identified by the colored badges on their uniforms) whose job it was to transport corpses to the crematorium. Bongartz warned them that they might be needed later that night.[18] Meanwhile, Commandant Weiter dispatched an SS corporal, Franz Xaver Lechner, to the cellblock to fetch Elser.

For over five years, Georg Elser had been kept in discreet seclusion. He'd spent most of his incarceration in Sachsenhausen's cellblock (the same building where Sigismund Payne Best had been held) before being moved to Dachau in early 1945. He was comparatively well treated, allotted three cells to accommodate himself, his special guards, and a workshop. Elser was a skilled craftsman (which had enabled him to conceal a massive bomb inside a pillar in the Munich beer hall where Hitler had been scheduled to speak), and occupied his time in captivity making furniture and zithers. Elser had been a very special prisoner, earmarked for a great postwar show trial in which the victorious Führer would expose the Allies' futile attempts to bring him down and parade the culprits before the world. The British agent Sigismund Payne Best and his colleague Richard Stevens would join Elser in the dock, arraigned as his accomplices. But with defeat now inevitable, that plan was moot, and Hitler would settle for revenge against those who had tried to kill him.

Lechner, accompanied by another SS corporal named Fritz, found Elser in his workshop next to his cell. "We've been ordered to bring you to the crematorium," said Lechner. "The chief of the block wants you to repair a door."[19]

Elser had often been called on to carry out repairs around the camp, and all camp inmates learned to obey orders instantly, without question, even when delivered at nearly midnight. Thinking little of it, he carefully swept up the shavings on his work bench and wiped clean his plane. Taking off his apron, he put on a jacket and followed the two SS men.

They left the cellblock and skirted around the deserted roll-call square. Passing through the iron wicket gate, they walked along the thoroughfare separating the concentration camp from the SS facility adjoining it. Nobody spoke; the SS guards were stone-faced, neither of them enjoying the deception they were practicing on Elser. Lechner, who had been a professional musician and admired Elser as a maker of instruments, felt nauseous and light-headed. Elser noticed nothing amiss.[20]

The crematorium stood at the end of the road in a pleasant, grassy glade of trees. There was a secluded patch of ground outside it where inmates were routinely killed, usually shot in the back of the neck. Inside the low brick building was a gas chamber. Several green-triangle prisoners emerging from the crematorium saw Lechner and Fritz and snapped to attention, caps in hand, to allow them to pass. They all recognized the zither maker. Inside the crematorium, SS-Oberscharführer Theodor Bongartz stood waiting. Returning Bongartz's "Heil Hitler!" salute and clicking their heels, Lechner and Fritz about-faced and left Elser to his fate.[21]

As they walked back to the camp, Lechner said to Fritz, "I'm sickened by this execution."

"Disgusting," said Fritz, staring at the ground.

"He was a good man . . ."

As they reached the gatehouse, they heard a shot ring out in the dark behind them.

Emil Mahl and his stretcher carriers hurried from the crematorium to find a corpse lying on the patch of ground at Bongartz's feet. They lifted Elser's body onto the stretcher and carried it into the crematorium.

Back in the cellblock, the remorseful SS-Unterscharführer Fritz returned to Elser's workshop. His eyes fell on the zither; he ran fingers across the strings, a shimmering chord filling the room. Feeling it was inappropriate now that the zither maker was gone, Fritz muted the strings. On an impulse, he picked up the instrument and went out.[22]

Returning to the crematorium, he found Elser's blood-stained body lying facedown on a trolley. The back of the skull was smashed in by Bongartz's bullet. Two other corpses similarly mutilated were waiting to be placed in the ovens. Without saying a word, Fritz placed the zither on Elser's body, then turned around and left. Shortly afterward the corpse was fed to the flames.

❖

While Georg Elser's fate was being secretly brought to its conclusion, the newly arrived Prominenten had been left waiting for several hours in the gatehouse. Finally, at around midnight, Commandant Weiter came in person to greet them.

With a show of hospitality, he introduced himself to each of them individually, even going so far as to try to kiss Vera von Schuschnigg's hand; she frostily withheld it. Weiter expressed his regret for the discomfort and delay they had been forced to suffer. "I am very sorry," he gushed. "Dachau is very crowded, and it has been most difficult to find suitable accommodations for such distinguished guests. I have done what I can, but even so

I realise that the quarters to which I shall now conduct you are far from being such as you expect and deserve, but really they are the best that I can provide. I hope you will forgive their shortcomings."[23]

The commandant summoned some prisoners, who gathered up the Prominenten's luggage and followed as Weiter led the way along the path by the roll-call square and past the kitchens—tracing in reverse the very route along which Georg Elser had been led just a little while earlier. Rounding the kitchen and administration building, they came to the cellblock.

Known informally as the Bunker and officially as the *Kommandaturarrest* (detention department), the cellblock was a long, narrow, single-story building spanning the width of the camp enclosure, discreetly shielded from the view of the rest of the camp by the building in front of it. It consisted of a central block containing the SS watch room, admissions office, and interrogation room; from this, two long wings extended out, lined on both sides with cells.

The Prominenten, most of whom had grown accustomed to squalid conditions in other camps, were pleasantly surprised by the Bunker. Unlike prison cells, the units were of varying sizes, and some were combined into sets of rooms; a few even had toilets, basins with running water, and parquet flooring. Were it not for the steel doors and the brutal decor, it might almost have been a rather down-at-heel hotel. What the Prominenten did not see—at least not yet—was the torment undergone by prisoners confined here. But they could guess.

Kurt and Vera von Schuschnigg, as the most distinguished prisoners, were given a cell with a second room adjoining it. Payne Best found himself in a cell with a communicating door to the one beside it, which was allocated to General Falkenhausen.

They had little inclination to appreciate their situation; all of them, especially those who had traveled the farthest, were half-dead with exhaustion and hunger. On top of his weariness, Payne Best was suffering badly from diarrhea (which he blamed on a bad sausage eaten at Schönberg the day before), so it was just as well that his cell was one of those with a toilet. In fact, he had dysentery and would take the better part of a week to recover.

Although the kitchens were closed, a prisoner orderly managed to rustle up some warm carrot soup, which Payne Best thought "not too bad."[24] Their hunger allayed a little, the Prominenten collapsed on their cots to sleep their first night in the notorious Dachau.

Ten

Traitors in Their Midst

Tuesday 10 April: Dachau

The next morning, Payne Best woke in his cell, feeling rested but still decidedly unwell. In daylight the cell seemed even pleasanter than it had at first sight. There was even a window. He turned the handle and opened it wide, letting in fresh air and the scent of spring flowers. There were bars on the outside, but nevertheless it was a proper window with a real view of a neat lawn and flowerbeds. There were even some garden chairs and a bench, where a pretty young woman was sitting chatting with an SS guard.[1]

Looking out at this quite pleasant sight—which would have been almost idyllic if it hadn't been for the SS insignia, the bars on the window, and the electrified fence a few yards away on the other side of the grass—Payne Best thought back on his tiny, dank underground cell at Buchenwald, with damp running down the walls and a little window near the ceiling offering a view of nothing, and felt thankful for small luxuries.

Breakfast consisted of black bread and jam. The Prominenten had hardly finished eating when a guard came along the corridor, ordering them to present themselves for inspection. They came out of their cells—which weren't locked—to find an SS lieutenant waiting for them in the passage.

He introduced himself as SS-Obersturmführer Edgar Stiller, the officer in charge of the Bunker. He advised the VIPs that they were free to move about the building, but within limits. "You may go out into the garden whenever you wish, and may associate with anyone you meet there. But be careful," he added severely. "You are absolutely forbidden to speak to any prisoners in this building who are not of your party. If you do so, the commandant will not fail to take appropriate action."[2]

The Prominenten would come to know SS-Obersturmführer Stiller well over the coming weeks, and their initial impressions of him were to be borne out by experience. He was dark haired, with deep-set, mournful eyes, a bony lantern jaw, and a heavy shaving shadow. By the standards of the SS-Totenkopfverbände (Death's Head Units), which were in charge of administering concentration camps, he was humane and conscientious. A former Austrian policeman, Stiller had served in Dachau since 1941, and one of his responsibilities was the social welfare of camp staff. With the arrival of the Prominenten, his principal function was now to act as liaison between the VIP prisoners and the SD, in whose custody they had been since leaving Buchenwald. Payne Best thought Stiller "a naturally kind-hearted and easy-going man but extremely weak and irresolute," who "had real sympathy for the prisoners in his charge and was ready to do what lay in his power to be of service to them."[3] Payne Best's assessment was undoubtedly colored by his personal experience and his prejudice in favor of Germans; other Prominenten were to have a quite different view of Edgar Stiller.

As he got his bearings, Payne Best realized why their cells were so pleasant: they were in a special section adjoining the central block of the Bunker, separated by a steel door from the rest of the long corridor, which was lined with the ordinary cells in which regular prisoners were confined, as Payne Best saw when going out through the side door to the garden.[4]

Kurt von Schuschnigg's view of Dachau was even more skewed by isolation; at first glance he thought it could have been "a well-kept country estate"; in his diary he described the "neat, solid-looking buildings, gravel paths bordered with flowers." Yet he realized that this section wasn't typical of the camp. Looking further, he saw "the watch-towers, the walls, the high-tension fences, the pompous inscriptions telling us that work makes a man free and that cleanliness is next to godliness . . . well, it is nothing new. In the eighth year of imprisonment one is no longer impressed."[5]

None of the Prominenten had yet seen Dachau's true nature. On the far side of the roll-call square, taking up most of the camp enclosure, were two long rows of wooden barrack buildings housing most of the concentration camp inmates. The wide, tree-lined thoroughfare between the rows was known colloquially as Liberty Street. Several of the barracks were used for purposes other than accommodation: a brothel, workshops, and the venue of the horrific medical experiments directed by Sigmund Rascher.[6] By April 1945 the barrack blocks were bursting at the seams with a population more than double what they had been designed to hold. More prisoners were arriving daily as the other concentration camps of the Reich were evacuated ahead of the Allied advance; the population was now approaching sixty-seven thousand men and women crammed into the barracks in the most appalling conditions. The prisoners, in their filthy, louse-ridden blue-and-white uniforms, lived cheek by jowl, starving, sick, and dying. There were no medicines and typhus was rampant, killing nearly fifteen thousand prisoners since January.[7]

In the secluded Bunker, the newly arrived Prominenten were shielded from all of this. Hjalmar Schacht, who had been part of the regime that had created this place of horror, "had the impression that this was indeed a camp for important prisoners and we saw that our building was entirely separate from the others."[8] Kurt von Schuschnigg, strolling in the garden, wasn't overly impressed by the "sad-looking patches of grass, a lettuce-bed, and in one corner the first timid narcissi." But looking back on his experiences since 1938, he was pleasantly conscious that nowhere—even at Sachsenhausen—had he and Vera and Sissy been so decently treated as they were here: "We are special prisoners," he wrote in his diary a few days after arriving.[9]

One of the first people Payne Best encountered after settling into his cell was a prisoner functionary named Paul Wauer, a Jehovah's Witness he had known in Sachsenhausen in 1940, when Wauer had been the camp barber.[10] Their reunion was emotional, and they had much to talk about. Wauer revealed that Georg Elser had been executed at the same time the Prominenten had arrived. Payne Best realized that this explained their long wait in the gatehouse. Wauer was upset; he had known Elser in Sachsenhausen, shaving him every day. The news of his death had passed through several sets of ears and lips before reaching Wauer and had picked up some false details: that Elser had been shot by a fellow prisoner who had also been killed immediately afterward, that the execution had been perpetrated in the garden outside the Bunker, and that the whole thing had been overseen by SS-Obersturmführer Stiller.[11]

Payne Best had no way of assessing the truth of this, but it sounded credible. He also heard (falsely) that Heinrich Müller's fatal order to Commandant Weiter had been delivered undercover to Stiller, who had relayed it to Weiter. Payne Best concluded that, despite his relatively lowly rank, Stiller was "possessed of more real authority than the commandant."[12] Given that he was now the man in charge of the Prominenten, this did not bode well, despite the soft nature Payne Best believed he detected.

Wauer's belief that Elser's murder had occurred in the garden was based on old Dachau practices. As pleasant as the new arrivals found the garden, Payne Best learned about its dark past from another prisoner functionary who served as the Bunker gardener, a former circus clown named Wilhelm Visintainer—"a most amusing little fellow."[13] He described how the garden had until recently been the venue for the execution of Bunker prisoners. There had also been a gallows at the far end, although most victims were shot. The executions had been discontinued and the gallows removed when some VIP prisoners housed in the Bunker objected. (This was Payne Best's first intimation that there were other important prisoners already there.) Visintainer told him that, in the process of turning the execution yard into a garden, over 150 pounds of pistol bullets had been dug up. The wall at the end of the garden was pitted with thousands of bullet holes. Visintainer added one last chilling detail: the condemned cells from which prisoners had been brought out to the wall or the gallows were the very ones now occupied by Payne Best and his companions.

During the first week, Payne Best's dysentery made him so weak that he could barely stay on his feet. And yet he enjoyed the time spent with his friends in the garden or the spare cell they used as a common room. He was nursed by Vera von Schuschnigg and Gisela Rohde, the wife of Dr. Lothar Rohde, a scientist suspected by the Gestapo of using his technical facilities for espionage. The Rohdes lived in the same section of the Bunker as the newly arrived Prominenten and were the only current occupants with whom the new VIPs were allowed to communicate. Vera and Gisela ("charming ladies") looked after Payne Best "with the utmost devotion." As voluntary prisoners, they were allowed to travel to Munich, bringing back food. Wauer obtained some charcoal tablets, which Payne Best "swallowed in vast quantities," and Lothar Rohde provided an electric warming cushion.[14]

Gradually Payne Best recovered, and on 14 April, the fifth day since arriving at Dachau, he was well enough to celebrate his sixtieth birthday with his friends. SS-Obersturmführer Stiller provided some bottles of wine, and a small but convivial party was held in the common room.[15]

❧

As they settled in, the Prominenten were kept entirely in the dark about the other VIPs in the Bunker. Although other prisoners were sometimes seen coming and going from their cells, they were forbidden to mix.

These mysterious Bunker VIPs included two Czech fascists, a film producer, an anti-Semitic journalist, several Yugoslavs and Italians (among them the grandson of revolutionary Giuseppe Garibaldi), and four clergymen, including the celebrated U-boat commander turned Lutheran pastor Martin Niemöller. There was a former Dutch defense minister, a one-time aide-de-camp to the Polish general in exile Władysław Sikorski, an aristocratic German family who had fallen foul of Hitler, and a distinguished French general of the Gaullist Armée Secrète.

There was one prisoner, however, who was of particular interest to Sigismund Payne Best. On his excursions into the garden, he would occasionally catch a glimpse of a familiar figure, far down the corridor, whom he recognized as Richard Stevens, fellow Secret Intelligence Service agent and Payne Best's former operational partner. They hadn't seen each other since the Gestapo HQ in Berlin after their capture at Venlo, more than five years earlier. Intrigued as he was, Payne Best obeyed the rules and made no attempt to communicate.[16]

That changed the day after Payne Best's birthday celebration, when a cask of beer was obtained and another small party was held in the common room. One of the guard corporals, SS-Unterscharführer Lechner, brought in one of his colleagues, and they played songs to the accompaniment of a lute. They told Payne Best how they had been professional musicians; both had been in the regular army and, after being wounded in action, had been drafted into the SS Death's Head Unit. Payne Best thought them "nice, well-behaved fellows." They treated the Prominenten very courteously and seemed to feel closer to them than to some of their fellow guards, some of whom Payne Best thought looked "pretty evil."[17] The Bunker was proving quite a cosmopolitan place—presidents and clowns, spies and lute players. Payne Best, despite his conversations with Wauer and Visintainer, had no idea that it had been Lechner who had marched Georg Elser to his death.

After the beer had been drunk and the party was breaking up, one of the guards whispered in Payne Best's ear, "Stay behind for a bit." The other revelers drifted away to their cells, until at last Payne Best was alone in the room. After a few minutes, Lechner reappeared; with him was Richard Stevens.

The two secret agents looked into each other's faces for the first time in five years. Stevens's eyes lit up instantly, and he rushed forward, flinging his arms around his old comrade. "I'm so glad to see you again. I'm so pleased, so glad," he repeated over and over. Standing back and looking Stevens up and down, Payne Best could see hardly any change in him; whereas Payne Best had aged and lost weight, his face becoming quite gaunt, Stevens looked fit and well.[18] Unlike Payne Best, who looked every inch the adventurous officer, Stevens looked more like a bureaucrat or a banker: stocky, with a large, fleshy nose and sagging jowls, a black, slug-like moustache, and slickly parted hair.

Once Stevens had finished saying how glad he was to be reunited with his old friend, they sat down to talk. Lechner furnished them with a bottle of wine and warned Stevens that he must not remain too long. SS-Obersturmführer Stiller and the Bunker command must not find out about this meeting.

The two men talked over their experiences since being captured. But despite Stevens's warmth, Payne Best harbored grave reservations about him. That very morning he had received a birthday gift from another prisoner being held secretly in the Bunker. Lieutenant Colonel John McGrath was a genial Irish officer who had served in the Royal Artillery. Having heard of Payne Best's arrival, McGrath had sent him, by way of a friendly guard, a basket of food supplied by the Red Cross. Inside, Payne Best had found a letter tucked among the packages.[19]

Although they'd never met, McGrath knew Payne Best by sight and reputation, having been a prisoner in the Sachsenhausen cellblock before his transfer to Dachau. He had tried to make contact with Payne Best there, but failed. In his letter McGrath told some of his story.

It was even stranger than Payne Best's. McGrath had been captured in June 1940 while serving with the British Expeditionary Force. Initially he'd been imprisoned in a POW camp in Bavaria. Keenly aware of the hostility toward the British felt by many Irishmen, the Germans had hatched a plan to exploit it. Fixing on McGrath as a potential recruit, they made him an offer. They wanted him to take over the running of a special camp for Irishmen that had been established at Friesack near Brandenburg. The idea was to persuade Irish prisoners of war to engage in espionage or sabotage missions against the British. McGrath rejected the proposal several times. Eventually he was persuaded by another British officer, Brigadier Claude Nicholson, who suggested that he could use his position to frustrate the Germans' objectives by encouraging the prisoners to go along with the German plans without actually putting them into practice.

In his letter, McGrath explained how he had followed Nicholson's advice, thwarting various German plans to turn the Irish POWs into saboteurs. Indeed, under his tenure a number of the men had escaped. Realizing what he was up to, the Germans had sent him to Sachsenhausen, where he was warned he would be shot unless he revealed the identities of those outside the camp who had helped with the escapes. He refused to name names, and eventually the Germans sent him to Dachau.[20]

McGrath's letter concluded with a stark warning: "In confidence I should tell you that I have absolutely no use for the man who was taken with you, Stevens. I think that he is the biggest Rotter that I have ever heard of." To Payne Best's wonder and dismay, the letter went on to describe an encounter with a young German officer who "was in the background of your case and knew everything," and who told McGrath all about Richard Stevens and the Gestapo:

> There can be no doubt that Stevens talked and talked and gave away everything he knew and of course as a result they continued to work on him. It appears that they failed to get anything worthwhile from you and more or less gave up as a bad job. When Stevens came here he was given almost complete freedom, out all day and go where he wished, even supplied with a bicycle, in fact he had everything a man could wish for. They again had him on a string as under expert direction of the Gestapo he was allowed to go to Munich and visit a girl there and stay out even to 2 a.m., and so this rotten story goes on from bad to worse and is too long to put on paper just now. I do not know if this man is mad or just a dangerous fool. Only a few weeks ago, here in the cells were some working girls charged with stealing. He wrote them letters, which were later recovered, and got into their cells and had intercourse with them. He got caught and it all came out. I have felt the situation very much. It is such a disgrace, and the man is such a liar that I do not speak to him more than I have to. I simply gave him Hell over these things, but I am afraid he has gone so low that he is beyond everything. I felt you should know the position and I know that you will respect my confidence.[21]

Payne Best was probably not wholly surprised by McGrath's words, although the details must have been a revelation to him. He had long feared his former SIS colleague did not have the mettle to stand up to interrogation, nor the moral fiber to endure years of solitary confinement.[22]

And now, here was that same man, greeting Payne Best as if they were beloved brothers and talking animatedly about their common hardships. It would never be known quite how much Stevens had betrayed his country. Whether Payne Best also complied with his Gestapo interrogators—and if so, how much—would likewise always remain obscure. But the doubt and suspicion added poison to the atmosphere surrounding the Prominenten and was a reminder of the deviousness of the Nazis.

The Dachau Bunker was home to a growing population of VIP prisoners. Shortly after the arrival of the Grüne Minna bringing Payne Best, Schuschnigg, and the others, a small group of distinguished Hungarians arrived, headed by former prime minister Miklós Kállay and including Miklós "Nicky" Horthy, son of Admiral Horthy, the regent. Hungary had formerly been a German ally, but in 1944 Kállay had foreseen Germany's defeat and made peace overtures to the Allies; Hitler responded by annexing Hungary and overthrowing its government. After imprisonment in their own country and a spell in Mauthausen concentration camp in Austria, Kállay and his entourage had been brought to Dachau.[23]

When Nicky Horthy arrived at Dachau he was still wearing the tweed jacket, gray flannels, and suede shoes in which he had been kidnapped by a team of Otto Skorzeny's SS commandos a year earlier. Yet he looked as immaculate as if he had just emerged from his tailor. Even his shirt looked clean and new. Like Payne Best, Kállay was impressed by the Bunker accommodations, with "pleasant cells with big windows, spring beds, an armchair, table, hot and cold water . . . and separate water closets. . . . The food was good, and we had hardly arrived when the guard asked me if I wanted light or dark beer from the canteen."[24] As he had no cash, Kállay went to see if he could borrow some from his neighbor in the next cell, who proved to be Molotov's nephew, Vassily Kokorin. The young Russian obliged.

Although only a stone's throw away from the rest of the camp, the life of the Dachau VIPs was a world away from that of the ordinary prisoners, who were starving, diseased, and dying in droves. But as time passed, some of the Prominenten began to grow restive. Payne Best fretted that, despite Gogalla's assurances that the VIPs would be kept at Dachau until liberation, the Gestapo did not intend to honor that promise. He wondered if there was some ulterior purpose in holding the Prominenten.[25]

Eleven

All in One Place

Sunday 15 April: Flossenbürg concentration camp

Wings Day listened to the rumbling and thudding of artillery in the distance. Each day it came closer. Yesterday he'd stood in the exercise yard with the young, clean-cut SS executioner, watching a long stream of American B-17 Flying Fortresses crossing the sky. "You see!" Day had said. "The Americans will be here very soon now."

The SS corporal had said nothing, simply gazing upward at the enemy planes tracing a mass of white condensation trails against the blue. "The Americans do not like the SS," Day said quietly to him, nodding toward the execution shed. "Perhaps if things go well for us, we might be able to say a word for you when the Americans come . . ."

Looking at Day, the SS man shrugged. "I don't like doing what I have to do, but duty is duty."[1]

That was yesterday. Day had felt sure that liberation was imminent. Today everything had changed. Early in the evening, the British Prominenten were ordered to get ready to move immediately. They trooped outside to find three vehicles standing in the yard: two three-ton canvas-topped trucks and a Grüne Minna. The British were joined by the Greeks and Russians who had traveled from Sachsenhausen with them, as well as fifteen other prisoners who had been held in the cellblock and other parts of the Flossenbürg camp, including Prince Philipp von Hessen and Dr. Josef Müller, whose face was bruised from a beating by the Gestapo.[2]

Dusk was gathering, and the hammering of artillery was now very close. Flossenbürg would be within the combat zone in less than twenty-four hours, and the SS personnel were beginning to evacuate the camp.[3]

Deciding that in the circumstances a show of resistance was in order, Wings Day confronted the evil-looking SS-Hauptsturmführer in charge of the cellblock's evacuation. "This is disgraceful," he said, indicating the vehicles. "I am a prisoner of the Luftwaffe, and have never been made to travel in such inferior transport. Go and tell the commandant that I object. We are not criminals."[4]

Although Day's RAF comrades—Jimmy James, Sydney Dowse, and Raymond van Wymeersch—spoke up in support, the German Prominenten were alarmed at this rash confrontation. But the SS officer seemed impressed by Day's confident authority and agreed to consult the commandant.

While this was going on, Jimmy James's attention had been drawn by one of the wretched inmates in striped uniforms who were watching the cellblock evacuation; the man was edging slowly toward the Prominenten. When the SS officer had gone, he approached the British and whispered, "I am Wadim Greenewich, British Embassy, Sofia." He explained hurriedly that he was scheduled to be shot to prevent his falling into Allied hands. Without pausing for reflection, Day, James, and Dowse pulled the man in among their group, put a Polish army greatcoat on him over his camp uniform, and covered his shaven head with an RAF cap.[5] Whatever happened, they were not about to leave a British citizen behind.

The SS-Hauptsturmführer returned with the commandant's reply: "If you do not get into the vehicles immediately, force will be used."

Oh well, it had been worth a try. The prisoners began embarking. Wanting to have a clear view of their location and route from the open rear, Day and James climbed up into one of the trucks—a wise choice, as the Grüne Minna proved to be the wood-burning type.

In convoy, the three vehicles drove out of Flossenbürg camp and down the country lanes toward Weiden. Over the next five days, thousands more prisoners would be brutally force marched along the same route.

When the US Army arrived on 23 April, eight days after the Prominenten's departure, only 1,500 prisoners—mostly those too sick to be moved—remained in the camp.[6]

The journey south was long, slow, and uncomfortable. During the night, one of the trucks broke down and its passengers had to be loaded into the other two vehicles. Twenty-one people were crammed into the Grüne Minna, which was designed to carry eight. SOE agent Peter Churchill was among them, sitting in stifling heat on the vehicle's fuel supply: sacks full of hard, triangular chunks of wood. It was too painful to sit for more than ten minutes at a time, so he alternated with standing in a half-crouch, trying not to bang his head on the roof as the van lurched and jolted.[7]

Conditions in the trucks were also bad; the prisoners were freezing cold and covered in thick dust. With several guards armed with machine pistols sitting among them, escape was impossible. Nevertheless, Jack Churchill, who was sitting next to Jimmy James, wrote a series of notes giving his name, his number, and the information that he was with a group of prisoners being moved from Sachsenhausen by the SS, tossing the slips of paper out of the back of the truck as it rolled along.[8]

When daylight came, the air attacks began. The road they were on ran through the immediate rear of the German army retreating from the west and was thick with military traffic. Intermittently, formations of Spitfires and Mustangs patrolled the road, strafing the columns of slow-moving vehicles. Each time the fighters roared over the trees, the SS guards leaped out of the truck and took cover in the roadside ditches. They remained true to their duty, never failing to cover the vehicles with their weapons even while they were taking shelter. The prisoners were left exposed to the machine-gun and cannon fire from the air.[9]

The violence being unloaded onto the ground from above grew more intense as the little convoy passed through Regensburg. They'd only just left the town when a massive air raid began. From the rear of the truck, Jimmy James watched as a vast stream of over four hundred Flying Fortresses, escorted by more than 250 Mustangs, bombed the marshaling yards and rail bridges around the town, the fighters peeling away to strafe nearby airfields. Jimmy noticed dozens of Luftwaffe planes standing on the airfields, useless for want of fuel.[10]

Late that night, more than twenty-four hours after setting out from Flossenbürg, the truck and the Grüne Minna drew to a halt before a "large and sinister-looking establishment."[11] Wiping the dust from his eyes, James saw a white building lit by floodlights, with high barbed-wire fences marching off to either side and guard towers in the distance.

He turned to the friendlier of the two guards. "What's the name of this concentration camp?" he asked in German.

The man answered cheerfully: "This is Dachau."[12]

There was a long wait while the Flossenbürg Hauptsturmführer arranged their reception. As they sat, Jimmy heard the sound of defiant singing coming from the Grüne Minna. In pain and half-dead with fatigue, but morally undaunted, some of the prisoners inside—including Peter Churchill, an Irish soldier of fortune named Thomas Cushing, and the Yugoslavian wing commander Hinko Dragic-Hauer—had struck up a rousing medley of old songs.

At last, the gates opened and the vehicles drove in. The prisoners disembarked under a heavy guard of SS troopers with snarling dogs and machine pistols. In the darkness, Peter Churchill spoke with Josef Müller; despite having escaped hanging in Flossenbürg, Müller was filled with foreboding. "I shall not be coming along with the rest of you," he said. "They are taking me to a special cell. I just wanted to tell you that if this is the end for me, as I fear, I shall think to the last of the lovely singing that you and your friends performed." Looking gray and tragic, he took Churchill's hand. "Goodbye, my friend."[13]

As they parted, Churchill was struck by the haunting realization that, even in this camp of tens of thousands of souls, "to die meant dying in solitude."[14]

The new arrivals were marched not to the Bunker but in the opposite direction. Skirting the roll-call square, they walked along the tree-lined central street. At the far northern end of the camp was a space containing several buildings: on the left were the vegetable gardens, and on the right was a rectangular barrack, smaller than the others and set apart with its own barbed wire fence around it.[15] It was to this building that the prisoners were marched.

Until very recently it had been Block 31, the camp brothel.[16] Conceived by Himmler as a means of encouraging industriousness, brothels had been introduced into several concentration camps in 1943. Hard-working prisoners could earn credits that could be used to buy tobacco and other luxuries, including visits to the brothel. (Jewish prisoners were excluded from this privilege.) The women who worked there were tricked into "volunteering" for it with promises of freedom afterward—promises that were typically not honored.

Dachau's brothel block had now suspended its business and been converted into accommodations for special prisoners. There were already prisoners living in it, mostly German Prominenten who had been moved from the Bunker.

As Wings Day and his men arranged their sleeping quarters in the small cubicle-like rooms, Day felt a hand on his arm. He turned to face an SS officer. He had a long, lantern-jawed face with deep-set eyes and a tight mouth. This was Day's first sight of SS-Obersturmführer Edgar Stiller. Unlike Payne Best, Day thought he looked cruel.

Stiller looked at Day's uniform. "You are the English Colonel, no doubt?"

"Yes."

Stiller had evidently heard about the confrontation with the SS officer during the embarkation at Flossenbürg. Tapping his holstered pistol to underline his words, Stiller said, "Here, an order is an order. There will be no complaints."[17]

Monday 16 April: Schönberg

Fey Pirzio-Biroli felt free for the first time in her long months of captivity. SS-Untersturmführer Bader, after a great deal of persuasion, had given permission for the Prominenten to go out individually for walks around the village.[18] It was exhilarating; the rolling green meadows around Schönberg were dusted with bright flowers, and birdsong filled the air. The villagers were kind to the prisoners, giving them gifts of food. Up here in the Bavarian forest, the war seemed very far away.

And yet Fey couldn't really enjoy it to the fullest; her mind was preoccupied by fears about her children. Corrado was only four and Roberto would have turned three in January, while Fey was in Buchenwald. Would she ever see them again, and, if so, would they remember her? She felt helpless, but tried not to be miserable in front of the other prisoners: "One had to carry on, I kept telling myself."[19]

During those days in Schönberg, one of Fey's close friends, Count Alexander von Stauffenberg, was suddenly hit by a devastating loss. Alex was a historian, the eldest brother of Colonel Claus von Stauffenberg, the July plotter. Although Alex had been entirely cut off from the conspiracy, he had been arrested by the Gestapo under *Sippenhaft*. His wife, Melitta—an extraordinarily gifted test pilot with the Luftwaffe—was arrested with him. She was doubly under suspicion, having previously been investigated for her Jewish ancestry. However, because of her vital importance to Germany's advanced aircraft development projects, Melitta had quickly been released and returned to duty.

She had never been able to accept Alex's continuing imprisonment and had tried to remain in contact with him. In early April, with the Allies closing in and fearing for his life in the hands of the SS, Melitta had set out in search of him.[20] Accompanied by her friend and fellow test pilot Hubertus von Papen-Koeningen, she took a Bücker Bü 181 Bestmann light aircraft and flew to Weimar, where she circled at low altitude over the Buchenwald camp. She'd done this a few times during Alex's captivity, and the layout was familiar. This time she was horrified to see that the Spruce Grove enclosure where she knew Alex had been held looked deserted, even though the rest of the camp was visibly still operational. Even from the air, Melitta could smell the charnel stink of the camp and see stacks of bodies. Fearing that Alex's might be among them, Melitta landed at Weimar and, with Papen-Koeningen's help, contacted the camp by phone and demanded information, claiming to represent Himmler. The VIP prisoners had been evacuated, they were told, and were believed to be at Straubing, near Regensburg.

Waiting until dusk to avoid American fighters, Melitta took off from Weimar, heading south. By 8 April, after several landings and brushes with death, she had discovered that Alex and the kin prisoners were at Schönberg. Rumor said that they were in the hands of a Gestapo execution squad.

Melitta took off early in the morning, heading for Schönberg, flying at treetop height to avoid being spotted by Allied fighters, following the line of the Danube and the railway. She flew over Straubing, and then, over the village of Strasskirchen, just thirty miles short of Schönberg, her luck ran out. She was spotted by the pilot of an American P-47 Thunderbolt fighter. Mistaking the Bestmann for a Focke-Wulf fighter, the American zoomed down to her level, slipped behind her, and fired two machine-gun bursts. A local worker on the ground saw the little light aircraft veer left and then spin into a field. Melitta von Stauffenberg was found alive but severely injured in the wreckage. Within hours she was dead.[21]

Fey was there when the news was brought to Alex four days later. Bader called him out of the classroom, and when he came back he was white with shock—"everything that remained of his past life had been destroyed." Fey "felt so sorry for this gentle and noble man."[22] Once Alex had recovered from the initial shock, he called Fey and his cousin-in-law Elisabeth von Stauffenberg to him, wanting to be with people who were close and understood his pain. Fey tried to comfort him, but he was beyond consoling; she realized that Alex needed her more than ever before. From that moment on, their already close friendship grew closer and more intimate.

During the next few days, the war began making its presence felt in Schönberg. With the front line growing ever nearer, refugees and retreating soldiers began pouring through the village. Conscious that the Prominenten were no longer secure, Bader announced that they must prepare to move.

Yet again the prisoners gathered their possessions and boarded the familiarly cramped and unclean buses while the Blums got into their car.

The SD guards resumed their stations on board, and the engines rumbled to life. With evening closing in, the small convoy rolled off through the wooded hills, this time heading west in the direction of Munich.

They drove through a night illuminated by air raids, the sky speckled with the flickering of flak bursts, and the landscape glowing with towns on fire and the flashes of bombs. In the dawn light the buses passed through Landshut, whose marshaling yards had been hit heavily the day before by elements of the same force that Jimmy James had witnessed bombing Regensburg.[23] The town was a blazing ruin; Fey and the others looked out of the bus windows at a scene from a nightmare. "Maimed horses and burning automobiles blocked the road; homeless people were wandering about aimlessly. Our buses passed slowly through, like a ghost train."[24]

Munich was the same. From a distance Fey thought the city looked intact, but she soon realized that the buildings were just hollow, burned-out shells, windowless and dead. Fey's family lived not far from here, and fearing for their safety she considered trying to escape in order to search for them, but after so long in captivity she lacked the courage to leave her friends.[25]

It was afternoon when the convoy pulled up in front of Dachau's gatehouse.[26] The prisoners were left in their vehicles while Bader went inside to report. Time dragged by—one hour became two and then three. Although it was only mid-April, the sun was blazing hot and the atmosphere inside the buses became unbearably oppressive.

Isa Vermehren was struck by the quiet submissiveness with which her companions awaited their fate. They sat in silence, which was occasionally broken by the voice of four-year-old Sybille-Maria, daughter of Ingeborg Schröder, who also had her ten-year-old son Harring with her. Ingeborg's misfortune was to be the daughter of a Wehrmacht officer who had joined a Russian-backed rebellion against the Führer on the eastern front. From time to time, Isa could hear Ingeborg's soft voice calming her little girl.[27]

As the hours dragged by, people became nervous and irritable, but they were forbidden to step outside to stretch their legs and get some fresh air. To their dismay and embarrassment, some of the prisoners had no choice but to relieve themselves where they sat.

At last Bader returned, accompanied by SS-Obersturmführer Stiller, and they were allowed to disembark. At first sight, Isa Vermehren thought Stiller looked "unpleasant in his whole demeanour."[28] The relationship between the two men would become a source of speculation among the Prominenten in the days to come. Stiller, as a first lieutenant, was superior in rank to Bader, a second lieutenant; nonetheless, Bader would sometimes behave as if he were in charge, taking advantage of Stiller's weaker personality. There might also have been a more sinister reason. While both were SS officers, Bader was also a Gestapo official. The Gestapo was feared by all, even by regular SS officers.

The prisoners were marched in through the gate. There followed another hour's wait in the hot sun on the edge of the roll-call square. Fey took little interest in her surroundings; depressed and dehydrated, she sank down and sat slumped on her suitcase.[29]

As they waited, Stiller suddenly reappeared and began aggressively ordering the German men to stand apart from the women and line up against the wall of the kitchen building. He told them that as Germans they were to be drafted into the Volkssturm, the improvised militia that had been scraped together some six months earlier for the last-ditch defense of German soil. Adolescent boys and old men had been swept into its ranks, armed with basic weapons, and sent to fight and die for the fatherland. Only men over sixty-five were exempt. Fey and the other women were appalled—these men were too starved and weak to fight anyone. As the men were marched away, their womenfolk cried. That they might die in some distant battle wasn't the only fear—for all they knew, this might be some cover for simply murdering the men here and now in the camp.

At midday, relief of sorts came to the women and old men in the form of coffee, and shortly afterward a meager lunch alleviated the depressed mood a little.[30] At about one o'clock Janot and Léon Blum were finally allowed out of the stifling heat of their car and escorted to the Bunker.

Later in the afternoon, a few others—including Markwart von Stauffenberg and Amélie and Fritz Thyssen—were also taken inside. As they were led through the narrow space separating the Bunker from the kitchen and maintenance block, they passed the little garden, where they were greeted by the sight of two eccentric figures standing somewhat forlornly with their baggage. One was a tall, thin man in civilian dress wearing a fedora and a monocle; the other was a German general in a scarlet-lined cloak.

Sigismund Payne Best and General Falkenhausen had been kicked out of their cells that morning. All the Bunker prisoners had been told to prepare to move to another location. The alert proved to be a false alarm, and the prisoners had returned to their cells—all except Payne Best and Falkenhausen, whose adjoining rooms had been set aside for Léon and Janot Blum.[31] Homeless and dejected, the two men waited in the garden with their luggage for hours.

Stiller promised to find them new accommodations. Payne Best, who was now on good terms with him, suggested that he abandon whatever orders he had regarding the Prominenten and simply let them stay until the Americans came. Stiller was visibly tempted. Payne Best could see that the SS officer was "pretty well scared out of his wits" by what the Allies might do to him, but even more scared of being caught disobeying orders. Without giving an answer or revealing what his orders were, Stiller went off, promising to find somewhere for them to stay that night.[32] It would be late evening before he arranged new cells for them in various parts of the Bunker.

Meanwhile, for Fey and the others left at the edge of the roll-call square, it was beginning to get dark when Commandant Weiter appeared and addressed them. There had been a misunderstanding, he said. The men would not be going to the Volkssturm after all; indeed, they would not even be separated from the women. With an unctuousness that struck Fey as absolutely insincere, Weiter expressed sympathy, saying that he understood how weary they must be after their journey. Fey didn't trust him an inch: "I had been too long around the SS to take any comfort."[33]

The women were finally reunited with the men and taken to their accommodations, which were in a pair of barracks in the SS complex outside the camp enclosure. Hungry and exhausted, they were given a good hot dinner, served by Russian prisoners from the camp. This unusual treatment immediately inspired rumors. Some people conjectured that the SS personnel were anticipating a surrender and hoping to show the Americans what good care they'd been taking of these important people. Other inmates went so far as to suggest that they would be exchanged for high-ranking German prisoners held by the Allies.

Whatever the precise nature of the SS's plans, one thing was certain. After years of being moved around, kept in separate places, shuffled and transferred, and then evacuated in a haphazard fashion, Hitler's VIP hostages were at last all together in one camp. Some 140 souls—spies, scholars, clerics, soldiers, wives, statesmen, celebrities, and innocent children from most of Europe's combatant nations—were close to discovering what their ultimate fate would be.

Twelve

The Exodus Begins

For the time being it seemed that the SS intended to keep the Prominenten in Dachau, although there were constant rumors that they would be moved.

In the Bunker, Dr. Lothar Rohde told Payne Best about three conflicting scenarios he'd heard through the grapevine, all of which seemed perfectly plausible. The first was that the Prominenten were going to Switzerland, where they would be handed over to the International Red Cross. The second was that their final destination was a château on Lake Constance, on the border between Germany and Switzerland. The third rumor was that they would be taken through Austria and then across the Brenner Pass into Italy.[1] These stories—none of which involved execution—were simultaneously reassuring and bewildering.

Meanwhile, there was no sign that they were going anywhere, and time was running out for the SS. The corridor through which the Prominenten had traveled from Sachsenhausen was tightening. Berlin was coming under siege, and the Russians were close to Dresden. Many of the places they had traveled through were already in Allied hands: Chemnitz, Bayreuth, and Plauen had fallen to the Americans; Buchenwald concentration camp had been liberated by elements of the 6th Armored Division of General George Patton's Third Army on 11 April. Now the US Seventh Army was pushing south while Patton advanced southeast, both armies rolling across Thuringia, Saxony, and Bavaria. Nuremberg and Stuttgart were under threat, and it would only be a matter of weeks—perhaps days—before the Americans reached Dachau and Munich.

The Germans' freedom of movement was also increasingly restricted in the east; the Red Army, having taken Hungary and Slovakia, was pushing across Austria. They had captured Vienna and would soon be moving toward the mountainous region in the western half of Austria. Meanwhile, the Allied forces in Italy were advancing northward toward the Italian Tyrol. The SS was running out of choices over what to do with its VIP prisoners.

As far as they were able, the Prominenten got on with life behind the wire. While rumors of an imminent move circulated, some prisoners tried to ensure that they remained in place until the Allies arrived. Payne Best's attempt to persuade Stiller to defy orders failed, but others took matters into their own hands. One of them was Wings Day.

The seasoned Great Escaper was always alert to possibilities. On the first night in Dachau's former brothel, there were two air raids nearby: one on an airfield to the north, and another on Munich itself.[2] Jimmy James was too tired to care and fell asleep while the building vibrated with the shock of the distant explosions. Day derived some pleasure from the SS's palpable fear of the approaching American forces.

Before he went to sleep, Day held a quiet conference with Mad Jack Churchill and SOE agent Peter Churchill. He told them he had no intention of being moved to yet another camp. If it looked like the SS was planning another transfer, Day would go into hiding and wait for liberation. He had found a trapdoor in the washroom ceiling, giving access to an attic space below the rafters; it was windowless and extremely constricted, but large enough for a man to hide.

Tuesday 17 April: Dachau

The morning after their arrival, Day and the others began getting to know the other prisoners in the brothel. They included John McGrath, the Irish colonel, who'd been moved from the Bunker. There were aristocrats, including Prince Friedrich Leopold of Prussia and Prince Xavier of Bourbon-Parma. There was also a contingent of clergy who had resisted Hitler, including the bishop of Clermont-Ferrand, Canon Johann Neuhäusler of Munich, and Martin Niemöller, the Lutheran pastor.

Jimmy James, shaking hands with Niemöller, was impressed by his "warmth and strength."[3] A short, slightly built individual in his midfifties, with a lively face framed by receding hair, wire-framed spectacles, and large ears, Niemöller had come to his vocation late in life: having served as a U-boat commander in the previous war, he had afterward become a Lutheran pastor. As a conservative, he had initially supported the rise of Hitler, only gradually becoming disillusioned by the growing persecution of Christians and Jews. Reflecting this, he would later write the short piece for which the world would remember him:

> First they came for the Socialists, and I did not speak out—Because I was not a Socialist.
>
> Then they came for the Trade Unionists, and I did not speak out—Because I was not a Trade Unionist.
>
> Then they came for the Jews, and I did not speak out—Because I was not a Jew.
>
> Then they came for me—And there was no one left to speak for me.

There were other Bunker prisoners who had been moved to the brothel to make space, including Payne Best's friends Margot and Erich Heberlein and Fabian von Schlabrendorff, the man who had tried to blow up Hitler's plane. Several Danes had also arrived from Flossenbürg with the British. Besides Captain Hans Mathiesen Lunding, who had been in the cell next to Admiral Canaris when he was executed at Flossenbürg, there were several members of the Danish resistance, as well as four members of the Danish section of SOE.

Of all the prisoners, the two who most impressed the British were General Sante Garibaldi and Colonel Davide Ferrero, two irrepressible Italian fighting men whose religion was inseparable from their fervent patriotism. Sante Garibaldi, sixty-nine years old, was the grandson of Giuseppe Garibaldi, the legendary revolutionary who had united Italy and was regarded as one of the founding fathers of the nation. Before the war, Garibaldi had been an entrepreneur and politician opposed to Mussolini. Based in France, he had tried in vain to form a Legion Garibaldi. Under Gestapo surveillance for some time, he'd been sent to Dachau in 1943.

Davide Ferrero was a tough Italian combat veteran. He was tall and muscular, with a florid complexion and dark curly hair. He'd been a highly decorated officer in the French Foreign Legion before joining the Italian partisans. Peter Churchill admired the way he sat among the hubbub of the crowded brothel calmly smoking his pipe, "for all the world like a champion golfer waiting patiently in a crowded club-house for his turn to tee off."[4]

Early that same morning, while the new arrivals were still getting their bearings, Canon Neuhäusler and the other clerics were told to pack their bags for an imminent move. After breakfast, Neuhäusler celebrated Holy Mass and the other clergy began preparations to depart.

Martin Niemöller, however, refused to go along with them. He was in a rebellious mood, adamant that he would not be taken to his own personal "Katyn"—referring to the murder of twenty-two thousand captured Polish officers by the Soviets in 1940. Niemöller had now been in captivity for eight years; one of his daughters had died, and a son had been killed. His nerves that Tuesday morning were taut as piano strings.[5] His wife, Else, was due to arrive in Dachau on Thursday, and she would be extremely worried if he had suddenly been deported. Niemöller insisted he would be staying put.

Others were getting edgy too. There were rumors that the Hungarian Prominenten had been taken away from the Bunker to be murdered en masse. The nerves of the prisoners in the former brothel weren't improved when they heard intermittent sounds of gunfire coming from somewhere in the camp. Many of them concluded that the long-feared mass slaughter of camp inmates was underway.

The Yugoslavian air force officer Hinko Dragic-Hauer was especially fearful. He had fallen foul of the Nazis after his country became allied to the Axis cause in 1941, having once earned high praise for discovering and denouncing a German spy. Dragic-Hauer tried to ingratiate himself by joining the Nazi Party and serving in an SS regiment, but the question mark hanging over him would not go away. On the capitulation of Italy in 1943, he reported sick with stomach ulcers. Believing that he merely wanted to sit out the war in safety pending an Allied victory, the Germans arrested him. Hearing the gunfire now, Dragic-Hauer begged Wings Day to lend him his RAF tunic. Day agreed, but was bemused that the Yugoslavian believed this tattered garment would somehow protect him.[6] Day told everyone not to worry; he was sure the shooting was only revolver practice. But it was far from reassuring when the crematorium chimney began belching smoke shortly afterward.

At five o'clock in the afternoon, SS-Obersturmführer Stiller came to the brothel and announced that the prisoners must prepare to move. Stiller was anticipating the arrival of the kin prisoners from Schönberg that day, and with the camp crowded to bursting, he was under pressure to keep his Prominenten accommodated. Space was running out, and as Payne Best had observed, Stiller was also deeply concerned about the arrival of the Allies. Arrangements had been made to begin moving the prisoners to another part of the Dachau sub-camp network, deeper inside German-held territory.

Day knew he had to act immediately on his plan to evade the move. Sydney Dowse elected to join him. Between them, with help from Peter Churchill and Mad Jack, Day and Dowse had collected a store of scraps of bread to see them through their period in hiding.[7] While the brothel was in upheaval, with prisoners collecting their belongings, Day and Dowse went to the washroom. The trapdoor was accessed by climbing over the shower cubicles. Safely inside, lying on the joists in the dark, the two airmen settled down to wait for liberation.

When Colonel Ferrero, the Italian partisan, heard about their plan, his unflappable calm vanished. He was even more horrified to learn that the two men were already in their hiding place. "For God's sake," he said to Peter Churchill, "tell them to come down. The dogs will sniff them out straight away. Even if they don't they'll die of the typhus epidemic that's already started and will get worse. Tell them we're going to Italy. I promise they'll be all right there. Once we're over the border the Partisans will liberate us!"[8]

It was now late afternoon, the kin prisoners from Schönberg had reached the camp gates, and the Prominenten who had been selected for departure—mostly consisting of the British, Italian, and Greek military prisoners—were already being assembled. Struck by Ferrero's warning, Peter Churchill realized the full folly of Day's plan. It wasn't dangerous only for him and Dowse but for all the Prominenten. Who could tell what Stiller might do in retribution if he discovered that two of his prisoners had disappeared?

Hurrying to the washroom, Churchill climbed up and lifted the trapdoor. Inside, huddled in the dark, he saw the pale faces of Wings Day and Sydney Dowse. He repeated Ferrero's message. They refused to move and resented having their plan interfered with by a foreign officer who had no business knowing about it. Churchill argued and cajoled, and eventually, with extreme reluctance, both men were persuaded to come out of hiding and rejoin their fellow prisoners.

For Day, the argument that tipped the balance was Ferrero's assurance that they were bound for Italy. He would be able to contact his partisan comrades, who would immediately come to their commander's rescue.

Assembled outside the brothel, the Prominenten were marched back the way they had come the night before, along the camp street to the roll-call square. The wide-open space was packed with tens of thousands of prisoners in striped uniforms, lined up in ranks for evening roll-call. As they marched past, the British POWs gave a thumbs-up to the starved skeletons, whose hollow eyes turned to watch them go by. Suddenly, from among them came a shout of "Raoul!".

Peter Churchill's heart skipped—"Raoul" had been his code name when he was running his SOE operation in France. Somewhere in that vast multitude was somebody who had known him—some French or British agent from that time. Churchill scanned the faces frantically, trying to see through the mass, willing the person to call out again. But the inmates, prompted by the shout, had begun murmuring among themselves, raising a buzz that drowned out everything else. Mad with frustration, Churchill could only imagine the despair of his friend lost in that mass of doomed humanity.[9]

At the gates, three buses were waiting—apparently the same ones that had just arrived with the kin prisoners from Schönberg. Here the brothel prisoners were joined by another group of thirty men, women, and children from the Bunker.[10]

Standing alongside the buses were their guards for the journey, led by the now familiar figure of SS-Obersturmführer Edgar Stiller, who would be overseeing their move in person. With him was a new face: an SS corporal called Ludwig Rottmaier. They were accompanied by twenty SD troopers from Bader's escort. Armed to the teeth, they encircled the prisoners and began herding them onto the buses, yelling at them the whole time.[11] It took only a few minutes to load the passengers and baggage. The buses started up. Soon, they had left the camp precincts behind and were on the main road to Munich.

Jimmy James reflected on the fact that today was his thirtieth birthday—his fifth in captivity; he wondered whether he would live to be thirty-one. He was sitting next to Fabian von Schlabrendorff, and they struck up a conversation. All the tight-lipped German would disclose about his past was that he had been implicated in the plot against Hitler. James discerned that "his aristocratic reserve concealed a story of suffering."[12]

As the convoy passed through Munich, the prisoners were deeply moved by the devastation they saw. There were no intact houses, just the jagged outlines of broken walls amid the piles of rubble. Trams with boarded-up windows were still running between the ruins, and people queued at the stops. To the prisoners, it was a marvel that anyone remained alive in this ghostly ruin. Peter Churchill wondered where these people lived and to what destination they could possibly be going in a tram.[13]

While daylight lasted, the sky was continually crossed by Allied aircraft, and twice the convoy stopped under the cover of trees. When night fell, the horizon was illuminated by fires and the flashes of explosions. The buses were heading more or less due south, and a rumor circulated that their destination was Innsbruck in Austria. With Ferrero's promises looking more and more remote and the Allied front receding over the northern horizon, Wings Day bitterly regretted having let himself be persuaded to leave his hiding place.[14] Moreover, Ferrero wasn't even here—along with Niemöller, the rest of the clergy, and several others, Ferrero and Garibaldi had been left behind in the brothel.[15]

By dawn the buses had left Bavaria behind and were in Austria; first light revealed a broad, deep mountain valley bathed in mist, with steep green hills cloaked in pine forest on either side rising to snow-capped peaks. This was the vale of the fast-flowing river Inn, in the northern fringe of the Austrian Alps—the region of the phantom Alpine Fortress, where the fanatics of the SS and the Nazi regime expected to make their last stand.

⁂

In Dachau, the remaining Prominenten continued to be shuffled around as the camp administration struggled to cope with overcrowding. Whenever any of them saw new faces, it was difficult to tell whether they were recent arrivals or had merely been secreted in some other part of the sprawling, teeming, stinking complex.

Payne Best was pleased to see the Heberleins when they were moved back to the Bunker from the brothel along with Hugh Falconer, Sigmund Rascher, and the enigmatic, suspicious young woman Heidel Nowakowski.

Of all of them, the one who felt most ill at ease was surely Dr. Rascher, returning as a prisoner to the scene of some of his most obscene crimes against humanity. Payne Best noted that Rascher and Heidel were taken to cells in the main corridor of the Bunker, and unlike most of the other Prominenten they were locked in. Payne Best also noticed that Vassily Kokorin, who had fallen in love with little Heidel, "almost went off his head with joy" when he saw her arrive in the Bunker.[16] However, she completely ignored Kokorin's greeting. It seemed she and Rascher had struck up a relationship.

Seeing the deep depression into which Kokorin now slid, Payne Best thought it just as well that the two lovers were isolated from the rest. He was concerned about Kokorin, who had attempted suicide more than once in Sachsenhausen. During the night, Payne Best went across the corridor to Kokorin's cell to check on him and found him sleeping like a baby. The next day Kokorin had completely regained his spirits and was full of good cheer. Whether he'd overcome his love for Heidel or convinced himself he could win her over was impossible to tell.

The childlike Kokorin had found a place in Payne Best's affections. The British agent thought him "a very loveable sort of boy, quite unspoilt and unaffected," who seemed to have the emotional life of a schoolboy. He even spoke like a child: "Stalin very beautiful man. He love my mother very much." In fact, it appeared that his mother was one of Stalin's many mistresses and the person the Soviet dictator liked and trusted most. "She go to him every day after supper," Kokorin once claimed. The family lived in a house on Red Square with eight rooms and two servants; if they wanted a car, it was provided for them by the Kremlin. Kokorin described Stalin as a "lazy" man who liked good food and drink and beautiful girls—a "beautiful character" who liked to laugh. Kokorin's uncle Molotov, on the other hand, was always busy. "He do all things that Stalin doesn't like and so people don't like him like Stalin."[17]

Payne Best asked him why on earth Stalin had allowed the son of a friend to face the danger of battle. Kokorin replied that Stalin trusted few people and relied upon the families of his most loyal associates to send on difficult missions. However, Kokorin had failed: "Stalin very cross that I am prisoner," he said, explaining that he had been expected to fight to the death. Like the other Russians, his future was far more uncertain than that of the other prisoners, for liberation meant danger. He would likely be shot or sent to a labor camp. He talked about escaping to America. Comparing Nazi and Soviet atrocities, Kokorin said, "German terror, ten, fifteen men. Russian terror ten–fifteen thousand men."[18]

The kin prisoners, in their barracks outside the wire, were not subjected to the same rotation and shuffling as those inside. Nonetheless, Fey Pirzio-Biroli's spirits were being eroded day by day. She and the redoubtable Maria von Hammerstein had acquired the rebellious habit of eluding the SS guards during air raids. Instead of going to the shelters, Maria and Fey would hide and remain behind in their barrack. But their nerve was wearing away. During one heavy raid, Maria went willingly to the shelter, leaving Fey alone in her bed. As the bombs thundered, Fey's courage failed. The noise and the solitude were unbearable, and she panicked, threw on her clothes, and ran to the shelter. A guard inside who saw the state she was in realized what had happened and smiled cruelly at her; she just stared at the floor, shaking uncontrollably.[19]

Her fears for her children escalated as the fighting drew closer. Germany was becoming an inferno of destroyed cities, torn-up countryside, and burning towns. Millions were being killed. In all this hell, what hope could there be for her little boys? They were so small, so innocent and fragile. Fey had to suppress the futile urge to escape from this place and go in search of them. She felt trapped and helpless and experienced an overwhelming rage against Hitler for what he had done to Germany and to her family.[20]

Occasionally there were vivid reminders of the nightmare beyond Dachau. One morning, Fey and a couple of her friends were in the yard outside their barrack when they saw one of their former female guards from Buchenwald pass by. Miss Rafforth had been a harsh jailer. Now the proud, imperious woman was reduced to a scarecrow, her uniform torn and disheveled, her face haggard. There was fear in her eyes as she described to Fey how Buchenwald had fallen to the Americans. There had been a fierce battle, but she had escaped and headed for Dachau. Some of her male colleagues had thrown away their SS uniforms and disguised themselves as civilians. Fey's stomach turned as Miss Rafforth described the cattle wagons into which the prisoners had been forced during the camp's evacuation, imagining the terror and starvation of all those innocent people. She couldn't understand the purpose of such sadism when Germany had so obviously lost everything.[21]

In the enclosed environment of the Bunker, though many gave in to depression, some of the Prominenten continued to live as if shut off from reality. This was especially so for those who were the most privileged, who had the most comfortable, spacious cells, furnished to approximate normal living conditions. Of these people, none was more comfortable than the two statesmen, Kurt von Schuschnigg and Léon Blum.

Schuschnigg's mind was occupied with great matters. Life in the Bunker was colorful but harmonious. "Nobody asks much about the past," he wrote in his diary. "Nobody is much concerned with the present; but everybody is worried about the future." It wasn't his immediate, personal future that exercised Schuschnigg's mind, but the future of the world. "We know that all will have been in vain unless people and peoples find each other again without resentment, without thoughts of triumph or revenge."[22]

He got on well with the German prisoners, spending "many happy hours" in their company. On Payne Best's birthday, 14 April, Schuschnigg and the British agent, along with the banker Hjalmar Schacht and General Falkenhausen, had sat out in the garden, enjoying the last light of the setting sun. Out of the blue, Schacht began reciting a passage from Homer's *Iliad* in fluent Greek, which all four men, cultured and traditionally educated, understood well. They joined in the recitation, moving on to Virgil and then Goethe, "until we stopped and found ourselves once more facing reality—Dachau and Adolf Hitler."[23]

Schuschnigg thought Hjalmar Schacht "one of the most intelligent Germans I have known," and wondered what guilt he must feel about having created the economic conditions that had enabled Hitler to thrive and make war on the world.[24]

Among all his companions, Schuschnigg was most intrigued and impressed by Léon Blum. They had met once before, in Paris in 1935, when Schuschnigg, as chancellor of Austria, had made a state visit. At that time, Blum had been a radical socialist who was yet to become prime minister. Had it been suggested then that Blum would next encounter the right-wing chancellor as a prisoner in Dachau (which was infamous even then)—let alone become friends—it would have seemed unbelievable. Nevertheless, Kurt and Vera von Schuschnigg spent many hours socializing with Léon and Janot Blum, and the conversation never failed to turn to politics, in which they found common interest, although very few shared opinions. "I must say that I am obliged to the Gestapo for having arranged this acquaintance with Léon Blum," Schuschnigg wrote, "in whom I have met a great European and—even more important to me—a fine and noble character. Perhaps that is the same thing."[25]

Of all things that Schuschnigg missed, he was most hungry for books—the one thing the Nazis had not allowed him to have during his captivity—and he was touched when Payne Best gave him his copy of the *Concise Oxford Dictionary*, the first book he had owned since losing his library years before. He and Payne Best had recognized each other when they first met—Schuschnigg's face was familiar from the many portraits that had appeared in the press in the 1930s, and the Nazi papers had printed many photographs of the captured British spies after the Bürgerbräukeller assassination attempt.[26]

On 18 April, the day after the group of Prominenten had been taken away in buses, SS-Obersturmführer Stiller and his subordinate Rottmaier returned to Dachau. They had left the prisoners at a location in Austria that, for the time being, was kept secret from the Prominenten still in Dachau. The two men had come back at Rottmaier's urging, neither of them wishing to get drafted into fighting for the Alpine Fortress.[27]

In the Bunker, there had been two notable new arrivals in the form of Josef Müller and Franz Liedig, who had been housed elsewhere in Dachau since arriving on the transport from Flossenbürg. Müller, who had no idea that he owed his life to his connections with the Vatican, was still mystified that he had not been executed with Canaris, Bonhoeffer, and the others. He and Liedig both looked worse for wear, having been starved and beaten—especially Müller. Payne Best felt so sorry for them, he gave them a half bottle of cod-liver oil that had been given to him by Mrs. Rohde, who worried about him being so underweight. They all had so little fat in their diet, the oil "tasted like nectar." Müller and Liedig polished it off in five minutes, declaring it the "best drink they had ever had."[28]

Conditions at Dachau were growing worse, with overcrowding becoming critical, disease spreading, medicines lacking, and food desperately scarce. When Canon Johann Neuhäusler and Chaplain Karl Kunkel walked the short distance from the former brothel block to the camp library in the administrative building, they were shocked at the number of corpses they encountered on the way. Most had died of typhus; name tags were attached to their toes.[29]

With everything falling apart at the seams, the SS personnel were increasingly on edge—scared of the approaching Allies, fearful of the mass of prisoners, and generally irritable and belligerent. On Thursday 19 April, the Prominenten received an unnerving reminder of the SS's lethal unpredictability. One of the clerical prisoners, Gabriel Piguet, former bishop of Clermont-Ferrand, was saying Mass in the former brothel block. Among the worshippers that morning was General Charles Delestraint, an elderly and courageous soldier and associate of Charles de Gaulle's exiled government. Delestraint had been instrumental in organizing the French Resistance around Lyon until his betrayal to the Gestapo. During the Mass, one of Stiller's senior underlings, SS-Sturmscharführer Fritz, barged in without warning, accompanied by another SS trooper.[30] Fritz ordered Delestraint to prepare to leave the camp within half an hour. He was to be taken by car with six other prisoners to a location near Innsbruck.

To most of the congregation, the intrusion was offensive, and some protested at the interruption of a religious service. As Delestraint was a devout Roman Catholic who had attended Mass every day, Fritz gave his permission for Piguet to give him Holy Communion, so that he could go with God's blessing.

Karl Kunkel helped Delestraint pack two suitcases. He was suspicious when SS-Sturmscharführer Fritz, taking one of the cases, said he would pick up the second in two hours' time, which contradicted his order that Delestraint would be leaving in thirty minutes. With no explanation, Fritz marched Delestraint away.

For the next few hours the worried clergymen made insistent inquiries to the camp authorities, but were met by silence. Later that day, Wilhelm Visintainer, the former clown who worked in the Bunker garden, brought them the shocking news. Delestraint had been taken to the crematorium and murdered.

Delestraint's death plunged the remaining Prominenten into even greater depths of insecurity and fear. They expected to be executed at any moment. Two days later, Payne Best thought his time had come when Stiller informed him that he was being transferred elsewhere. He wondered whether his illicit encounters with Richard Stevens were the cause. When he said a hurried farewell to his friends, they all looked as if they would never see him again.

Returning to his cell to pack, Payne Best met Martin Niemöller, who assured him he was only being transferred to the former brothel.[31] Relieved, Payne Best was just about to leave for his new quarters when the air-raid alarm sounded, forcing him to seek refuge in a shelter. The bombing force comprised 111 American Flying Fortresses unloading hundreds of tons of bombs onto the Munich marshaling yards; it was a haphazard, imprecise raid, bombing through heavy cloud with the aid of ground radar.[32] The intensity was such that the shelter rocked like a storm-tossed ship, and Payne Best was nearly blown off his feet. It was the second heavy raid in less than forty-eight hours.[33]

Afterward, he set off with an SS guard and a prisoner carrying his baggage. On the way to the former brothel they passed a number of barracks surrounded by barbed wire and guarded by sentries armed with machine pistols. His SS guard explained that the precautions were due to typhus.

There were a few emaciated figures lying within the enclosures but Payne Best couldn't see whether they were alive or dead.

In his new accommodations, Payne Best missed the freedom of the Bunker garden. The brothel's barbed wire enclosure had only just enough room to walk two abreast.[34] He was soon acquainted with the population of Prominenten, which consisted mostly of a mixture of Soviets, Scandinavians, and Italians. Among them were General Garibaldi and the charismatic Colonel Ferrero. The Soviets were very friendly and kind; the Scandinavians tended to keep to themselves but were friendly all the same. The Russians were excited at the news of Kokorin's presence in Dachau and told Payne Best how Stalin's son had died in Sachsenhausen.

Léon and Janot Blum had also been moved to the brothel building. Payne Best was impressed by their dignity and their exemplary kindness and bravery. They were friendly toward all their fellow prisoners and behaved as if their guards simply didn't exist. "Never for a moment did they show the slightest sign of fear or even that they were conscious of being prisoners."[35]

All the other Prominenten were acutely conscious of their situation, and many were becoming annoyed that nobody on the Allied side seemed to be concerned about them. Where was the rescue attempt? The soldiers among them were certain that if a battalion of paratroopers were to land in the vicinity of Dachau or Munich, they could quite easily fight their way to the camp. As far as Payne Best could tell, the camp guards were the only troops in the immediate vicinity, and they weren't fighting soldiers.[36]

Payne Best had often discussed with Dr. Lothar Rohde the possibility of establishing contact with American forces on the Danube. Rohde claimed to know Germans who would be willing to make an attempt to get through the lines to contact them. If Payne Best were to write a letter, that would convince the Americans of the German emissaries' authenticity. Payne Best was doubtful. Could Rohde be trusted? All Payne Best knew of him was what Rohde himself had told him. They reached a compromise, whereby Payne Best permitted the use of his name and provided an SIS code number by which he could be identified.[37]

Soon after his move to the brothel, Payne Best received a message from Rohde, saying that one of his men had "almost certainly" managed to reach the Americans. Rohde was now planning to go too. He was allowed to make trips outside the camp, accompanied by Stiller's corporal, Ludwig Rottmaier. Rohde had talked to Rottmaier, who was morbidly afraid of being drafted to the front lines, and he had agreed to come with him. Together, the two of them should be able to get through the lines easily enough. Rohde bided his time, waiting for an opportunity.

Meanwhile, a few days after Rohde's agent was believed to have reached the Americans, Payne Best noticed a great increase in the number of Allied aircraft flying over, apparently carrying out reconnaissance. All the Prominenten grew excited, believing that deliverance could not be far away.[38]

Thirteen
Into the Redoubt

Tuesday 24 April: Dachau

It was around 3:30 in the afternoon when Payne Best heard the roar of fighters flying over the camp. He was in the middle of packing his belongings. Earlier that day Stiller had visited and warned the Prominenten in the brothel that they were being evacuated from the camp. They should be ready to leave by five o'clock.

For several days, Allied firepower had been getting uncomfortably close to Dachau. Even the prisoners who had been praying for liberation began to fear that they might be engulfed in a bloodbath that would make no distinction between friend and foe, innocent and guilty. For the first time, they could make out the front line on the horizon, marked by the thunder and smoke of artillery barrages, creeping relentlessly toward them. It seemed that the camp itself—a major local hub for the SS, with its transport, technical, and barrack facilities—had become the focus of the fighting. The air-raid sirens hardly stopped anymore, night or day; likewise the noise of Allied planes was always there, whining in the distance or screaming overhead. Running out of strategic targets, the Americans were throwing most of their effort into tactical support of the front line.[1] The air and ground shook with the concussion of bombs. The tension among the civilian Prominenten grew unbearable, and the SS guards, caught like prey in the closing jaw of the Allied advance, aged visibly with each passing hour, scurrying aimlessly about the complex as if instinctively looking for a way out.[2]

Payne Best left off packing and went to the window, intrigued by the unusually loud and close roar of the fighters overhead. He counted six glittering shapes diving and swooping over the camp, firing their machine guns at some unseen target on the ground, beyond the buildings in the SS complex, raising flickers of flame and smoke. General Sante Garibaldi joined him at the window. He knew the layout of the camp well and reckoned they were attacking the transport park.

Eventually the fighters either ran out of ammunition or decided they had done their job. They banked away from the pillars of smoke and flame, climbing, dwindling to black specks against the sky, engines fading to a faint whine drowned out by the hubbub of the camp.

Shortly afterward, the prisoners in the brothel received word that the five buses slated to take them away had been destroyed in the raid. The move was postponed to the following day. The prisoners' hopes rose, and Payne Best began to believe that Rohde's agent really must have succeeded in getting his message through.[3] The destruction of the transports might be the prelude to a rescue bid.

The next afternoon—Wednesday 25 April—Payne Best, Garibaldi, and most of the other Prominenten stood near the window, looking and listening for the fighters to return. Replacement vehicles had been obtained, and they were scheduled to leave at five o'clock. If there was to be a rescue, either it would have to happen now, or the vehicles would have to be destroyed. Karl Kunkel wrote anxiously in his diary, "We continue to hope for low flying fighter planes . . . but the weather is unfavourable."[4] As the hours ticked away toward five, there was no sign.

At five o'clock a guard came in and ordered them to take their luggage outside, where two trucks were waiting. With heavy hearts, they began carrying their cases and boxes out of the building and loading them up. These were just the baggage trucks; buses were on the way for the prisoners. As they were hefting their luggage up onto the truck beds they heard the familiar hum of incoming low-flying fighters.

As one, the Prominenten, with Payne Best in the lead, raced back into the building and crowded at the window. This time an even larger force of fighters—perhaps as many as ten, Payne Best reckoned—dived down on the transport park, plastering it with machine-gun and cannon fire. They were big twin-engine planes, possibly RAF Mosquitos or American P-38 Lightnings.[5] Again flames shot up and pillars of black smoke rolled into the sky.

Once more, word came back that three of the five prepared buses had been destroyed and thirteen people had been killed or injured—whether SS troops or inmate laborers was unclear.[6] It seemed there would be no move today either. Payne Best and his friends danced in exultation. At this rate, the Americans would be here before the SS could muster the wherewithal to move their VIP hostages elsewhere.

Intelligent people who had been in Gestapo hands for so long should not have underestimated the determination and resourcefulness of the Germans, especially when backed into a corner. The celebrations were short-lived. Around six o'clock another order came through: prepare to move immediately. The joy in the brothel was doused as if by a bucket of water. Two buses had survived the air attack, and three trucks had been rushed in from Munich to replace the ones destroyed. Not only would the move still go ahead, for some it would involve a long journey into the unknown on hard benches in the cold, open backs of the trucks.[7] All they were told was that their destination was somewhere in the Tyrol, in the Alpine Fortress.

As they set out for the camp gates, following the baggage trucks on foot, the brothel Prominenten were joined by others who had only lately moved in with them. One was Pastor Martin Niemöller, who had been persuaded to accept that he wouldn't be allowed to wait any longer for his wife. Canon Johann Neuhäusler and Chaplain Karl Kunkel had walked over to the Bunker to see him and ask if he would come with them. (The kin and Bunker prisoners were being left behind for the time being.)

During their time together at Dachau, the clerics—most of them from very different Christian churches, some of which hadn't been at all friendly to each other—had formed a tight-knit ecumenical community, and they intended to stick together come what may. Niemöller agreed so long as they were sure that the terrifying SS-Untersturmführer Bader would be staying behind at Dachau.[8]

Niemöller wrote a postcard to his wife, Else:

> The deportation south is beginning. Our destination is unknown to us. Be brave for our children's sake. And may the faithful God protect you! In his Kingdom we will see each other again, if it is not meant to be on this earth. I'm calm inside, but around me reigns chaos. . . . Greetings to our friends, kiss the children, I remain thankful for everything. Lovingly and forever your Martin.[9]

Dozens of "old" Prominenten—VIPs who had been in Dachau before the others arrived—were joining the transport. Besides Garibaldi and Ferrero, they included the fifty-five-year-old claimant to the Spanish throne, Prince Xavier of Bourbon-Parma, who had served as an officer in the Belgian army until May 1940 and later joined the French Resistance, in which he'd served until his arrest in July 1944. Another was Prince Friedrich Leopold of Prussia, apparently arrested for listening to the BBC. There were also Joseph Joos, a leading Roman Catholic newspaper editor; the Austrian writer Konrad Praxmarer; and Richard Schmitz, a Christian Socialist who had briefly been vice chancellor of Austria and had served as mayor of Vienna until Germany annexed the country. All the long-term Dachau Prominenten wore regular striped camp uniforms, having only been assigned to the VIP category within the past two days. A few, including Schmitz and Joos, wore civilian suits that had been disfigured with ugly black-and-white strips sewn on.[10]

The march from the brothel commenced with Lieutenant General Aleksandros Papagos at its head. The Prominenten didn't even glance at the SS guards. Many of the ordinary inmates stood at attention as they went by, but most formed a heaving blue-and-white sea of humanity, unwashed and starved, congregating to see the VIPs depart.[11]

Payne Best thought Prince Xavier and Richard Schmitz looked "thin and worn," but Prince Friedrich Leopold, who had been working in the camp canteen for a long time (a job that provided many opportunities for acquiring extra rations) was in very good shape. The prince had an indomitable spirit and was something of a celebrity within the camp, affectionately nicknamed "Pat" by the prisoners. As the Prominenten passed the crowds, prisoners surged forward at the sight of Pat, all trying to shake his hand in farewell.[12]

Karl Kunkel held his purple priest's gloves in his hands as he walked, giving his blessing to the many who stepped out of the crowd shouting, "Monsignor, Monsignor!" Others shouted "Schmitz!" to the former mayor of Vienna. Comrades lined the route, friends shook hands, and priests embraced Bishop Piguet. Joseph Joos noticed how the SS did nothing to prevent this impulsive demonstration of shared humanity, as if even they realized that condemned men are entitled to a last taste of human kindness. Everyone presumed that these prisoners were being taken to their doom.[13]

Schmitz walked with a heavy heart. As a leading member of the Austrian Christian Social Party, he was vehemently anti-Nazi and one of the few people who had proposed armed resistance to the German takeover of Austria.[14] Having been in Dachau for seven years, he now feared the worst. He'd been told that his name was on a "special list" of prisoners compiled by Himmler himself. Two days ago he'd been told he was to be "deported," a term that invariably meant death.[15]

Joining this ragtag group of civilians, soldiers, clerics, and princes were the two prisoner functionaries from the Bunker: former clown Wilhelm Visintainer and Paul Wauer, the barber, who had somehow managed to pull strings in order to take their chances with the Prominenten.[16] Wherever they might be going, and whatever risks they might face, to Visintainer and Wauer it seemed preferable to waiting here in this seething, teeming hive of disease and starvation. Reaching the roll-call square, it was easy to understand their reasoning. The entire front of the maintenance and kitchen block was piled with corpses. The stink was stomach turning.

The Prominenten were not the only ones leaving. Thousands more prisoners, in a state of total exhaustion, were being herded out of the camp on foot, beaten and whipped by the SS as they walked. On Himmler's orders, the general evacuation of Dachau was beginning; these poor souls—many of whom had already been marched hundreds of miles from other camps—were beginning the final death march.

Just three vehicles were waiting at the gatehouse for the Prominenten: the two surviving buses, which looked quite comfortable, and a plain military truck, which did not. Payne Best, who was walking with Prince Pat, deliberately made for the nearest bus. He felt far too weak and ill to withstand a journey by canvas-topped truck. But as he was about to board, SS-Obersturmführer Stiller barred his way.[17]

"You are to travel in the lorry," he said.

Payne Best protested, pointing out his age and how ill he had been. It was undeniable that despite his smart appearance he was extremely thin and frail, his cheeks hollowed out and his eyes sunken. But Stiller was adamant; Payne Best must go on the truck. With extreme reluctance, he gave way. He discovered later that Richard Stevens was already on the bus, and Stiller was sticking doggedly to his orders to keep the two spies separate, unaware that they had already met and talked several times.

Climbing up into the truck with some difficulty, Payne Best found himself a place on the bench close to the rear, where he could at least see out. Josef Müller and Franz Liedig took seats beside him—almost like a replay in reverse of the moment when they and Ludwig Gehre had been taken from the Grüne Minna by the Gestapo outside Weiden. Both had survived the fate intended for them then. Perhaps that was a good omen. Several senior Russian officers were on board, with whom Payne Best had been on very friendly terms in the brothel—they'd taken him into their circle, inviting him to their rooms to smoke and drink and talk at length about politics and the war. They were all anti-Stalinists who had given themselves up to the Germans and could anticipate certain execution if repatriated to the Soviet Union. When Vassily Kokorin climbed aboard, Payne Best introduced him to them. They had heard of his presence in Dachau and had been intrigued to meet such a highly connected figure, lowly as he was in military rank and despite his closeness to Stalin. To Payne Best's disappointment, as soon as he was among fellow Russians Kokorin "went Slav," disappearing into his native culture so thoroughly that Payne Best "scarcely saw anything more of him."[18]

It was about eight o'clock on a bright, pleasant spring evening when the convoy, with the truck leading the way, followed by the buses, and with the two baggage trucks bringing up the rear, finally got moving.[19] As their bus drove away from the camp complex, Pastor Niemöller said to Canon Neuhäusler—purposely speaking loudly enough for Stiller to hear—"Johannes, now we don't leave Dachau via the chimney after all."[20]

Others did not have this consolation. The kin prisoners and some of the Bunker prisoners—including the Schuschniggs—had been left behind in the increasingly distressing, disintegrating environment.

The two churchmen were less exultant when they witnessed the utter devastation of the once stately city of Munich. It was in an even worse state than it had been a week earlier when the Great Escapers had passed this way. Already razed, the central districts and the areas near the marshaling yards had been hit again and again, bombs pouring into the devastation, obliterating whatever remained standing and churning up the rubble from previous assaults. The little convoy passed through the remains of streets where the piles of stone and brick were still smoldering, strewn with broken timber and dusted with glass shards and the soiled detritus of human life. Smoke hung in the air.

As a young man before World War I, Sigismund Payne Best had lived in this city. A talented violinist, he had abandoned a career in business to pursue music and had come to the University of Munich to study musicology. He knew the city center like an old friend, knew every street and alley and building. Now all he could see was a bank of rubble, with the gutted shells of buildings beyond. The truck bucked and swayed as the driver picked his way through the wreckage, lurching over scattered masonry and filled-in bomb craters.[21]

Leaving the city behind, Payne Best looked to see which direction they would take. Would they swing southeast in the direction of Hitler's lair at Berchtesgaden, where there was rumored to be a last stand by the SS and Hitler Youth? Would they turn west toward Lake Constance on the Swiss border? A river ran parallel with the road, which Payne Best identified as the Isar.[22] That must mean they were on the road to Wolfratshausen—south. And south could only mean Innsbruck and the Alps.

In fact, Payne Best was mistaken. The river was not the Isar, but more likely the Leitzach. They were heading southeast toward Rosenheim.[23] It was late evening by the time they reached the town, which happened to be the birthplace of Hermann Göring. Standing on the west bank of the river Inn, Rosenheim was a sizeable place, a pleasant Bavarian settlement of gabled townhouses and churches topped by weathered onion cupolas. But the Prominenten saw nothing of it in the pitch dark. As the convoy drove through, the air-raid siren began its rising moan. The driver of the leading truck was alarmed by the sound and took a wrong turn, coming up short at one of the bridges over the Inn, which had been blown away, leaving behind a stump of broken masonry.[24]

The large vehicles struggled to turn around in the narrow street. The passengers in the truck were ordered to get out—apparently the guards had a notion that the Prominenten would help direct the maneuver. All the SS drivers appeared to be completely incompetent, struggling to turn their vehicles, and the howl of the sirens was punctuated by furious curses, the guards yelling at the drivers to hurry up and get them the hell out of there before the enemy planes arrived and they were all killed.

Payne Best noticed a patch of open ground next to the road with a wood beyond. In the dark, with the guards so distracted, it would be easy to slip quietly among the trees and escape. He resisted the urge. He had to consider the retribution Stiller and Bader might exact on the other prisoners if any of them escaped.[25]

Eventually the vehicles were turned around and the Prominenten resumed their places. The drivers retraced their route and found the right road leading out of town. They had scarcely cleared the outskirts when the first bombs landed, filling the night with light and thunder.

They drove on through darkness, heading south toward Austria. The road wound and climbed into the foothills of the Alps, following the river Inn. Payne Best's bony, undernourished backside suffered badly on the hard bench, especially as the driver clumsily negotiated the twists and turns in the road, at one point hitting a roadside wall so hard Payne Best thought the vehicle would tip over. Daylight was likely to bring a worse ordeal; the Americans and British were subjecting all routes into the Alps to sustained attacks, trying to stem the flow of German troops and matériel into the mythic Alpine Fortress.[26]

Traveling far more comfortably in one of the buses, Karl Kunkel watched the scenery go by and feared what fate lay in wait beyond the mountains. "We make a stop in the alpine upland," he wrote in his diary. "The giant moonlit mountains are beautiful, where the glaciers are shimmering. They look so peaceful. Will they be the death of us? We all know it: we are being deported as hostages. Maybe the war will last a long time for us still."[27]

Canon Neuhäusler knew this region well. Shortly after midnight, they passed through the small villages of Niederndorf, Oberaudorf, and Mühlbach, which had once been part of his parish. "I bless the living and the dead of my former place of work," he wrote in his diary.[28]

Richard Schmitz hadn't seen his homeland for many years. He was deeply moved to be back, and his heart leaped to see the dawn light revealing the familiar landscape of the Austrian Tyrol.[29] Soon enough the skyline of Innsbruck appeared—beautiful against the backdrop of the broad, steep Alpine vale in which the city lay, in a wide bend of the river Inn, hemmed in by thickly forested slopes.

The convoy crossed the river and rumbled through the sleeping early morning streets. Everyone aboard, somehow convinced that this was their destination, looked out to see where they would halt. To their surprise, they passed right through the southern outskirts into an expanse of flat countryside. Payne Best wondered whether they were bound for the Brenner Pass and Italy, as Ferrero had claimed. A short distance beyond the city, the convoy turned off the main road onto a track and came to a halt before a gate in a high wire fence, guarded by SS sentries. A painted sign proclaimed this to be Reichenau Work Education Camp. The sentries opened the gates and the convoy rolled in. The Prominenten had reached their mysterious destination.

Fourteen
SS-Sonderlager Innsbruck

Thursday 26 April: Reichenau, Austria

The truck's tailgate crashed down. Aching and weary, Payne Best lowered himself to the ground. Around him, the others disembarked from the vehicles, looking in bewilderment and dismay at their new surroundings. It was a camp, but not like any they had seen before. There were no watchtowers, and it was small, with only a dozen or so buildings. And it seemed eerily deserted.

Situated in a hamlet just outside Innsbruck, nestling against the south bank of the Inn, Reichenau Work Education Camp had been founded by the Gestapo as a holding center and forced-labor camp for the "workshy" of Austria. It had lately been cleared out and reallocated to the vast system of outlying sub camps administrated from Dachau. Now renamed SS-Sonderlager Innsbruck, it was focused largely on one purpose: to hold the VIP prisoners evacuated from Dachau.[1] The beautiful background of the Alps to the north and south made a strange and striking contrast with the bleak camp, like a vast fortress wall enclosing it. Payne Best might have been heartened to know that on this very day back in Dachau, Lothar Rohde would finally succeed in making his escape with the help of Rottmaier.[2] But even if he succeeded in reaching the Americans in person, what good could it possibly do now?

After disembarking, the Prominenten were led into the guards' canteen next to the gate. They were given bread and sausage, along with the ubiquitous German acorn coffee. It was still early morning, and after a night of relentless movement and stress the prisoners were too tired to do anything but slump at their tables and couldn't bring themselves to care much what happened to them. They were left dozing for a few hours and were eventually ordered outside.

Rising to their feet with some difficulty, they walked out into a beautiful spring morning. The sky above the mountains was blue and bright, and the air was already as warm as midsummer. The spires of Innsbruck could be seen clearly against the green mountain slopes. Noticing a foul smell, Payne Best realized that the enclosure opposite the canteen was a latrine. He saw a man with "straw-coloured hair, dressed in khaki shirt and shorts" go in. Someone looking that peculiar couldn't be anything other than an Englishman, so Payne Best went to introduce himself.

The straw-haired prisoner turned out to be none other than Mad Jack Churchill. Payne Best had never met him, but had seen the reports of his capture in the German newspapers. It had been mistakenly trumpeted as a major coup, the commando leader being supposedly a close relative of the British prime minister.

This surreal meeting of two of Britain's celebrated special operatives, representing the fields of espionage and special forces, outside a concentration camp toilet in a stunning landscape on a beautiful day was brought to an abrupt end. The two men managed only a brief chat—filling each other in on how they came to be here—before one of the guards ordered Payne Best to return to the flock.[3]

Jack Churchill returned to his barrack to report that a large new group of Prominenten had arrived. Wings Day, Jimmy James, and the Great Escapers, along with Peter Churchill, the other military prisoners, and Wadim Greenewich, the former passport officer from the Sofia embassy, had been in Reichenau for eight days. They had arrived in the early morning after a beautiful mountain dawn. SS-Sonderlager Innsbruck—so hastily renamed that the old work camp sign was still on the gate—literally stank. The latrines were little more than open pits whose reek became intolerable in the spring sunshine, the stench pervading much of the camp. The barracks were infested with mice and rats, and the mattresses and bed linen crawled with lice.[4]

There had been barely fifty regular inmates in the camp when Day and his companions first arrived, and the place felt depressingly forlorn. SS-Obersturmführer Stiller, disgusted by the conditions, spent hours arguing with the local authorities and contacting Dachau by telegram and telephone, fruitlessly demanding alternative accommodations.[5] Giving up, and fearing that he might be drafted into the defense of the Alpine Fortress, he had returned to Dachau. That first night, the prisoners had tried to raise their spirits by singing in ironic celebration of their new home, but their revels were interrupted by loud banging on the wall from their SD guards, billeted in the next room. A voice came through the thin partition: "Shut your traps! How do you expect people to sleep with that filthy row?"

Jack Churchill banged back. "You shut yours!" he shouted. "It's about time you heard some decent singing now that your marching songs have led you to defeat."[6]

They sang on into the night.

Reichenau had turned out to be like Flossenbürg writ small. The regular inmates—relatively few in number—were driven out at dawn on working parties and returned exhausted after dark barely capable of standing up. They were starved and beaten and generally treated worse than animals.

During the following days, Wings Day had pondered their situation. Although the SS command structure was disintegrating and discipline slacking, the possibility of a sudden decision by the SS or Hitler to massacre the Prominenten was growing more likely, not less. The closer the Allied advance came, and the more tightly the Nazis were backed into a corner, the more probable such an outcome became. Day's instinct, honed by years in the prisoner resistance networks of POW camps, was to escape at the earliest opportunity.[7]

The problems with this line of thought became more pronounced when the transport from Dachau arrived on 26 April, bringing dozens of clergymen, lawyers, demoted royalty, and other motley individuals. These people, some of whom he had met briefly in the Dachau brothel or fleetingly at Flossenbürg and Sachsenhausen, struck him as being of a very different kind than his little group of British and Allied military men. They were not "escape minded." Most had been tortured or terrorized during their captivity, and with a few exceptions their experiences had reduced them to a passive state of mind in which they could think of only two possible outcomes: submission to the SS or liberation by the Allies.

Moreover, most of them had at some time or other been far closer to death than they were now, and they were reluctant to countenance risks. If only a few men escaped, retribution would likely fall on the rest, as Ferrero had pointed out, but a mass escape by all of them would be practically difficult and virtually impossible to motivate the other prisoners for. Chances might improve if they were taken over the border to the Italian South Tyrol, where they would be surrounded by Ferrero's partisan friends. However, to Wings Day that seemed a remote prospect, and he felt growing doubts about the reliability of the Italian's assurances that the partisans would save them.

After the new arrivals had moved into their accommodations, Payne Best went across to the barrack in which Wings Day's group were billeted and introduced himself. Having already met Mad Jack, he was now introduced to SOE agent Peter Churchill and the Great Escapers—Wings Day, Jimmy James, Sydney Dowse, and Raymond van Wymeersch—as well as some of General Papagos's officers, four Irish soldiers, and two Polish airmen, Jan Izycki and Stanislaw Jensen, who had served in a special duties squadron of the RAF.

Payne Best was delighted and enthralled to meet them—particularly the Britons—and spent all day with them. Not only was it the first opportunity he'd had in five and a half years to talk freely, man-to-man, with people of his own nationality and kind, but he felt thrilled to encounter men whose courage and fighting spirit had made them heroes among their fellow prisoners. Although they were all extremely kind and friendly to the aging spy, in his heart Payne Best felt ashamed that, while these men had broken out of prison camps time and time again, "I had done nothing but sit in my cell leading the well-fed life of a prize poodle."[8] Rather than regaling him with their adventures, Wings Day and his friends quizzed Payne Best about his own experiences in the Sachsenhausen cellblock. He suspected that they were only pretending to take an interest, which added to his sense of inferiority in their presence.

Supper was brought by one of the camp inmates. Contained in what looked to Payne Best like garden watering carts, it was the standard concentration-camp fare of watery stew made with beets and vegetables. Then to bed. The camp was so thinly populated that each person had a whole bunk. Payne Best, who seemed immune to bites, was the only one who slept untroubled by lice. The following morning, generals Falkenhausen and Thomas, his neighbors in the bunk room, complained bitterly of being eaten alive.[9]

Payne Best spent the next day exploring Reichenau. The long-term inmates were a strange assortment. As far as he could gather, most were captured members of the French Resistance, all clothed in rags. Many were women whose spirits were very far from broken—they treated their guards with disrespect, talking back to them quite brazenly. Noticing the Prominenten, they shouted out taunts about the newcomers' obtrusively well-dressed appearance.

There was another set of prisoners whom Payne Best spotted working in a fenced-off kitchen garden. Greenewich managed to talk to them and discovered that they were American airmen, captured after being shot down. Why they were not in a regular prisoner of war camp was a mystery to the Prominenten. The SS treated the Americans abominably, and they were in a state of starvation. It was heartbreaking to see their skeletal forms working the garden plots with painful slowness, as if the slightest movement cost them energy they could scarcely summon.[10]

Like almost all of their contemporaries, the Prominenten were unaware that these were just a few of the hundreds—if not thousands—of American and other Allied prisoners of war held, abused, and in many cases murdered by the SS in concentration camps.[11]

Thursday 26 April: Dachau[12]

After the departure of the second transport, dozens of Prominenten still remained in Dachau, including some in the Bunker, some in the former brothel, and most of the kin prisoners in their barracks in the SS complex.

Caught between the hope inspired by the relentless advance of the Allies and the fear of increasing agitation and panic among the SS, the prisoners didn't know which way the cards would fall—rescue or a reckoning. The constant thunder of bombs and shells and the flashes and rolls of smoke on the horizon suggested that liberation might do them no good if the battle rolled right over Dachau.

In his room in the Bunker, Kurt von Schuschnigg opened his diary and looked over the entries for the past few days. "Nobody can tell us what is going to be done with those of us who remain in Dachau," he had written a week earlier, after Wings Day's transport had left. "It is said that we, too, will be evacuated. Another rumour says that the International Red Cross is going to take over the entire camp. That, of course, would be ideal, but I have learned my lesson about rejoicing too soon and I refuse to believe it."[13]

Two days later, on Sunday 22 April: "We are waiting."

On Wednesday 25 April, the second transport had departed. "We are still waiting," Schuschnigg wrote.

The following day: "The Americans are closing in on Munich. We are still waiting."

Later the same day Schuschnigg turned back the page and added one word:

"Evacuation!"[14]

That morning, SS-Obersturmführer Edgar Stiller had begun assembling the third and final transport of Prominenten from Dachau. It was a complicated task, made more difficult by Dachau's disintegrating command structure. For days the Americans had been held in check at a line approximately twenty-five miles to the north. The evacuation of thousands of prisoners each day had thrown the whole place into convulsions, and SS personnel had now begun to desert. One group made a run for it after carefully burning a stock of Red Cross parcels the SS had seized for themselves.[15] Organizing transport in this increasingly febrile, chaotic situation was a battle in itself.

The Prominenten remaining inside the camp—besides Kurt, Vera, and Sissy von Schuschnigg—included Léon and Janot Blum, Erich and Margot Heberlein, and Fritz and Amélie Thyssen, as well as Gertrud Halder and a few kin prisoners, including Countess Gisela von Plettenberg and Isa Vermehren. Also remaining in the Bunker was Dr. Sigmund Rascher, who had special reason to fear being "liberated" by the Allies.

In the hospital barracks, which, being outside the wire, were more exposed to the activities of the complex, the kin prisoners had been subjected to dreadful sights in these last days: trainloads of evacuees coming from Buchenwald had died en route and arrived as corpses, and thousands of half-dead souls had been force marched out of the gates and down the road to the south. Fey Pirzio-Biroli wondered what purpose there could be in this appalling, futile sadism. She and her fellow prisoners had imagined that Dachau was all but surrounded, that there was nothing left to do but wait for the Americans.[16] When the order came for yet another move, Fey could scarcely believe it. "Prepare to leave!" yelled Bader's men. "Bring only what you can carry in your hands!"

Wearily, the kin prisoners scraped together their most precious belongings, which they bundled into improvised rucksacks made from blankets. Fey was exhausted, and the trudge through the SS complex to the camp gate was purgatory. They passed row after row of emaciated inmates lined up ready for the death march, watching in bewilderment as the strange procession of Prominenten went by like a caravan of nomads, with sacks on their shoulders and pots, pans, and bowls dangling and clanking as the SS guards urged them along.[17]

A similar procession wound its way from the Bunker to the gatehouse. Each person took only what he or she could carry. Mothers led their children by the hand. When they reached the roll-call square, the Prominenten were confronted by a vast mass of prisoners, all arranged in columns, marching to the gatehouse under SS guard like the ghosts of a defeated army, trudging in flimsy down-at-heel shoes or wooden clogs, raising a deep reek of unwashed bodies in soiled clothing. "Here and there we could hear the rise and fall of hushed talk," Schuschnigg recorded. "It sounded like the last murmur of a storm or perhaps its first warning roll."[18] There would be no transport waiting for these poor souls, just a long and grueling march, which many of them would not survive. Any who lagged behind or fell aside would be shot. Schuschnigg was aware that many of them were Austrians—people he had once governed (and, as a fascist, in many cases oppressed).

The SS shepherded the Prominenten toward a narrow aisle held open alongside the exodus, and they passed out of the gate. As the vast and the tiny groups passed each other, Schuschnigg noticed that "a worn-out hand stretched out from the mass. Here someone called, there a familiar face smiled tiredly." Hands were raised in salute. "They are our friends," Schuschnigg wrote later, "human beings—men and women—Austrians." The memory of this contact with his people would remain with him: "It was perhaps the most impressive moment of all these years."[19]

Outside the gates three buses and a truck were lined up waiting. There was bustle everywhere, with SS troopers coming and going and motorcycles and cars speeding across the freight yard of the railhead nearby. The prisoners' luggage was piled up, with the guards' bags stacked next to it. There was also a pile of ammunition boxes. A truck stood near the service buildings being loaded with large boxes, which the guards said contained their food supply, although none of the Prominenten ever saw that truck again.[20]

By the time the kin prisoners reached the gates, the vehicles were already almost full with prisoners from the Bunker, and they had to be squeezed in wherever there was room. Fey was heaved in over the tailgate of the truck, already so overloaded that people had to stand between the benches, stooping over to keep from banging their heads on the bars holding up the canvas.

All three buses and the truck were jammed to bursting before all the prisoners were aboard, and there were no other vehicles to be had. Stiller's SS guards separated out some of the younger men and sent them to join the ordinary prisoners still filing out of the gates and shambling through the complex. Among those dispatched in this way was Reinhard Goerdeler, the twenty-two-year-old son of Carl Goerdeler. He was dragged away from his mother and sisters and sent away with the doomed mass. Maria von Hammerstein's son Franz was also taken, as was twenty-four-year-old Markwart von Stauffenberg Jr. Major Dietrich Schatz, the loyal Nazi officer who had protested so loudly and indignantly at being locked in a cell at Regensburg, also went on the death march.

Fey watched with pity as the young men were led away, accompanied by a special detail of Stiller's men to guard them. She wondered if she would ever see any of them again. The vehicles were kept waiting while the columns went by. Fey saw several prisoners, too weak to march, fall to their knees. The SS guards yelled at them, belabored them with rifle butts, and if they still couldn't rise shot them in the back of the neck. The young kin prisoners were healthier and fitter than most, but if they flagged or wandered, they might expect a bullet like the rest. Fey fought down the urge to be sick. She wondered what the SS could possibly be intending for so many ruined people.[21]

Himmler's plan was to herd them into the Ötz valley in the Austrian Tyrol, where they would work in a fighter-jet test facility; as it turned out, only a handful would ever make it to Austrian soil.[22]

It was around midnight by the time all the Prominenten had been accounted for and the way was clear. Fey was distressed to see that "the despicable Bader" ("who prisoners think is capable of anything") was traveling with them in addition to the more civilized Stiller. Sitting near her were Kurt von Schuschnigg and Vera, with Sissy drowsing on her lap. It was too dark to recognize anyone else, and people were silent. Not so in the luggage truck, where Isa Vermehren sat among the bags and cases with several SS guards and the functionary prisoners Wilhelm Visintainer and Paul Wauer, who had volunteered to go with the second transport but had been held back at the last moment. Visintainer had now been asked to come along to serve as a cook, but he had a terrible feeling that he would not survive the journey. He'd been in Dachau for a long time and had seen a great deal of the terrible secret atrocities that had gone on there. "I know too much," he kept saying to Isa, "and they know that I know it."[23]

Driving out of the SS complex and heading south, the convoy overtook the endless weary lines of humanity. Marie-Gabriele von Stauffenberg caught a glimpse of the five young Prominenten marching with them, and like Fey she wondered what would become of them.[24] It took about an hour for the convoy to reach the open road and pass the head of the marching columns.

In the darkness the Prominenten were spared a clear sight of the ruins of Munich. Thereafter, they had a much harder time than those who had traveled in the two previous transports. The little convoy moved slowly but steadily southeast toward the Alps, following the same route through Rosenheim that the second transport had taken. The roads were packed with endless lines of refugees and prisoners. There was a constant drone of aircraft overhead, and every town they passed through had been devastated.[25] Climbing into the mountains, the roads grew narrower and steeper, and although they couldn't see the landscape the Prominenten could feel the chilly Alpine air. The overloaded vehicles had to stop frequently; sometimes the going was so difficult that the prisoners had to get out of the struggling vehicles and walk alongside. On one occasion they had to help push the truck to the top of a steep incline.

During one of the stints of walking, Fey took the opportunity to talk with Kurt von Schuschnigg, who was probably the most celebrated of all Hitler's hostages. She found him rather reserved and economical with words and sensed that he went to considerable lengths to conceal and rise above his suffering. And yet his lively mind took a keen interest in the world despite his long separation from it. Given his seven years as a prisoner, Fey expected his knowledge of world events to be outdated, but she found he was absolutely up-to-the-minute, with an acute understanding of the problems facing Europe once the Nazis were defeated. Russia's current incursion into Europe troubled him—once they were here, they would not willingly leave.[26]

Schuschnigg confessed to Fey that he sometimes suffered from depression, and she guessed that his wife must be a great comfort to him. Fey found Vera steadfastly cheerful and kind. The two women talked at length as they trudged up the mountain road, Vera with Sissy in her arms, telling the story of the child's birth while her husband was imprisoned and how she had followed him to Sachsenhausen. She confessed that it had been after the move to Flossenbürg, where they were no longer secluded from the horrors, that she had begun to suffer with her nerves; their building was not far from the execution shed, and she would often hear guards ordering prisoners to strip, followed by cries for help and mercy, then gunshots, then silence.[27]

As an ambassador's daughter, Fey was keen to mingle with the great and good. During another of the many uphill walks that night, she introduced herself to Léon and Janot Blum. To her gratification, Blum immediately recognized her maiden name—Hassell—and recalled her father, Ulrich, the former German ambassador to Italy, who had been executed in September 1944 for his part in the July plot. Fey noted how elderly Blum looked, and that he walked with a limp caused by his sciatica, leaning on a stick. She was struck by how modest and unpretentious the Blums were and by Janot's devotion—like Vera von Schuschnigg's—in sharing her husband's incarceration. Despite his Jewishness, Blum bore no animosity toward the German people—they had been taken over by the disease of Nazism, he felt, as had many others in Europe, including his own compatriots. As a socialist, his view of Europe's future was less gloomy than the right-wing Schuschnigg's. International cooperation would be the key, and grand ideologies like Nazism and Fascism were to be shunned.

At long last, the strenuous climb ceased, and the downhill leg of the journey began. Dawn revealed the breathtaking Alpine scenery—a balm for tired eyes. Fey was so exhausted she could hardly stay upright on her bench seat.

On a fresh, bright spring morning, with the air growing as warm as summer, the transport passed through Innsbruck and drew up outside the gates of Reichenau. They swung open, and the vehicles rolled into the camp. Fey barely had the strength to climb down from the truck. She found herself in a malodorous gravel courtyard, where a crowd of several dozen people stood watching. Fey recognized among them people she had known in the schoolhouse at Schönberg. The two groups of prisoners greeted one another joyfully. To Fey it felt like a "surprise birthday party," and the guards allowed it to go on unhindered.[28]

Old friends were reunited and many new acquaintances were made. The prisoners of war from Sachsenhausen—who had been more isolated than most from their fellow Prominenten—saw many new faces and were particularly pleased to meet Kurt and Vera von Schuschnigg and the Thyssens, their former secret neighbors from the Sonderlager.[29]

Peter Churchill made a head count, and reckoned—slightly inaccurately—that there were now 132 Prominenten representing twenty-two nationalities.[30] Wings Day, who had been keeping a register of all the VIP prisoners, was now able to complete it, coming to the slightly different total of 136.[31] In fact, there were 139 men, women, and children, each one of them a priceless but extremely endangered hostage of the Third Reich. Having been all in one place only once before—and very briefly—the Prominenten were all together in one group for the first time.

⁂

In fact, not quite all of the Prominenten were at Reichenau. After the third transport left Dachau, one person remained behind in his cell in the Bunker: SS-Hauptsturmführer Dr. Sigmund Rascher. The building had been evacuated, and while chaos reigned elsewhere in the Dachau complex, the two long, bleak corridors lined with steel doors were eerily quiet.

Earlier that day, noticing the commotion surrounding the departure of the other Prominenten, Rascher had inquired of SS-Scharführer Lechner—the music lover who had taken Georg Elser to his ignominious death and been so friendly to Payne Best—whether he would be accompanying them. Lechner presumed that he would and told him so. And yet as time passed and the noise outside Rascher's cell settled down, nobody came to release him. Hours ticked by.

It was around seven o'clock in the evening and the third transport was still outside the main gates when the telephone rang in the Bunker. Lechner answered it and heard the chilling voice of SS-Oberscharführer Theodor Bongartz, manager of the crematorium and Georg Elser's executioner. He instructed Lechner to move all other prisoners except Rascher from the cellblock into the garden. That was impossible, said Lechner; he was the only guard on duty. Some of the Prominenten were going out to the buses, and there were thousands of ordinary inmates waiting to depart in the roll-call square.

A short while afterward, Bongartz turned up at the Bunker. He was an unpleasant sight at the best of times: a smooth-skinned, demonic face with a long, curved nose, thick eyebrows, a downturned slash for a mouth, and eyes as hard and bright as wet stones. Accompanying him was the notorious Emil Mahl, the crematorium administrator. A deceptively ordinary-looking individual with a long upper lip and balding pate, Mahl was known as the hangman of Dachau. Obtrusively loading his pistol in front of Lechner's eyes, Bongartz once more ordered him to evacuate the Bunker of all inmates except Rascher.

Again Lechner refused because it wouldn't be possible to guard them securely. Having seen the situation for himself, Bongartz understood Lechner's predicament. He ordered the corporal instead to remove Rascher from his cell and take him to one at the extreme eastern end of the corridor—behind a heavy steel door separating it from the rest of the block. By this time, Lechner could have little doubt what Bongartz intended to do.

Rascher was startled by the approach of rapid footsteps and his cell door squealing open. He rose, and Lechner led him out of the cell and along the corridor, with Bongartz and Mahl following close behind. They passed through the steel door into the empty seclusion of the far wing, where Rascher was pushed into the farthest cell and locked in. Bongartz told Lechner he was no longer required.

Lechner went back through the steel door, closing it behind him. He knew exactly what to expect. Putting his eye to the peephole, he saw Mahl open the food hatch in the cell door, and Bongartz point his pistol through it. Three gunshots rang deafeningly loud in the enclosed space. Bongartz leaned close to the hatch and said, "You pig, now you've got what you deserved." (His contempt most likely sprang from Rascher's betrayal of the regime, rather than any qualms about the atrocities he had committed.) The two men opened the cell door and walked in. Bongartz kicked the corpse, then ordered Mahl to stoke up the crematorium.[32]

It was grotesquely fitting that Sigmund Rascher's life should come to an ignoble end at the hands of his fellow SS men, in Dachau, where he had callously taken the lives of so many innocent prisoners in the name of research. Despite the horrifying things Rascher had done, Sigismund Payne Best had mixed feelings when he learned of his death. He believed Rascher undoubtedly deserved to die for his crimes—and would have been hanged anyway if he'd survived to fall into Allied hands—and yet Payne Best felt a pang of sorrow for his fellow prisoner, "for we had been through much together and always he had behaved with gallantry and been our loyal comrade."[33] Such were the strange attachments that could form among human beings in an extremity of shared adversity.

Fifteen
Out of the Reich

Friday 27 April: Austria

The last light of a glorious sunlit day was fading over the Alps as the long convoy of buses and trucks left the broad valley of the Inn, passing between the two rearing mountain walls forming the steep vale of the winding river Sill.

In their vehicles, the Prominenten looked back on their day with a mixture of regret and longing. For most of them it had been full of surprises, and for some delight and joy had been mingled with terror. They had had one single day all together in the camp at Reichenau, meeting and getting to know new people, reunited with old friends and familiar faces. And then it had all come to an end in yet another rush to embark on yet another move.

This time they had received even less notice than usual. It had been coming on to evening when SS-Obersturmführer Stiller had gone among them ordering them to their transports. Within fifteen minutes they were being herded aboard a fleet of half-a-dozen buses and trucks, some of which had been brought from Innsbruck, with a supply truck trailing behind.[1]

It took a long time to load up, and people grew fractious. Payne Best, determined not to spend another moment on a truck's hard bench, got into an argument with Stiller, who still intended to keep him separate from Stevens, the wily spy having managed to get himself onto a comfortable bus in quick time. Payne Best pointed out firmly that, as Stevens was ten years his junior, *he* could endure the wooden bench this time. Payne Best was backed up by Colonel John McGrath, and Stiller gave way. Stevens was relocated and Payne Best sank gratefully into a soft, luxurious seat. Imprisonment had made him so thin, he almost feared his bones would push through his flesh if he had to sit on any more hard surfaces.[2]

Besides stress and disorientation, a pall of foreboding had been cast over this latest chapter in their odyssey. That day, SS-Untersturmführer Bader and his squad of twenty SD troopers, who had been mysteriously absent, reappeared in Reichenau.[3] Unlike the thirty or so SS Death's Head guards Stiller had brought with him from Dachau, who despite their title were relatively stolid and restrained, Bader's men were perceived as executioners. They were a death squad, and the prisoners feared them. Wilhelm Visintainer, hearing one of the Prominenten express a fear that they could be held in Reichenau for months, said, "Don't worry, they will shoot us before that." Looking at Bader's killers, Jimmy James thought Visintainer could well be right.[4] Payne Best also found it difficult to believe that the SS intended to let the Prominenten live when a squad whose sole function was the extermination of unwanted prisoners had been assigned to them.[5]

The feeling of foreboding had been reinforced that afternoon, after Bader's arrival and before the evening order to embark, when the Prominenten were suddenly locked inside the barracks. For two hours the camp was quiet, and then they were let out again. Later they discovered that three Austrian resistance leaders had been hanged. When the Prominenten resumed mingling, there was a renewed sense of impending death, which hung over them as they boarded their transports.[6] Wings Day and Jimmy James noticed boxes of hand grenades being loaded into the SS supply truck; a few of those tossed into the overcrowded vehicles would finish off the hostages very quickly.[7] Some, indeed, were loaded onto the buses: Isa Vermehren, boarding a bus with her precious accordion, noticed at least one box of grenades being brought aboard.[8]

Fey Pirzio-Biroli boarded the same bus as the Schuschniggs and Blums, Martin Niemöller, and Bogislaw von Bonin, as well as many of the kin prisoners. Fey had spent much of the afternoon at Reichenau frantically seeking out fellow German prisoners who might have information about her sons. She could only assume they were still in the hands of the SS but had no idea where or in what circumstances. All she got for her pains was the deeply troubling information that the SS kept some children in special institutes, and that sometimes they had their names changed and were given for adoption to loyal Aryan Nazi families. Fey had eventually given up inquiring; not only was she getting nowhere, she could sense that her fellow prisoners didn't want to be bothered with worries beyond their own situation.[9]

Peter Churchill rode in the same coach as Fey. He too had spent some of that day searching for news of a loved one, Odette Sansom, his lover and French counterpart in his SOE operation, betrayed and captured with him in France. His search had been prompted by Isa Vermehren; hearing that there were two men named Churchill among the Prominenten, Isa introduced herself to Peter and asked whether he had a wife in Ravensbrück, where Isa had been incarcerated for a while. She described a Frenchwoman she had known there, who went by a pseudonym imposed by the SS, "Frau Schurer." This woman had claimed her real name was Odette. Churchill was certain from the description that it must be her. Isa said she was in "excellent health and spirits" as far as she knew, but that one of the other Prominenten, Wilhelm von Flügge, one of the Canaris resistance circle, might know more; he had been imprisoned in the men's compound at Ravensbrück and had known Odette better. Churchill already knew Flügge, who had been billeted in the same barrack at Reichenau.

He found Flügge in the barrack room and showed him the snapshot of Odette he carried with him. Was this the Frau Schurer he had known?

Flügge studied the photograph, but shook his head and gave it back. "I'm sorry," he said. "This is not the woman I knew." Seeing the look of dismay on Churchill's face, he asked to see the picture again. "Yes, yes," he said. "It might be she. . . . People can change so much in prison. . . . Forgive me, my dear Churchill." With that, he handed back the photograph, stood up, and walked unhappily out of the room.[10]

Churchill sat alone, his mind filled with fear and foreboding that threatened to grow into despair. All the painful uncertainty he had felt since being parted from her by the Gestapo came rushing back. The war would soon be over and one way or another he would find out what had really been done to her, and he both yearned for and dreaded that discovery. He told himself that fretting would do no good to either Odette or himself. He tried to focus on the thought that if she was still alive, at least he would be in a position to care for her and help her forget whatever traumatic experiences had so changed her that she was no longer recognizable from her picture.[11]

For Kurt von Schuschnigg, his day at Reichenau had been a sweet sorrow. For the first time since his imprisonment, his feet were back on Austrian soil. He tried not to look too closely at the scenery, because the emotions he felt threatened to overwhelm his self-control and shatter his rigid sense of dignity.

Among the crowd at Reichenau, he had been reunited with many old friends and was especially pleased to shake hands once again with Richard Schmitz; Schuschnigg was shocked at how elderly and worn the former mayor was after years of captivity. "In meeting these men and old friends," Schuschnigg wrote in his diary, "I cannot avoid thinking of those hundreds and hundreds of other people who suffered a similar fate during all these years." He reflected that though some, like himself and his family, were still alive, "more, far more, are no longer among the living. Our personal experiences become small and unimportant measured with the endless misery around us."[12]

The convoy drove through the night alongside the winding river Sill, following its course ever higher into the Alps. The overloaded buses, never making more than fifteen miles per hour, struggled on the steeply climbing roads, which were crowded with Italian slave laborers and escapees from the death marches heading home on foot.[13] At the same time, German refugees and war-weary soldiers were trickling in the opposite direction.

Prominenten and displaced Italians alike were heading for the Brenner Pass, the narrow mountain defile linking Austria with Italy. For Stiller, this journey was a desperate search for a place in this phantom Alpine Fortress to hole up and await orders regarding the fate of the hostages. All around, the German lines were collapsing, and to retreat from one Allied advance was to rush toward another.

The gateway to Italy had been subjected to repeated Allied bombing in an effort to prevent a German retreat to the Alpine Fortress. Approaching the pass, the road was crammed with refugees traveling in both directions, soldiers, and a logjam of buses, trucks, and assorted military vehicles. The traffic was packed so tightly that one of the SS guards lost half his arm when two of the vehicles grazed one another.[14]

Despite the uncertainty about their fate, some of the British Prominenten—who were traveling in the same bus as Fey and the Schuschniggs—managed to whip up a jubilant atmosphere. The indomitable military men were heartened by the coming end of the war and lifted their spirits in song. Isa Vermehren, aboard the same bus, got out her accordion and led them in chorus after chorus, with the Irish sergeant Thomas Cushing leading the singing and playing percussion on pots and pans. The result was like a combination of an English seaside excursion and a Berlin cabaret.[15]

The convoy reached the beginning of the Brenner Pass sometime near midnight, with a bright moon illuminating the mountains and casting haunting shadows among the ruins of the hamlet of Matrei am Brenner. At that moment, the bus in which the songfest was taking place broke down, bringing the convoy to a halt. It had been towing a heavy passenger trailer and simply couldn't cope with the load on the steep roads.[16]

As the bus sat stranded on the roadside, Fey watched the eerie moonlit figures of the refugees walking by through a landscape that seemed to her eyes bleak and desolate.[17]

❧

While the convoy was laboring up the Brenner Pass, the last evacuations were leaving Dachau. By late the next day, the camp would be echoing to the sound of its air-raid sirens, heralding not the threat of Allied bombers this time but the happy approach of American ground forces. Commandant Weiter and his staff had fled the camp, notionally following the call from RSHA chief Ernst Kaltenbrunner to assemble in the Alpine Fortress, but also with the more immediate concern of saving their own skins.[18]

During the night of Saturday 28 April, an international committee of prisoners was formed to organize the camp in preparation for the arrival of their liberators. The Americans finally reached Dachau the following afternoon. The first to enter the camp were soldiers from the 3rd Battalion, 157th Infantry Regiment, 45th Infantry Division, part of General Alexander Patch's US Seventh Army. Additional units from the 42nd Infantry Division reached Dachau the same afternoon.

They found a hell on earth. Before they even entered the camp they discovered railway freight wagons packed with the corpses of over two thousand men, women, and children. Inside the camp they found more dead bodies, stacked everywhere in massive heaps. There were thirty-two thousand survivors remaining, many of whom were close to death and would not survive long after liberation.

The GIs who saw Dachau would never entirely recover from the experience. "It made us sick to our stomach," wrote one American officer, "and so mad we could do nothing but clinch our fists."[19]

Saturday 28 April: Brenner Pass

It was now the early hours of the morning, and the convoy still sat by the roadside, waiting for a replacement for the broken-down bus. It was cold, the spring weather of the Inn valley having given way to the permanent wintry chill of the high pass.

Inside the bus, the British prisoners were still enjoying their singing. Isa Vermehren squeezed out the melancholy opening chords of "Boulevard of Broken Dreams," the sentimental romantic lament sung by Constance Bennett in the 1934 movie *Moulin Rouge*. Suddenly, from the darkness inside the bus, Kurt von Schuschnigg's sharp, furious voice cut in: "How can you sing in this grave hour?"[20]

The British officers could have answered his question easily enough but didn't bother. Instead they lapsed into silence, and the anxieties that had been allayed by their singing crept back into their minds.[21] They sat and looked out at the pale moonlit rubble of the destroyed village and the spectral refugees walking through it, weighed down with packs and bags, some pushing handcarts, a few lucky enough to have acquired horses and mules.

In the silence, Peter Churchill, sitting near the front of the bus, overheard a muttered conversation between one of Bader's scar-faced guards and the driver. They were talking about the carnage they imagined must be happening at that moment in Berlin. The guard grew angry and said that if the Führer was killed in the fighting he would take vengeance on the Prominenten. "I'll mow down these bastards like nine-pins," he growled.[22] Churchill and most of the others had already discerned these feelings in the faces of the SD troopers, and it was chilling to hear them expressed. They could only hope that Hitler would stay alive for the time being.

This wasn't the only such conversation; Colonel Bogislaw von Bonin and the industrialist Wilhelm von Flügge overheard a fragment of quiet talk between two SS sergeants. One asked, "What are we going to do about those who still have to be liquidated?" The other said, "Well, we were ordered to put the bomb under the bus either just before or just after the . . ." The rest of the sentence was inaudible.[23]

The clergymen Karl Kunkel and Johann Neuhäusler disembarked from the bus to take a look around. They spoke with some of the retreating German soldiers and were told that it was a very bad idea to go any farther south; the Americans were already at Trento, a little over ninety miles to the south, and advancing rapidly. Rather than going back to the bus or ambling about the eerie ruins, Kunkel and Neuhäusler took the opportunity to slip into the welcoming embrace of a local inn, the Weisse Rössl, one of the few structures still standing. The innkeeper gave them wine, bread, and sausage, and when he heard of their plight, urged them to stay with him or simply run away. Neuhäusler replied that he was intent on sharing the ordeal of his fellow prisoners until the very end, no matter what gruesome denouement it might entail.[24]

A few of the British officers got permission to step off the bus and stretch their legs. Payne Best wandered among the ruins of a bombed-out concrete bunker. Air raids were an almost nightly occurrence at this strategic bottleneck, and a rumor circulated that the Prominenten had been deliberately halted here in the hope that there would be another one—their guards would execute them all and blame their deaths on the bombing.[25]

Wings Day and Mad Jack Churchill, unaware of the rumor, stood at the roadside earnestly debating the possibility of making their escape. In the end they decided against it; besides the risk of retribution for their fellow prisoners, they were already traveling along the only feasible escape route.[26]

Walking back to the bus, Day found SS-Obersturmführer Stiller standing by the door. "I hope you had an interesting walk, Wing Commander," he said sardonically. Day took it as a sneer rather than an inquiry.[27]

Day had the impression that neither Stiller nor Bader had much idea what they were doing or where they were going. Their division of responsibility was notionally simple. Stiller was responsible for the transport, accommodation, and general custody of the hostages and was therefore in command. Bader had only one role: to carry out whatever final orders Berlin handed down. It was expected to be execution. The standing order from the top was not to let the Prominenten fall into Allied hands under any circumstances. However, all communication with Berlin had been lost, and the SS officers' bewilderment and confusion presented an extreme risk that they would simply slaughter the prisoners as the only way of fulfilling their standing order.

Of the two, Bader, as a practiced, hardened killer, seemed the more likely to turn the evacuation into a mass execution at the least excuse. Stiller was in a more invidious position. Payne Best was not the only prisoner to suggest that he disobey his orders and take the convoy to Allied lines; Richard Stevens had put the same suggestion to him. As they were leaving Dachau, Stevens had said to Stiller, "If you've got any sense you'll steer the convoy towards the nearest United States unit and hand us over unharmed." But it wasn't that simple; Stiller didn't need Stevens to point out that if he were caught by the Americans in his SS uniform, "they'll string you up from the nearest tree." Stiller considered Stevens's suggestion, then replied, "Let us see what we come across on the road."[28]

And here they were, on the road, broken down in the middle of the night. The likelihood of Stiller taking the prisoners to the Allies had shrunk to a virtual impossibility since Reichenau. Although he technically outranked Bader, Stiller was less strong-willed, and his SS men could not be relied upon to follow orders with the verve of Bader's executioners.

Finally, at about 1:30 in the morning, a replacement bus arrived from Innsbruck. It took another two hours for the prisoners to be transferred and the last stragglers to be rounded up and herded aboard.

With dawn just beginning to lighten the eastern sky over the towering Alps, the convoy reached the top of the pass and began the long descent into the Italian Tyrol.

Sixteen
The Sunrise Conspiracy

German forces in Italy were stronger than one might have guessed from the troops retreating through the Brenner Pass, and the Allied forces were not as far advanced as rumor had it. The soldiers who spoke to Karl Kunkel and Johann Neuhäusler at Matrei am Brenner had been misinformed; the Americans were still well short of Trento and were having to fight hard for every gain.

Operation Grapeshot, the Allied 15th Army Group's spring offensive, had begun on 6 April, attacking from a line that ran from just north of Pisa on the west coast of Italy to Ravenna on the east coast, passing south of Bologna and north of Florence. A force of over nine hundred thousand troops of the US Fifth Army and the British and Commonwealth Eighth Army was launched on a massive offensive aimed at driving into Lombardy and Veneto across the broad plain between the northern fringe of the Apennine mountains and the southern edge of the Tyrolean Alps.

While a small part of Fifth Army pushed up the narrow west coastal plain and the British Eighth Army attacked north from Ravenna, the main American strength was aimed up the center, straight across the plains toward Bologna, Modena, Verona, and Lake Garda.

The Americans met resistance along the river Po, but within a few days spearheads were driving northwest toward Brescia and northeast toward Padua and Venice. In the center, the US 85th and 88th Infantry Divisions, flanked on the left by the 10th Mountain Division, advanced due north for Verona and Lake Garda, straight toward the area of the South Tyrol where Hitler's VIP hostages were being taken by their guards.[1]

On 26 April, while the last transports were leaving Dachau and heading south into the Austrian Alps, units of the 85th "Custer" Infantry Division were passing easily through the German lines north of Verona, on the southern foothills of the Tyrol. But the 10th Mountain Division, tasked with advancing to the Brenner Pass, met the toughest resistance it had encountered since leaving the Apennines. The Germans had blown up vital tunnels, and on 28 April the 10th Mountain realized that it would not be possible to take the north end of Lake Garda by land.[2] And without securing the lake, which lay like a long spearpoint embedded in the valley leading to Bolzano and the Brenner, the main thrust of their advance would be impossible.

That Saturday afternoon, while the hostage convoy was making its way down from the head of the Brenner Pass, a regiment from the 10th Mountain Division took Lake Garda using DUKW amphibious vehicles supported by artillery fire from the British 178th Medium Regiment. However, it would take another two days to move the division to the head of the lake so that it could begin its advance up the valley toward the first major town, Trento.[3]

Progress had slowed, and so long as a war zone stood between the Prominenten and the Allied lines, their lives were in imminent danger.

❖

That same day, 28 April 1945, was a historic one for the Italian people. On this day, the life of their former leader and self-styled duce came to a bloody and degrading end. Benito Mussolini and his mistress Claretta Petacci were shot by partisans at a country house near Lake Como, in the northwest corner of Italy close to the Swiss border. They had been captured the previous day while trying to reach Switzerland, where they hoped to secure safe passage to Spain. Their corpses were later taken south to Milan, where they were displayed on the pavement of the Piazzale Loreto before being hung upside down from the girders of a wrecked Esso gas station, the whole event captured on film for the world to see.

At the same time, with what remained of German-occupied Italy in its death throes, momentous events were unfolding that had life-or-death implications for the Prominenten. The secret conspiracy between German and Allied commanders to bring the war in Italy to an end was drawing to its denouement.

Since March 1945, SS-Obergruppenführer Karl Wolff, supreme SS and police commander in Italy, had been engaged in secret negotiations with the Allies, offering to arrange a unilateral surrender of German forces. These covert talks had been conducted through several emissaries in various obscure locations on the borderlands of neutral Switzerland and German-occupied Italy. They also involved two cloak-and-dagger operations in which Wolff himself crossed into Switzerland in civilian disguise to talk directly with the American spymaster Allen Dulles in Bern.[4]

Regardless of his ulterior motives—not least his own survival and self-aggrandizement—Wolff took considerable personal risks in seeking to achieve his goal. At the behest of Dulles, he had gone to the extraordinary length of installing an OSS radio operator in the attic of the SS Italian headquarters so that he could remain in permanent contact with both Dulles and the supreme commander of the Allied armed forces in Italy, Field Marshal Harold Alexander. The man selected as the radio operator was a Czech known only by the name "Wally," who had been an inmate in Dachau. Wally was provided with an SS uniform and a large supply of cigarettes and set to work. He put up his antenna and established radio contact with Allied HQ at Caserta. The only evidence to indicate his presence to Wolff's SS headquarters staff was a sign outside the room warning, "Admission only with special permission of the Obergruppenführer!"[5]

Dulles and Wolff had discussed the matter of political prisoners. Dulles asked how many were being held in Italy. Wolff didn't know, but guessed there were "several thousand" of many different nationalities. Dulles asked what would happen to them in the event of a German collapse or surrender. "There is some danger that they will be killed," said Wolff, confirming what the OSS had already heard: that secret orders had gone out from

Hitler or Himmler to kill all political prisoners rather than let them fall into Allied hands alive. "Will you obey these orders?" Dulles asked.

Wolff got up and walked up and down the terrace outside the meeting room. After some moments he returned and gave his answer: "No." He swore on his honor that he would not obey any orders to have the prisoners killed.[6] However, this was not the same as swearing to protect them; the order to dispose of the Prominenten would not be issued to him, but directly to SS-Obersturmführer Stiller.

Karl Wolff's approaches to the Allies in general, and to Dulles in particular, were already known to several senior German officials and military commanders, who supported him to a lesser or greater extent depending on how they perceived his actions as affecting their own personal circumstances.

Among those who knew was Luftwaffe Field Marshal Albert Kesselring, who had been commander in chief of Army Group C, the German force in Italy, until his transfer to take charge of the western front in March 1945. His replacement, Colonel General Heinrich von Vietinghoff, and Vietinghoff's deputy, General Hans Röttiger, also knew, as did the head of the Luftwaffe in Italy, General Maximilian Ritter von Pohl, and Franz Hofer, the Nazi Gauleiter of the Tyrol and Vorarlberg. Finally there was Otto Rahn, the German ambassador to Italy.

Of all these senior men, General Pohl, General Röttiger, and Ambassador Rahn were the most consistent in their support of Wolff's efforts to bring peace quickly. Others, less well-disposed to Wolff, soon became aware of his clandestine excursions into the enemy camp and began to cause trouble. Ernst Kaltenbrunner remained determined to resist the enemy to the last, and when he heard of Wolff's conspiracy he informed Himmler and threatened to tell Hitler. Himmler was appalled by Wolff's flagrant insubordination and warned him not to leave Italy again. To emphasize the dire seriousness with which he viewed the matter, he had Wolff's family taken into custody.

Wolff's continuing contacts with the Allies—dubbed Operation Sunrise by the OSS—were taking him into increasingly dangerous territory.[7]

The early, hesitant stages of Sunrise, immediately following the meetings in March 1945, were characterized by delay and vacillation. The Germans couldn't specify exactly what they wanted from the Allies and were terrified of being accused of treachery. The Americans and British were suspicious of German motives and recognized the possibility of being drawn into a Nazi plot to destabilize the alliance with the Soviet Union. On the other hand, the Allies believed the Nazi propaganda about the Alpine Fortress and were extremely anxious to reach a resolution that would prevent their having to fight a costly campaign to overcome such a formidable obstacle.[8]

The transfer of Albert Kesselring robbed Wolff of his most powerful ally, while his replacement, Vietinghoff, was a stiff old aristocrat who lacked the initiative or temperament to disobey orders or take independent action. Wolff had no alternative but to drag his feet in his negotiations.[9]

But the more Wolff delayed, the more he lost his leverage with Dulles and the Allies. By early April, the military situation had deteriorated so badly for the Germans that a local capitulation in Italy had lost some of its attraction for the Allies. With 15th Army Group's offensive gaining ground, German Army Group C was being forced to abandon one vital position after another.

Nonetheless, there were some encouraging developments for Wolff. Disillusioned with the Führer's inability to realize the scale of the rout, Gauleiter Franz Hofer, whose 1944 report had been instrumental in building up the concept of the Alpine Fortress, was coming around to the idea of a negotiated solution. On 13 April, Wolff was suddenly and inexplicably summoned to Berlin by Himmler. On arrival he quickly discovered that his superiors knew about his trips to Switzerland. Kaltenbrunner was furious, Himmler less so. Hoping to activate his own secret plans for a settlement with the Western Allies, Himmler couldn't make up his mind whether to punish Wolff or make use of his contacts in Bern himself. Finally, unsure how to proceed, he allowed Wolff to present his case directly to Hitler.[10]

There followed two days of meetings in the Führer bunker on 17 and 18 April. In Hitler's present state of mind, these encounters could easily have turned fatal for Wolff. Lesser men would have been shot for treachery, but Hitler praised Wolff's enterprise in making "top level" contact with the Americans. However, when Wolff tried to gain Hitler's endorsement to continue his talks, the Führer advised caution. He was convinced the fragile alliance between the Western Allies and the Soviet Union was on the verge of breaking up; when that happened and the Allies were disunited, Germany would be able to choose which side it wanted to deal with.[11]

On 19 April, while most of the Prominenten were languishing in Dachau and the first small group were finding their feet at Reichenau, Wolff returned to his headquarters on Lake Garda, disenchanted with Hitler and more determined than ever to make a local deal with the Allies.

Unfortunately for him—and for the safety of the VIP hostages—Dulles's advisers from the Combined Chiefs of Staff had become convinced that Wolff's maneuverings were part of a Nazi plot to push the Western Allies into a conflict with the Soviets. They clearly shared Hitler's view of the alliance. Moreover, they were increasingly confident about the 15th Army Group's advance. General Vietinghoff's forces were still resisting fiercely, but the momentum was decisively in favor of the Allies.

The leading German protagonists in Operation Sunrise met on 22 April at Vietinghoff's headquarters at Recoaro, in the mountains east of Lake Garda, while American forces were fighting against stiff German resistance on the river Po. It was decided that Wolff should return to Switzerland. There was no clear agreement about what he was going to propose to Dulles, because each of those present had different demands. The main thing, whatever Wolff decided to put to Dulles, was to do it quickly and drive as hard a bargain as possible. Wolff left for Switzerland on Monday 23 April, taking with him Lieutenant Colonel Victor von Schweinitz, a staff officer in Vietinghoff's command, and Wolff's own adjutant, SS-Sturmbannführer Eugen Wenner.

It was a wasted trip; Dulles was under orders not to parley with the Germans. In any case, they had almost no negotiating leverage remaining. With the Allied assault across the Po, the German Fourteenth Army had suffered a grievous blow from which it would never recover, while Tenth Army was effectively neutered. Although certain regiments still fought fiercely in places, Army Group C could no longer offer a realistic resistance to the superior Allied forces hammering against it. Moreover, partisan attacks were breaking out all over the German rear, and Wolff's headquarters was compelled to retreat from Lake Garda to Bolzano.[12] Wolff had no choice but to return to Italy, leaving Schweinitz and Wenner behind to continue negotiations.

Just before midnight on Friday 27 April—while the Prominenten were being driven up to the Brenner Pass—Wolff reached his new headquarters in Bolzano. In the early hours of the following morning, he attended a meeting at Vietinghoff's headquarters with Vietinghoff, his deputy Hans Röttiger, Gauleiter Franz Hofer, Ambassador Otto Rahn, and Wolff's debonair SS liaison man, Eugen Dollman. Wolff told the gathering that there was now no realistic alternative to unconditional surrender. Hofer was appalled at the prospect, and after a violent row stormed out of the room. The meeting broke up after daybreak, with no agreement between the conspirators.

In the meantime, Wolff waited to hear from his two emissaries in Switzerland.[13] He did not have to wait long; at noon that day, Schweinitz and Wenner boarded Field Marshal Alexander's plane at an airfield near Annecy in France, headed for Allied Forces Headquarters in Caserta, Italy. Schweinitz was carrying General Vietinghoff's written authority to surrender.

Had they known of it, the Prominenten would undoubtedly have greeted this development with cheers. With the exception of a relatively small number of hardened and perceptive cynics, most would probably have looked to their immediate future with optimism, anticipating a speedy liberation. What they would not have realized—perhaps with the exception of partisan leader Colonel Ferrero—was the violent, boiling chaos into which the country was dissolving.

Officially the Germans in Italy were offering their surrender. On the ground, in the cauldron of the front line, it would not be so simple, with individual elite German units simply ignoring the surrender and Italian partisans producing an epidemic of violence, not only against the Germans but against each other.

In such a situation, 139 VIP hostages traveling into the maelstrom in the hands of fanatical Nazi guards who had sworn to murder them if Hitler was defeated were like a clutch of baby chicks wandering onto a busy highway.

Seventeen
Appointment with Death

Saturday 28 April: Brenner Pass

An SS trooper on a motorcycle rode down the winding mountain route leading from the pass. He went at a slow pace, weaving past the traffic of retreating German troops heading up toward Austria, Italian refugees walking down, and vehicles going both ways. A dozen or so yards behind him, the convoy of buses rolled slowly along at a steady fifteen miles per hour. Every now and then the motorcyclist revved his engine and raced ahead, reconnoitering the route. At every road junction he stopped and held up a hand. The convoy would halt, and Bader and Stiller would disembark to confer with the outrider. There was a great deal of pointing, headshaking, and shrugging. Eventually the two officers boarded again and the convoy resumed its journey.[1]

It seemed to the Prominenten that the two SS lieutenants had little or no idea where they were supposed to go. They were out of touch with Berlin and, with a man as volatile as Bader and a commander like Stiller who lacked the character to take charge of him, that didn't augur well for the safety of the hostages.

Some Prominenten were convinced they knew their destination. Fey was told by Markwart von Stauffenberg—"Uncle Moppel," as she called him—that they were definitely going to the town of Bolzano, about fifty miles south of the Brenner Pass, where the Waffen-SS was planning to stage its last stand. He'd heard a rumor in Reichenau that the local Gauleiter of

Innsbruck had already gone there. Fey's heart sank: "What irony if, having survived so long, we should be killed in the last battle of the war!"[2]

At least the scenery was a compensation. The morning sun revealed a deep, narrow valley of steep green hills and rocky outcrops, folded and creased like a loose garment stitched with bands and patches of pines and studded with isolated Alpine farms. Above the green tree line were glimpses of sharp rocky peaks capped with snow. The valley descended steeply from the high pass, the road winding among the folds.

Kurt von Schuschnigg gazed with the sentimental eyes of a man coming home. He was a Tyrolean by birth and upbringing, born in 1898 in the valley above Lake Garda, and he knew every town and village. In his childhood, all of this land had been Austrian. Tyrol had once been a historic princely state at the heart of the Austro-Hungarian Empire. After the defeat of the Central Powers in 1918, the empire had been broken up, Austria reduced to a rump, and the southern half of Tyrol had been given to the Kingdom of Italy under the Treaty of Saint-Germain. Schuschnigg still thought of it as his homeland and only with reluctance acknowledged that "politically speaking" South Tyrol was Italian soil now.[3] It was a place of mingled cultures, and almost every settlement and locale had two names, one German and one Italian.

It soon became apparent to Schuschnigg that, wherever they were going, it was certainly not Bolzano. Just after the village of Franzensfeste,* the deep vale leading down from the Brenner Pass began to open out. The convoy turned left, through a gap in the mountains leading to the Puster-Thal, a broad Alpine valley running west to east through the Dolomite range. Schuschnigg knew that following the Puster valley would eventually lead back into the Austrian East Tyrol; he mentioned this to Payne Best and others, which opened a whole new avenue of speculation.[4]

By nine o'clock that morning, the weather was wet and gloomy, sheets of rain pouring into the valley and turning the forested highlands into a misty haze. The convoy had traveled about thirty miles and was just

* Italian: Fortezza

beyond the village of Welsberg-Taisten,† when the lead vehicles turned off the main highway onto a road signposted for the lakeside resort of Pragser Wildsee.‡ After a few yards, they bumped over a railway crossing and immediately pulled to a halt.[5] Yet again, the prisoners watched Stiller and Bader get out and stand in the rain debating what to do. Eventually the buses were reversed out of the side road and back onto the highway, where the drivers pulled over and switched off their engines.

They were in a landscape of Alpine meadows, sloping up on either side to thick stands of pine forest. The railway ran alongside the road, both of them disappearing in the distance behind a curtain of haze and forested slopes.

It was a peaceful setting, in which a person might find comfort and lose his sense of danger. This was an illusion. Northern Italy was erupting in a frenzy of murder and recrimination after five years of war. The execution of Benito Mussolini—which happened later that day—was just one part of it. Three days earlier, on 25 April, the National Liberation Committee in Milan—the umbrella organization for the Italian resistance movement—had declared a general insurrection, calling on partisan units across northern Italy to commence intensive attacks in the German rear areas.[6] Villages, towns, and cities were becoming the scenes of pitched battles between resistance fighters and German police and military units. Partisans roamed the countryside exacting bloody revenge on Nazis, fascists, and any suspected collaborators. Often their methods were every bit as sadistic as those used by their onetime overlords. The competing partisan factions were also fighting each other. In this atmosphere of retribution, and with the SS and SD troopers keen to be rid of or revenged on their captives, the lives of the Prominenten hung more precariously in the balance than ever.

Pastor Niemöller had noticed that some of their guards were getting drunk on hooch foraged from a village along their route. He warned

---

† Italian: Monguelfo-Tesido

‡ Italian: Lago di Braies

Wings Day that drunkenness among the SS was often a prelude to the perpetration of an atrocity. Niemöller wasn't the only one who had this feeling of foreboding. Day couldn't help noticing that the Prominenten who had spent long periods in concentration camps were becoming "very jittery" as the buses sat by the side of the road, waiting.[7]

Their worst fears were allayed somewhat when Stiller addressed them. He explained, almost apologetically, that the Pragser Wildsee hotel, to which he had hoped to deliver them, had turned out to be occupied by three Luftwaffe generals and their staffs, and he would have to find alternative accommodations. But because the vehicles were precariously low on fuel, he was running out of options. They would have to stay here for a time, while he explored the possibilities.

Despite the prisoners' anxiety about their guards, this announcement provoked loud protests. Forgetting the dire peril they were in, the Prominenten began voicing their more immediate concerns. When would they be given breakfast or at least a drink? All they'd had since the previous day was coffee and marching rations. The women were concerned about the children and the elderly. Everyone was irritable and tired after their exhausting journey and fed up with the seemingly directionless wandering. The military men in particular—including a number of generals who had commanded large forces in the field—were disgusted by Stiller's and Bader's disorganization. The whole thing was a pointless shambles. Faced with rebellion, Stiller left the buses to consult with Bader again.[8]

Meanwhile, the prisoners were permitted to get out and stretch their legs. The rain had stopped, but it remained wet and cold. The SS and SD guards lined both sides of the road at ten-yard intervals, machine pistols at the ready.

Payne Best had taken the opportunity several times to speak with Stiller alone, inquiring about his plans and gauging his mood and character, neither of which impressed him. Now, strolling about on the road, he struck up conversations with some of Bader's SD troopers, having made their acquaintance during the period in the schoolhouse at Schönberg. He had absolutely no doubt that these men would shoot the prisoners if ordered to do so, yet among those he spoke to he detected little eagerness for slaughter. At least one of them thought it would be a good idea to start by killing Stiller and Bader. Payne Best tried to encourage this idea, but it didn't seem likely to catch on.[9]

To Payne Best's mind, a more likely prospect would be to try again to encourage Stiller to defy his orders and save the Prominenten, in the hope of receiving favorable treatment when he was captured by the Allies—as he inevitably would be sooner or later. Having put this to him at Dachau, Payne Best had made no headway, and he fared no better now. Stiller was a scared man, and not inclined to overrule Bader. Although Stiller's thirty SS men outnumbered Bader's SD troopers, the latter were more motivated and more prone to sudden violent action. Most of Stiller's men weren't murderers; many were former Wehrmacht soldiers who'd been forced into the SS.[10]

Hoping to put pressure on Stiller, Payne Best talked to Hjalmar Schacht and Fritz Thyssen as they promenaded beside the buses. As "the plutocrats of our party," Payne Best proposed that they offer Stiller a hefty bribe—say one hundred thousand Swiss francs—to take all the hostages to Switzerland. Both men shook their heads at the idea. They refused to have any part in such a dangerous scheme. Payne Best tried to persuade them, but failed; perplexed and angry at their timidity, he gave up.[11]

Some of the prisoners were getting frightened, stuck here beside the road with their armed guards lined up in that ominous fashion. A rumor spread that a Gestapo order had been found on one of the buses, instructing the SS officers to shoot all the hostages when they reached their destination. As the waiting dragged on, it was starting to seem as if they had reached the end of the line.[12]

Meanwhile, curious Italian peasants had begun to drift toward the roadside scene. They were kept back by the guards, but they waved to the strangers and began to recognize some of the well-known faces among them, guessing that some kind of intrigue was going on.[13] The convoy also became an object of curiosity to people passing by on the road. A truck full of German troops drove past and jeered at the prisoners, shouting abuse.

They appeared to think the Prominenten were *Parteigenossen*, members of the Nazi Party desperately fleeing the approaching Allies.[14] The irony was not lost on the prisoners.

Eventually the spectacle provoked a breakthrough. Some civilians on bicycles came along, heading toward Niederdorf,* a village about a mile ahead. They recognized Kurt von Schuschnigg, and when they reached the village they reported what was going on to the local authorities. By chance, an Italian quartermaster from the high commission at Bolzano happened to be in Niederdorf that day. Anton Ducia, an engineer by profession, was responsible for the billeting of German forces in this part of the South Tyrol, as well as looking after the many civilian refugees. Hearing of the plight of the busloads of VIP prisoners, he came out to investigate.[15]

Ducia was a well-dressed man in early middle age, with an alert, intelligent, and good-natured face. He introduced himself to Schuschnigg and spoke to Stiller, offering to provide food and accommodations for the prisoners in Niederdorf. Stiller, apparently fearing that control of the situation was slipping out of his grasp, was reluctant to let this Italian take a hand. Determined to help, Ducia traveled back and forth between the roadside party and the village several times, making inquiries and provisional arrangements and trying to persuade Stiller. What neither Stiller nor the Prominenten knew was that Ducia, besides working as an administrator for the Nazi occupiers, was secretly a leader in one of the local Italian resistance networks and therefore had reasons of his own to take an interest in the plight of the hostages.

Stiller's authority was beginning to evaporate in the face of an obviously sensible plan. The Prominenten, individually and in groups, began taking matters into their own hands. Blithely disregarding the German guards, Canon Neuhäusler led a small group of fellow clergyman to Niederdorf, intent on finding whatever supplies they could lay their hands on to feed the women and children. Not even Bader's SD men so much as raised a finger in objection.

---

* Italian: Villabassa

In the confusion of the moment, another small group of prisoners took the opportunity to melt away from the crowd. General Sante Garibaldi and Colonel Davide Ferrero discovered—or possibly Ferrero knew already—that an Italian railway worker who operated the nearby crossing and lived in a little Alpine-style cottage beside it was a low-level partisan leader, with a rank equivalent to a sergeant or corporal. Garibaldi and Ferrero invited Peter Churchill, along with their two Italian orderlies, Amici and Bartoli, to accompany them on a visit.[16]

Slinking away from the convoy, they were welcomed into the railwayman's cottage, where they were regaled with a huge breakfast. The simple country fare seemed like a banquet to Peter Churchill, who hadn't eaten so well in a very long time. Back at the convoy, Isa Vermehren saw a freshly slaughtered lamb carcass being carried into the cottage and wondered what was going on.[17]

With the situation slipping through his fingers, Stiller confronted his increasingly unruly prisoners and promised them that he would not keep them waiting there. With that, he headed for Niederdorf, apparently intending to resolve the crisis.[18]

The town of Niederdorf was really little more than a village on a winding river with a beautiful baroque church and several charming hotels and hostelries catering to the tourist trade. Until lately it had been a quiet little place, busy only during the holiday months, but was now overrun with refugees and soldiers. Stiller found the neat central square gridlocked with military traffic and the sidewalks thronged with people. He couldn't find either a telephone or a telegraph office to communicate with his superiors. When he approached a Wehrmacht detachment and asked for assistance, its leader refused to help an SS officer. With the structure of the German armed forces crumbling, the enmity between the Wehrmacht and the SS was coming out, and the terror inspired by Himmler's elite was losing its power over ordinary soldiers.

It was only when he walked into the town hall—a building of gray stone and white stucco in one corner of the square—that he found a receptive ear. The mayor listened to Stiller's account of his predicament, and after protracted negotiations he finally gave a promise that some of the prisoners could be accommodated in the town hall. Others would have to be housed in local hotels and private houses.

However, when Stiller spoke to Anton Ducia, the Italian quartermaster admitted he had reached an impasse. Every hotel in Niederdorf was full and every type of accommodation in the region was taken up by army staffs, their support groups, and medical posts, as well as civilians from bombed-out hospitals and schools. The Puster valley and South Tyrol were fully booked.[19]

In desperation, Stiller invoked the name of Franz Hofer, the Nazi Gauleiter, the most powerful civilian in the area, directly responsible to Heinrich Himmler. Hofer had promised Stiller accommodations for up 160 prisoners and sixty guards at the Pragser Wildsee hotel. Ducia was galvanized by the mention of the Gauleiter's name, and Stiller underlined the point, reminding Ducia that he had several dozen volatile SD and SS men under his command. He added, "If accommodation isn't found for these prisoners, I fear the worst may happen."

Ducia knew he had to act swiftly and decisively. A speedy evacuation of the Luftwaffe generals occupying the Pragser Wildsee was imperative. He assured Stiller he would sort the matter out. In the meantime, the mayor promised to attend to Stiller's immediate needs for that evening.

Back at the railway crossing, the unhappy occupants of the five buses continued to endure an uncertain and uncomfortable wait in the cold and damp. Most of them had returned to their seats, preferring the cramped conditions over getting soaked to the skin. It was eleven o'clock in the morning when the clergymen returned from Niederdorf with coffee, margarine, and cheese, enough to provide a frugal meal for some of the needier prisoners. But for the rest, the long hours ticked away and the hunger pangs grew.

In the railwayman's cottage, only a hundred or so yards away, there was an atmosphere of celebration, conspiracy, and intrigue—Peter Churchill, Sante Garibaldi, Davide Ferrero, and their Italian orderlies having enjoyed a veritable feast provided by their partisan host. After a while, one

The entrance to Sachsenhausen concentration camp near Berlin where some of the VIP hostages were imprisoned before being transported to Dachau.

A rare photo of British Secret Intelligence Service agent Sigismund Payne Best at Sachsenhausen concentration camp in 1943. (Private Papers of Captain S. Payne Best, OBE; Imperial War Museum)

John "Mad Jack" Churchill was a British commando renowned for going into battle armed with bagpipes, a longbow, and a broadsword. In 1940 he killed a German soldier with his bow. Churchill was captured in 1944 while fighting in Yugoslavia with Tito's Partisans.

Harry "Wings" Day: Shot down in 1939, Day was a major planner, organizer, and participant in the Great Escape, which he survived. His role in rescuing the Prominenten has not been fully acknowledged.

Sydney "Laughing Boy" Dowse was shot down in his Spitfire in 1941. He was a survivor of the Great Escape and was later imprisoned in Sachsenhausen concentration camp, where he made another escape attempt. (Ian Sayer Archive)

Bertram "Jimmy" James: Shot down in 1940, James was involved in several escape attempts, including the Great Escape, which he survived, and later one from Sachsenhausen concentration camp. (Ian Sayer Archive)

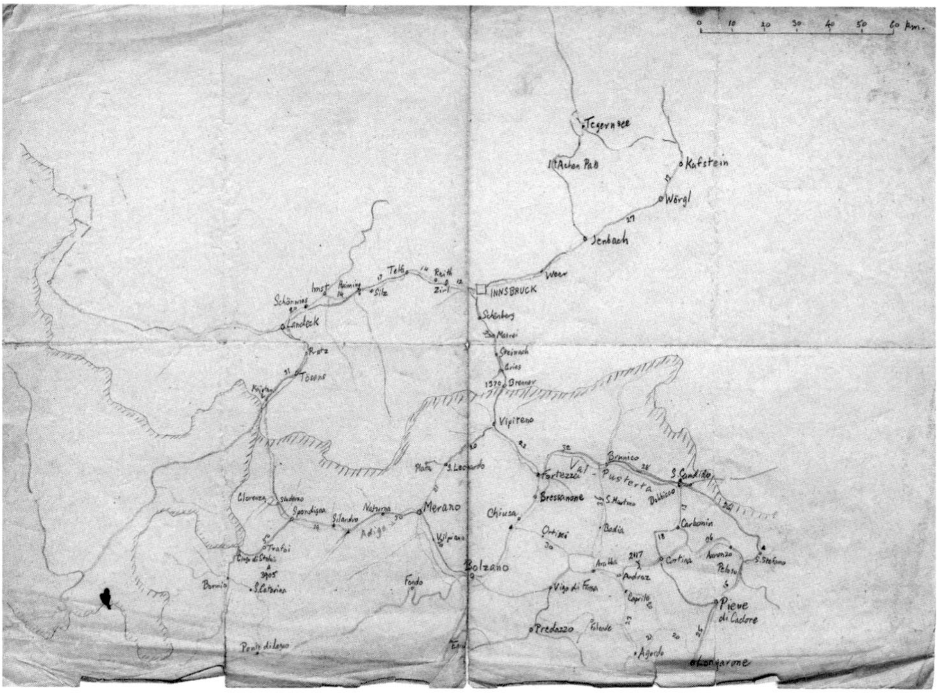

Jimmy James's handwritten "Escape Map," which he compiled during the fateful journey to the Tyrol. (Ian Sayer Archive)

The Bunker (on the right) at Dachau concentration camp, where some of the VIP hostages were accommodated before they were taken to the Tyrol. The yard in front of the Bunker had been used for executions. (Ian Sayer Archive)

Georg Elser attempted to kill Hitler with a bomb in 1939. Imprisoned in Dachau, he was finally executed in April 1945.

Richard Stevens was another British Secret Intelligence Service agent captured in 1939 together with Sigismund Payne Best. For several years he was imprisoned in Dachau in a cell near Georg Elser.

Georg Elser's cell in the Bunker. He was taken from here and executed in the camp crematorium following instructions contained in the Müller Order. (Ian Sayer Archive)

Gestapo chief Heinrich Müller issued several orders in April 1945 believed to relate to the execution of VIP hostages.

A page from an Enigma intercept decoded by British Intelligence. This message confirms the execution of Georg Elser and seeks further instructions relating to the VIP hostages. (National Archives, Kew, London)

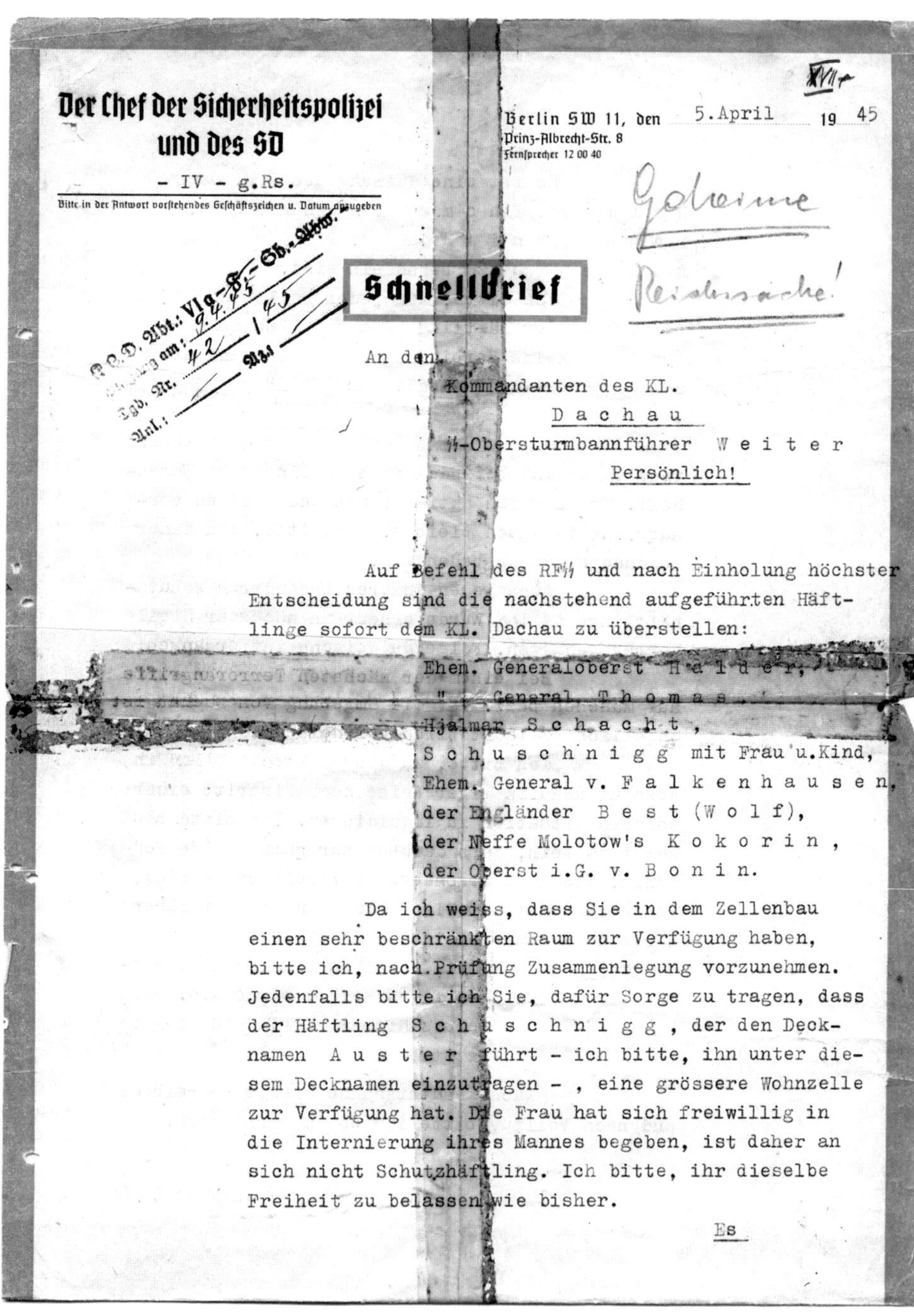
Der Chef der Sicherheitspolizei
und des SD
- IV - g.Rs.
Bitte in der Antwort vorstehendes Geschäftszeichen u. Datum anzugeben

Berlin SW 11, den 5.April 1945
Prinz-Albrecht-Str. 8
Fernsprecher 12 00 40

XVII

Geheime Reichssache!

R.S.D. Abt.: VIa-B-Gb.-Abw.
Eingang am: 9.4.45
Tgb. Nr. 42 / 45
Anl.: / Bl.

Schnellbrief

An den
Kommandanten des KL.
Dachau
SS-Obersturmbannführer Weiter
Persönlich!

Auf Befehl des RFSS und nach Einholung höchster Entscheidung sind die nachstehend aufgeführten Häftlinge sofort dem KL. Dachau zu überstellen:

Ehem. Generaloberst Halder,
" General Thomas,
Hjalmar Schacht,
Schuschnigg mit Frau u.Kind,
Ehem. General v. Falkenhausen,
der Engländer Best (Wolf),
der Neffe Molotow's Kokorin,
der Oberst i.G. v. Bonin.

Da ich weiss, dass Sie in dem Zellenbau einen sehr beschränkten Raum zur Verfügung haben, bitte ich, nach Prüfung Zusammenlegung vorzunehmen. Jedenfalls bitte ich Sie, dafür Sorge zu tragen, dass der Häftling Schuschnigg, der den Decknamen Auster führt - ich bitte, ihn unter diesem Decknamen einzutragen - , eine grössere Wohnzelle zur Verfügung hat. Die Frau hat sich freiwillig in die Internierung ihres Mannes begeben, ist daher an sich nicht Schutzhäftling. Ich bitte, ihr dieselbe Freiheit zu belassen wie bisher.

Es

There are thought to have been several orders issued by Heinrich Müller relating to the hostages. The

Es ist eine Weisung des RF$$, dass H a l d e r , T h o m a s , S c h a c h t , S c h u s c h n i g g und v. F a l k e n - h a u s e n gut zu behandeln sind.

Ich bitte, auf jeden Fall besorgt zu sein, dass der Häftling B e s t (Deckname W o l f) keine Verbindung aufnehmen kann mit dem dort bereits befindlichen Engländer S t e - v e n s .

v. B o n i n war im Führerhauptquartier tätig und befindet sich in einer Art Ehrenhaft. Er ist noch aktiv Oberst und wird es voraussichtlich auch bleiben. Ich bitte, ihn daher besonders gut zu behandeln.

Auch wegen unseres besonderen Schutzhäftlings "Eller" wurde erneut an höchster Stelle Vortrag gehalten. Folgende Weisung ist ergangen:

Bei einem der nächsten Terrorangriffe ~~auf München bezw. auf die Umgebung von Dachau ist~~ angeblich "Eller" tötlich verunglückt.

Ich bitte, zu diesem Zweck "Eller" in absolut unauffälliger Weise nach Eintritt einer solchen Situation zu liquidieren. Ich bitte besorgt zu sein, dass darüber nur ganz wenige Personen, die ganz besonders zu verpflichten sind, Kenntnis erhalten. Die Vollzugsanzeige hierüber würde dann etwa an mich lauten:

> "Am .... anlässlich des Terrorangriffs auf ..... wurde u.a. der Schutzhäftling "Eller" tötlich verletzt."

Nach Kenntnisnahme dieses Schreibens und nach Vollzug bitte ich es zu vernichten.

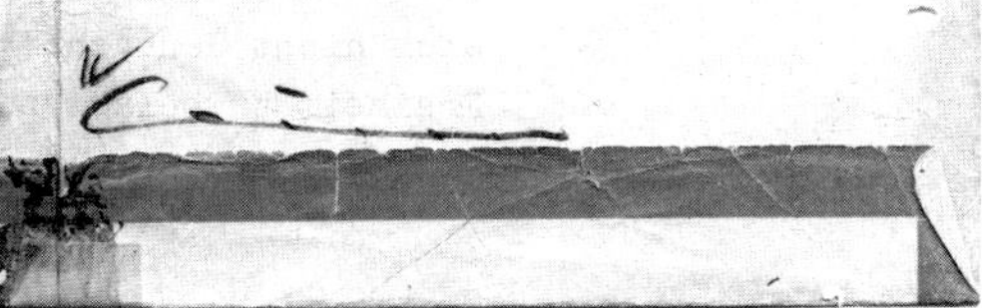

original of the only surviving one was discovered by Ian Sayer during the research for this book.

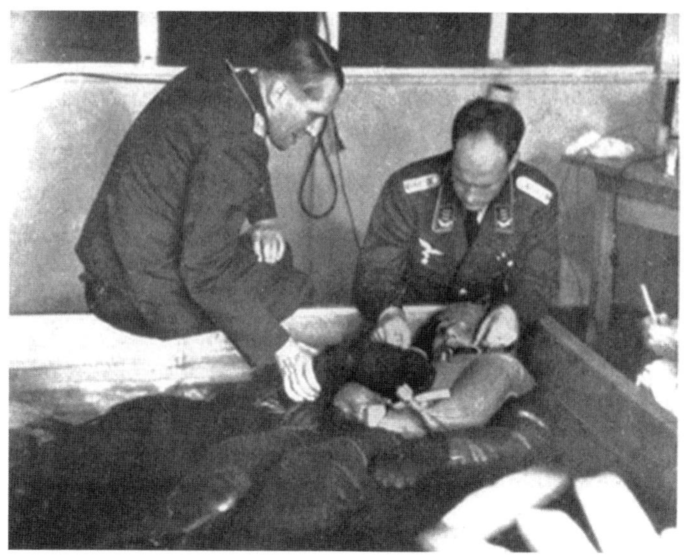

Dr. Sigmund Rascher (right, in Luftwaffe uniform) conducts an ice water experiment at Dachau. Rascher was later an SS officer and VIP hostage.

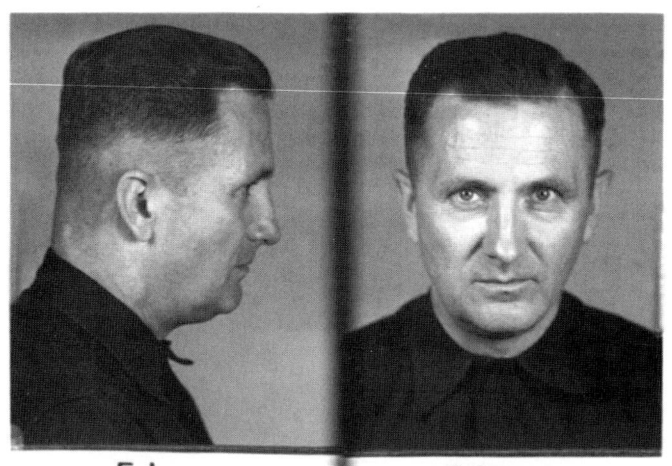

Edgar Stiller was the SS officer responsible for the VIPs imprisoned in the Dachau Bunker. In April 1945 he assumed responsibility for the transport of the 139 VIP hostages to the Tyrol. (National Archives)

Fey Pirzio-Biroli with her sons Roberto and Corrado. On her arrest by the SS, Fey was separated from her boys, and throughout her captivity knew nothing of their fate.

Hjalmar Schacht was a former president of the Reichsbank and Nazi Minister of Economics. Arrested for alleged involvement in the Hitler bomb plot, he was later tried at Nuremberg but acquitted. (Ian Sayer Archive)

A former prime minister of France, Leon Blum was voluntarily accompanied by Jeanne Levylier ("Janot"), whom he married during his imprisonment in the concentration camp at Buchenwald. (*L'Ours*)

General (later Field Marshal) Aleksandros Papagos was commander of the Greek army. In 1943 he began a resistance movement and was taken hostage. He later became prime minister of Greece.

The enigmatic Heidel Nowakowski: Some of the hostages thought her to be a spy and others a "lady of the night." The true story is told here for the first time.

Isa Vermehren: A pre-war comedienne and accordion player, she became a "kin prisoner" when her brother defected to the British. Later she became a nun. (Ian Sayer Archive)

Niederdorf: The scene of the denouement between the SS and the Wehrmacht on Monday 30 April 1945. (Ian Sayer Archive)

Church of Saint Stephen at Niederdorf, where some of the hostages attended Mass on Sunday 29 April 1945. All prayed for deliverance from their anticipated impending execution at the hands of the SS. (Ian Sayer Archive)

Hotel Pragser Wildsee immediately after the liberation of the hostages. (Imperial War Museum)

A lone soldier stands guard at Pragser Wildsee following the liberation of the hostages. (National Archives)

A large group of former VIP hostages gather in front of the Pragser Wildsee following their liberation by US forces. (National Archives)

Emma Heiss-Hellenstainer, owner of the Hotel Pragser Wildsee, and VIP hostage Prince Friedrich Leopold of Prussia. (National Archives)

Fritz Thyssen (in long coat) was a former financier of the Nazi regime who opposed the war and was later imprisoned. His wife, Amelie, remained with him in captivity. Sigismund Payne Best is standing to the right of Thyssen. (National Archives)

Pastor Martin Niemöller contemplates his good fortune at the Hotel Pragser Wildsee after having been liberated by US forces. (National Archives)

British SOE agent Peter Churchill and his fiancée, Odette Sansom, in 1947. He survived because he was thought to be a relative of Prime Minister Winston Churchill. (Central Press/ Getty Images)

Lieutenant Colonel John T. English, commander of the US 339th Infantry Regiment, holds little "Sissy" Schuschnigg (the daughter of the former Austrian chancellor) while her mother, Vera, and British secret agent Sigismund Payne Best look on. (National Archives)

Martin Niemöller, former World War I U-boat captain turned pastor, who opposed the Nazi regime's control of the churches, thanks his liberator Lieutenant Colonel John T. English. (National Archives)

of the orderlies, Bartoli, emerged from the cottage and walked back to the buses, where he discreetly approached Wings Day and Mad Jack Churchill. "With General Garibaldi's compliments," he said. "My master wishes to see you in the cottage there as soon as you can manage."[20]

Bartoli walked back to the cottage, and a few minutes later, Day and Churchill unobtrusively wandered away from the convoy in that general direction. Quietly they slipped in through the door.

They found their fellow officers seated around the kitchen table, on which there were flagons of wine and a half-eaten roast lamb. Garibaldi, playing the host, invited the two Englishmen to sit. He welcomed them profusely in Italian, with Peter Churchill translating, and invited them to partake in the lamb and Chianti. "Gentlemen," said Garibaldi. "I have asked you to come here so as to give you the picture of the situation as we see it, and also because Colonel Ferrero promised we should find means of escape once we reached Italy."[21]

Day recalled this promise vividly, and how bitterly he had regretted being influenced by it and abandoning his and Dowse's plan to hide in the roof space at Dachau.

"Fifty yards away in the wood over the level crossing," Garibaldi went on, "lies freedom." He relayed the information he had received from the railwayman: The pine forests nearby were crawling with South Tyrolean partisan units, numbering about a thousand men. The railwayman could provide several cars to convey the officers present in this room to them.

"The position, therefore, is as follows," said Garibaldi. "If we join the partisans, who have invited me to be their leader, we could then surround the convoy and rescue all the prisoners. On the other hand, our absence might jeopardise the lives of the people left behind. In that event I can arrange for the partisans to surround us without our being with them." Garibaldi paused while Peter Churchill translated his proposal, then said, "Wing Commander Day, may I have your views, please?"

Day felt a rush of enthusiasm and relief at the thought of escape and action, but he kept a level head. He paused, and said, "On the whole I think the second plan is less risky for the majority. We have a number of women and children with us, and also some elderly people. They must be protected from harm. I feel, therefore, that we should stay with the convoy so that we can overpower the SS when your partisans attack."

Garibaldi turned to Jack Churchill. "And now your opinion, please?"

Mad Jack gave Garibaldi his habitually belligerent look. He was made of different stuff than the other men present and had no scruples about the risk to the other prisoners, or indeed about securing their liberty. "I think we should escape while the going's good," he said.[22]

"Thank you," said Garibaldi. He then asked for the views of Ferrero, the seasoned guerrilla leader.

"I agree with Wing Commander Day," said Ferrero.

Garibaldi looked at the faces around the table. "Gentlemen, the majority votes for the second course of action."

At Day's suggestion, it was agreed that the attack should take place the following night, Sunday 29 April, by which time the Prominenten should be in more secure accommodations and therefore safer. An attack on the convoy on open ground would probably result in more casualties among them than among the SS. When the attack began, the conspirators around the table, together with Sydney Dowse, Jimmy James, and the other British would attack the SS men from behind.

Garibaldi drew the meeting to a close. "We are all agreed on the plan, which I shall now set in motion. I thank you all."

Leaving the cottage, Peter Churchill found himself admiring Garibaldi and Ferrero's selflessness; they could simply have melted away into the countryside to join their partisan comrades, leaving the other prisoners to their fate. Churchill wondered how he would have acted in a similar situation, returning to a German-occupied England after years in captivity and finding an army of British partisans at his beck and call. Would he have acted as the Italian officers had?

Mad Jack thought differently. As they walked back through the rain to the convoy, he told Day it was a pity they had missed a great opportunity to escape. He wasn't overly troubled, however—he confided to Day that was planning to "beat it" that night and strike out on his own.[23] Returning to their buses to find that several small groups of Prominenten—mostly younger men—had taken it upon themselves to walk into Niederdorf, Day and Jack Churchill decided to do the same, and they set off on foot.[24]

While Stiller struggled to organize accommodations in the town, yet more random parties of prisoners were wandering off. Bader went into Niederdorf to try and assert some control. He stormed from place to place, raging, and threw one party of clerical prisoners, including Karl Kunkel, out of a tavern where they'd found shelter.[25]

Out in the street, Kunkel saw General Georg Thomas and the young lawyer Fabian von Schlabrendorff, accompanied by the Englishman Sigismund Payne Best, walking into the village.[26] Payne Best was intrigued by Schlabrendorff, one of the handful of people who had actively participated in assassination plots against Hitler, resisted Gestapo torture, and yet lived. The three men, bored and extremely hungry, had come looking for sustenance. As they walked along the street toward the center of the village, picking their way through the crowds of refugees and German soldiers, someone called out "Thomas! Thomas!" A German general who had been standing nearby came rushing forward and embraced Thomas; they were old friends.[27]

Karl Kunkel, watching this encounter, noticed SS-Obersturmführer Stiller looking on. The expression on Stiller's face was transparent—he knew he was losing control.[28]

Walking on, Payne Best and Schlabrendorff bumped into Anton Ducia, who rounded up several more of the wandering Prominenten and took them to the Goldener Stern hotel, where they could get food. Payne Best's joy and excitement at being in a real hotel again was almost overwhelming. It was clean and warm, and they were quickly taken care of by the friendly, solicitous woman owner. Having washed, the prisoners were led to a long table where they were served liver and mushroom stew by Tyrolean waitresses in bright, pretty dresses. Would the gentlemen like wine? They absolutely would, and soon they were laughing and talking like a band of holidaymakers.

Back at the convoy, there was neither joy nor laughter. The majority of the Prominenten had remained aboard their stationary buses—those who were too intimidated by the guards or not fit or healthy enough to walk the distance through the cold rain to the village. There were others who chose not to abandon their weaker companions at the roadside. Besides the cold and discomfort and hunger, fear was spreading among them.

After the breakup of the meeting in the cottage, Peter Churchill had returned to his bus to find a small insurrection taking place. An SD guard on one of the other buses had been drinking schnapps, as had most of his comrades, including SS-Untersturmführer Bader. This man had downed most of a bottle and—with help and encouragement from some of the prisoners—had fallen into a stupor. One prisoner had extracted the guard's wallet, which contained a folded-up document issued by Himmler's office in Berlin. It gave orders for the execution of twenty-eight named Prominenten, including all the British officers and other military prisoners.[29]

Eighteen
Plan of Execution

Saturday 28 April: Niederdorf

The discovery of the order created a dramatic stir among the Prominenten who had remained with the convoy. It was confirmed by Wilhelm von Flügge, who reported that he had been dozing aboard his bus earlier and had overheard Stiller and Bader talking about orders they had received "to execute prisoners when the right moment arrived."[1]

Kurt von Schuschnigg and his family had more than just hearsay to concern them. SS-Untersturmführer Bader had actually shown him an execution list. Schuschnigg described it in his diary as "a list of the people who are to be done away with, on Himmler's special orders. My wife's name and my own are on the list, neatly printed in black and white. I knew of the list at Dachau, and I suppose we are shown the document now to subdue our spirits."[2] Far from being terrified by this information, Schuschnigg was too numb to feel anything.

In the meantime, various conversations between the Prominenten and their guards had revealed a wide, and possibly widening, gulf between two broadly different groups. On the one hand were the fanatical Nazis, totally in thrall to their Führer, who were livid at the imminent defeat of their beloved fatherland. This group included most if not all of Bader's men, hardened and brutal thugs who would carry out summary executions without a second thought. The others, consisting of at least some of Stiller's men, were of a more sympathetic disposition—men who had never really relished some of their more disagreeable functions in the past and were beginning to worry about their prospects in the future.[3]

There was no doubting which camp SS-Untersturmführer Friedrich Bader belonged in. The big question mark was over his unwilling partner—and technically his senior officer—in the ambivalent form of SS-Obersturmführer Edgar Stiller. Payne Best had gained the impression that Stiller "not only could not do anything but did not much want to, and it looked rather as though he were adopting only passive resistance to Bader's wish to liquidate the whole lot of us."[4] To him, Stiller was an insipid, weak, and totally untrustworthy individual who mostly just wanted to survive. It had been on this basis that he had attempted in vain to get Schacht and Thyssen to bribe him.

There was at least one German among the Prominenten who was willing to take action. As soon as he heard of the execution order found in the guard's wallet, Colonel Bogislaw von Bonin decided to find a telephone and make contact with the headquarters of Colonel General Heinrich von Vietinghoff, the commander in chief of German forces in Italy.

Although only a colonel, Bonin had served at the very top of the army general staff; not only was he accustomed to dealing with senior commanders, he was personally acquainted with Vietinghoff. Formerly an operations officer in the Afrika Korps and chief of staff in XIV and LVI Panzer Corps, Bonin had later served as chief of the operational branch of the army high command. Neither Stiller's nor Bader's men felt inclined to hinder this impressive figure when he descended from his bus and set out along the road to Niederdorf, accompanied by Wilhelm von Flügge.[5]

In town Bonin and Flügge went into the Hotel Bachmann, an inn in the main square, which was packed with people. Among the crowd they spotted Stiller and Bader at a table with some other SS men, filling their faces with sausages and beer. Bader glared furiously at the two Prominenten but, after a tense pause, went back to his food. Bonin and Flügge moved on to the Goldener Stern hotel, where they found some of their fellow Germans—along with Sigismund Payne Best—dining in considerable luxury. Bonin was so hungry, and the food before him so inviting, that he decided to delay his mission for a little while and sat down to eat.

Halfway through the meal, General Georg Thomas came in, full of news. The general he'd been talking to in the street was an old and very close friend of his and happened to be the town major* of Niederdorf. He was eager to do whatever he could to help resolve the plight of the hostages. It was a precarious situation. With the partisans' general insurrection in progress, there was chaos and fighting everywhere. At the same time, the German high command in Italy was in delicate negotiations with the Allies to bring about a cease-fire. Payne Best pointed out to Thomas that the German general commanding this operational area would be held responsible by the Allies if any harm came to the hostages.

Thomas admitted that he didn't personally know the commander in chief, Vietinghoff. Bonin, seeing his moment, stepped in. After some discussion, it was decided that Bonin and Thomas should both go with the town major and try to arrange for Bonin to telephone Vietinghoff.[6]

After they had gone, the luncheon party was joined by Wings Day and Mad Jack Churchill. Like Bonin and Flügge, they had tried the Hotel Bachmann and found it bursting at the seams with people, including fellow prisoner General Papagos and his party having "a whale of a meal." Unable to find anywhere to sit, Day and Churchill had crossed the road to the Goldener Stern, where they found a group of Scandinavian, Yugoslavian, and Hungarian Prominenten, as well as some of the German kin prisoners. The latter were accompanied by Flight Lieutenant Sydney Dowse, who had developed a romantic attachment to young Gisela von Plettenberg.[7]

After lunch, Day learned of Bonin's efforts to make contact with Vietinghoff. He approved of the idea, considering Bonin "a very live and very nice wire"; Day had been thinking to himself ever since the Brenner Pass that if he'd been one of the German generals he'd have seized this "heaven sent opportunity to get rid of this murderous gang of SS guards."[8]

---

* *town major*: In a war zone, an officer in charge of the administration of an occupied town

However, although Day was pleased that the German prisoners were finally taking some decisive action, he was not about to throw his lot in with them. As far as he was concerned, Payne Best was welcome to help with their attempts to negotiate, but Day didn't consider himself "an active prodder." He believed that the best solution was immediate rescue, not passively waiting for some negotiated deal. As dangerous as it was, he much preferred Garibaldi and Ferrero's attack plan.[9] For the time being, the conspirators were keeping this scheme secret from the other hostages.

Eventually the various little groups of Prominenten finished their lunches and—with remarkable obedience—walked back along the forest-lined road to the spot near the railway line where the buses were parked. For some, all their worldly belongings were aboard those vehicles, and they wouldn't willingly leave them behind.[10] Others may have been to some degree institutionalized by their long imprisonment, habituated to captivity. There was also the constant concern that if even one person were to abscond, their guards might inflict disproportionate retribution on those left behind.

By the time the wanderers had returned to the buses, it was late afternoon and the other hostages were growing ever more restless and despondent. Stiller was struggling to keep them under control. Having lasted all day with nothing but a cold breakfast of cheese and bread, their patience was at an end, and they demanded to be driven into the town. Stiller repeatedly told them that arrangements for their accommodation would be made before long. They reminded him of his promise not to keep them waiting in the cold and rain, and eventually he offered to take just the women and children into Niederdorf. The men would have to sleep on the buses.

Canon Neuhäusler roundly rejected this proposal on behalf of everyone present.[11] Stiller told him petulantly that if any men wanted to go into the town they could walk there themselves. Since some of the men—such as Léon Blum—were too old and frail to walk and were suffering in the purgatory of the cramped buses, Neuhäusler rejected this absurd suggestion too.

In the end, Stiller caved in and gave the order for all five buses to be driven into Niederdorf. Their engines started up and, with a gray and gloomy day turning into a dismal, dark evening, they pulled away along the road. With the inevitability of a farce, the tail-end bus ran about a hundred yards then stalled and ground to a halt. It had run out of fuel. Another bus had to come back and tow it to the town after dropping off its passengers. Payne Best, aboard the stranded bus, was consumed with anxiety and impatience at the delay, longing to find out whether Thomas and Bonin's bid to get the Wehrmacht involved had borne any fruit.[12]

By the time the last of the buses rolled into Niederdorf it was nearing midnight. The older Prominenten were in a bad way. Léon Blum was almost prostrate from fatigue, pain, hunger, and cold.[13] The VIPs' arrival caused a stir in the small community. The South Tyrolean people had never seen anything quite like it before. One of the Prominenten, the politician Hermann Pünder, described the scene: "Thin gentlemen wearing general's trousers with civilian jackets and floppy hats, women with long military boots, shivering people without coats, at best with a warming neckerchief, old gentlemen with grubby rucksacks on their backs."[14] The locals felt sympathy for this ragtag collection of unfortunates, and the mayor had managed to persuade some of them to find space for the Prominenten.

The accommodations varied greatly, and some were luckier than others. Most of the able-bodied had to make do with straw palliasses on the upper floors of the town hall. These hostages—including all the most active military men—were the main security risk, and Stiller set a strong guard throughout the building; his and Bader's men covered the entrances and exits and were posted at key points inside. Other Prominenten, mainly the women and children, had been found beds in a variety of hotels and guesthouses.[15] The luckiest were those assigned rooms in Niederdorf's finest hostelries. That night, the Bachmann and Ebner hotels played host to the most illustrious among them, including Kurt and Vera von Schuschnigg, the Greek generals, and some of the Hungarian ministers. Léon and Janot Blum and the Thyssens were put up by the local parish priest in his house. Fey Pirzio-Biroli and some of the other young women were provided with mattresses on hotel floors.[16]

Payne Best's bus, towed into town long after the others, was met by Anton Ducia, who had assisted the mayor in arranging billets. Payne Best struck lucky—he was invited by General Falkenhausen to share a room he had arranged for himself and General Thomas at the Hotel Bachmann. His comfort was also assured by one of Colonel John McGrath's Irish soldiers, Corporal Andy Walsh, who had appointed himself Payne Best's personal servant, carrying his luggage up to the room. Eager to speak to Thomas or Bonin, Payne Best was disappointed to learn that nothing had been seen of either of them since they had gone off together at lunchtime.[17]

Having heard that there was wine to be had if one charmed the hotel's female owner, Payne Best and Colonel McGrath set off in search of the kitchen. There, amid the bright lights and bustle and clash of pots and pans, they bumped into two of their guards. One, whose name was Fritz, had been a quartermaster sergeant in Dachau and was one of Stiller's more humane men. Or so Payne Best had believed. His companion was one of Bader's SD men; they had been at the wine and were both well along the way to drunkenness. Thinking this would be a good opportunity to get information out of them, Payne Best engaged them in conversation. McGrath, who didn't speak German, walked off and left them to it, missing out on one of the most extraordinary dialogues of the war.[18]

The SD trooper was glassy-eyed and on the verge of passing out, whereas Fritz was alternating between inebriated melancholy—rambling tearfully about his poor wife and children—and truculent assertions that the enemy would never take him alive.

"You're a good fellow," Payne Best told him. "You've always behaved well towards us."

Fritz fixed him with an unsteady look. "I look on you as a dear friend," he slurred. "Let's drink to *Brüderschaft*!"

Payne Best joined him in a toast to brotherhood, and assured him, "I shall put in a good word for you when you fall into the hands of our troops."

This provoked a blustering outburst. Fritz boasted extravagantly about how many Tommies he would kill, repeating that they'd never capture him alive. Eventually his bragging wore itself out and he said, "Yes, I know you're my friend and would help me—*if you were alive*." Fumbling at the breast pocket of his tunic he took out a typewritten paper and flourished it. "Here is the order for your execution. You won't be alive after tomorrow."

Payne Best tried to conceal his shock. "What nonsense is that?" he said. "Surely no one is going to be such a fool as to shoot any of us at this stage of the war! Why, the whole lot of you will be prisoners yourselves in a day or two."

That provoked another round of bluster from Fritz about how the SS would never be beaten and never surrender. At this, his semiconscious SD friend roused himself and started muttering, "Shoot 'em all down—bum, bum, bum—bump 'em all off is best." He began fumbling at the catch of his pistol holster.

Fritz shook his head. "No, it's quite certain," he said, flourishing the paper. "See, here it is in black and white." He waved it in front of Payne Best, who couldn't read all of it, but made out just enough to see that it was indeed an order issued by the RSHA in Berlin, containing a list of VIP prisoners who must not be allowed to fall into Allied hands and must therefore be executed if there was any danger of this occurring. Payne Best managed to read some of the list, which included Schuschnigg, Blum, Niemöller, Schacht, Müller, and generals Falkenhausen, Thomas, and Halder. It also included Major Richard Stevens and, indeed, Payne Best himself.

He made a show of incredulity. "You surely don't mean to tell me that Stiller would be such a fool as to carry out this order?" He told Fritz how sure he was that Stiller would hold on in Niederdorf and hand over the hostages to the Americans when they arrived.

"Stiller!" Fritz spat contemptuously. "Don't you make any mistake about it. It's Bader who runs this show, and he says he's going to liquidate all the prisoners."

Bader, Fritz added, had been in possession of these orders for the past three months. It was a fixed, preordained plan: The Prominenten would be hostages or they would be dead. There would be no liberation. "Bader always carries out his orders," said Fritz.

Payne Best asked whether Fritz would participate when the time came—would he gun down a man with whom he had just drunk to *Brüderschaft*?

"Ja, Herr Best, but what can I do?"

Fritz described how the following day all the Prominenten would be driven to a hotel in the mountains nearby, where they would be herded inside and shot with machine pistols, and the hotel set on fire. "I don't like it at all," he said. His objections were not so much to the slaughter but to the intended method. He knew from experience that the standard-issue MP40 machine pistols the guards all carried were not efficient killing weapons—they were inaccurate and the rounds were not powerful enough. "A lot of people won't be dead when the place is set on fire," he said.

He paused, lost in thought while Payne Best digested this piece of information. Eventually Fritz went on: "Herr Best, you are my friend. I will tell you what we will do. I will give you a sign before they start shooting and you come and stand near me so that I can give you the *Nackenschuss*—a shot in the back of the neck. That is the best way to die—you won't know anything about it. I'm a dead shot—never miss."

Fritz described in detail the neck-shot method—how the pistol was aimed at the base of the skull, how the muzzle must not touch the skin or the victim would flinch, which would spoil the aim. The bullet must enter at precisely the right spot in order to kill instantly. Fritz was highly experienced at the *Nackenschuss*. "I can do it without looking, almost." He pulled his Walther P38 from its holster and gestured unsteadily with it. "Just turn round and I'll show you."

Payne Best hastily declined the offer. "Don't be silly! How can I see what you do behind my back?"

Fritz nodded. "You," he said to his SD pal. "Turn your head so I can show Herr Best how to give the *Nackenschuss*."

His friend was too far gone—he stared stupidly at Fritz and muttered again, "Bump them all off . . . bum, bum bum . . ." He gave a wild sweep of his arm, sending the wine bottle and glasses crashing to the kitchen floor. Then he laid his head on the table and started snoring.

By now Fritz was too drunk to concentrate and he began rambling again about his innocent wife and little ones, who had no idea of the thousands of people he had killed. He moved on to the subject of how this terrible war had been inflicted on the world by the Jews in England and America and the Führer was a good, peaceful man.[19]

Deciding that the time had come to withdraw, Payne Best left Fritz and his sleeping friend and went back upstairs. Falkenhausen was alone in their room; there was still no sign of Thomas or Bonin. Not wanting to add to the fears already rife among the hostages, Payne Best kept quiet about his conversation with Fritz. If the other Prominenten knew the attitude growing among even Stiller's supposedly more peaceable men, it might escalate the fear into outright panic. Had Payne Best known what was going on elsewhere among his fellow British prisoners, he'd have had even more cause for concern.

Niederdorf town hall was turning into a mix of international hotel and hive of plots. Up on the top floor, General Sante Garibaldi had established what was, in effect, his own partisan headquarters. All evening, members of the local resistance, posing as ordinary civilians calling to pay their respects to their famous countryman, had been coming to meet him and receive orders.[20]

Observing this, Jimmy James—who had now been briefed on Garibaldi's attack plan—was impressed by the sight of him holding court. He had, as if by magic, discarded his striped concentration camp garb and replaced it with the light blue uniform of an Italian general, with all his decorations displayed. Somehow he had succeeded in preserving the uniform throughout his imprisonment. A splendid figure, he oversaw the preparations for the attack with an imperious but good-humored expression on his broad face, with its prominent thick nose and teeth that protruded slightly when he smiled.

Since hearing about Bonin's plan to negotiate their release with Vietinghoff, Garibaldi had decided to postpone the attack temporarily. Wings Day and the other British officers had agreed somewhat reluctantly, insisting that the postponement should be brief. James, for one, wanted action; he didn't like the thought of "sitting around waiting to be massacred by the Bader gang."[21] They were also uncomfortable with the idea of relying on the Germans to free them. Day had made many German friends during his captivity and respected the German people, but he didn't believe that their word could be relied on in such a tense situation—especially when it involved generals who were currently still fighting the Allies.[22]

Adding to the powder keg, Stiller's and Bader's men had learned of Bonin's plan and resented it. The idea of one of their prisoners reaching over their heads to a general of the Wehrmacht did not sit well with the SS men. Payne Best's friendly drinking companion Sergeant Fritz had commented on Bonin, "We should have shot that traitor first."[23]

There was also friction brewing in the town hall among the Hungarian VIP prisoners and the German kin prisoners. Whereas former Hungarian prime minister Miklós Kállay and former secretary of state Andreas Hlatky had been accommodated at the Hotel Bachmann, ex-minister of the interior Baron Péter Schell had sought lodgings in the town hall alongside the British POWs, whose straw mattresses were laid out in the council chamber and banquet hall. The six remaining Hungarians—senior army officers and Nicky Horthy's secretary—had had no accommodations provided for them. They came into the town hall carrying cases and valises bulging with their prized collections of wine, cigars, and fine food.[24]

Finding that there was no room for them or their possessions and no spare palliasses, they went to the chamber where some of the male kin prisoners had settled and began forcibly evicting them. All the enmity between the deposed Hungarians and their former German allies bubbled up. The kin prisoners, who were mostly not fighting men, quailed in the face of the aggressive army officers.

Wings Day was told about the confrontation and immediately went to intervene. Accompanied by Baron Schell, he marched into the chamber, which was crowded with prisoners and stacked with the Hungarians' belongings. Day called loudly for attention and firmly told the Hungarians, "Get out at once, or I will personally see that you and your luggage are chucked into the street." Baron Schell backed him up, berating his countrymen for their shameful behavior in their own language, using—by the sound of it—much stronger terms. It had the desired effect. The Hungarians gathered up their things and retreated to a different room, where the only beds were piles of loose straw.[25]

Across Niederdorf, the various Prominenten eventually settled for the night. Many of them felt relief at being able to lie down after so long sitting upright, even if it was only on straw. But there were some who were aware of the real, palpable tension rising. Captain Peter Churchill, like most of his fellow Britons, was one of them. He had spent part of the afternoon in a long and fascinating conversation with Fabian von Schlabrendorff, who had told him the story of his army career and his involvement in a bomb plot against Hitler in 1943. Churchill, who liked and admired the German, realized what an act of trust it was to confess this. As they parted, Schlabrendorff said, "We are not out of the wood yet, Churchill, and I feel that tonight may be a danger spot."[26]

There was one man among the hostages who was not willing to put up with the tension, discomfort, and confinement any longer. Colonel Jack Churchill had made up his mind to do something about it right away.

He and Jimmy James were sitting on their straw palliasses in the council chamber when suddenly Mad Jack said in his clipped, abrupt manner, "I'm off, Jimmy. I've had enough of this lot. You coming?"

As a Great Escaper, Jimmy James's instinct for absconding was strong, but he was also accustomed to systematic planning. "No," he said. "Not this time." He reasoned that the war would almost certainly be over before they had stumbled their way over the first mountain.[27]

Mad Jack was unimpressed by this argument. He'd had enough of the way Payne Best and his German friends seemed to dominate everything, talking and planning and never actually doing anything. Jack Churchill was an aggressive fighting man who had enjoyed an extremely active war. Nine months of imprisonment—a great deal of it in solitary confinement—had frayed his patience and temper beyond endurance. It wasn't just being stuck here that bothered him; he had a yearning to get back into the fight, and time was rapidly running out.[28]

He talked the matter over with Wings Day and received the same answer: Day declined to join him, although his reasons were not the same as James's. For one, Day had promised Garibaldi that the British officers would help overpower the SS guards when the partisans made their attack. More importantly, he was the de facto leader of the British prisoners (with the exception of Payne Best, who went his own way), and his absence would definitely be noticed immediately, with dire consequences for the other hostages.[29]

Although he wouldn't go with him, Day approved of Churchill's attempt and gave him assistance. He and Jimmy James provided some spare warm clothing and Day walked with him part of the way. They left the town hall and walked along the square, turning left by the Hotel Bachmann onto the dark, narrow street leading to the edge of the little town.[30]

As a justification for helping Mad Jack escape, Day planned that if ever there seemed a real imminent danger of the SS shooting the British prisoners, he would announce to Bader in front of his men that Colonel Churchill had escaped with a list of every man in the SS and SD squad, and that if they murdered the prisoners, they would be executed as war criminals the moment they were captured.[31] In truth, this was a feeble plan concocted to excuse Churchill's action. Several people had rejected the idea of escape on the grounds that it would risk bringing down the wrath of Bader on those who remained, in particular the children, women, and old men. On that night in Niederdorf, with the SS facing apocalypse and many of its members drunk with bloodlust, the danger had never been greater.

At the railway line on the edge of town, Day wished Mad Jack good luck and watched him walk away into the darkness across the tracks, heading for the fringe of the thick pine forest.

When Payne Best heard later about Jack Churchill's escape, he was angered and disgusted. "It was, I think, a cowardly action, such as even the bravest man is sometimes guilty of." Peter Churchill also disapproved and remonstrated with Day.[32] They feared for the consequences if and when the SS discovered Mad Jack's absence. In truth, the escape was not cowardly but selfish, born of Jack Churchill's inability to control his impulse to rejoin a war that was already ending.

As Day watched him disappear into the darkness, he didn't know that Mad Jack had no intention of contacting the Allies on the prisoners' behalf or of doing anything other than helping himself.

Day returned to the town hall. Walking in through the front door, he was alarmed to find the entrance hall barred by a cordon of fifteen of Bader's SD troopers with their machine pistols at the ready.[33] Bader himself was pacing up and down, obviously in a bad mood. Peter Churchill happened to walk in at the same time as Day. Bader strode up to him. "Where is your cousin?" he demanded.

Peter Churchill was accustomed to the Germans' erroneous belief that he was Jack's (and indeed Winston's) cousin. He knew nothing of his namesake's escape and simply shrugged. "I have no idea," he said. "Perhaps he's already upstairs and fast asleep."[34] Beside him, Wings Day tensed, thinking quickly. Were they searching for Mad Jack already? Surely he hadn't been gone long enough for his absence to register.

"Well," said Bader. "We have reserved a special room for you British officers in a nice house across the square."[35]

Day didn't like the sound of this but, keeping his outward cool despite the sense of imminent danger, he said, "We don't want any special rooms. We'll doss down with Colonel Churchill and all the others. We've already made our arrangements."

Bader was nonplussed by this bland response and seemed unwilling to press the matter. He walked away.

Once Bader was out of earshot, Miklós Kállay, who had overheard the exchange, came and whispered to Peter Churchill, "In God's name don't go to any special room tonight. They're gunning for you. I feel it in my bones."

"Thanks," said Churchill. "But don't worry. We feel it too."

Trying to act as unconcerned as possible, Day and Churchill made their way up the main stairway of the town hall. Day didn't know what to think. It would have been easy enough for Bader to check upstairs to see if Mad Jack was there. Had they already captured him, and was Bader simply looking for confirmation that Day had been involved? More than anything, Day felt sure the SS must know about the Garibaldi meeting and would guess that the British contingent must be involved. Was the idea of putting them in a house together a way of isolating—and ultimately liquidating—the threat?[36]

There was a renewed vigilance among the SS and SD guards (those who were still sober, at least). Stiller and Bader were apparently determined to reimpose order after the day of misrule, and their men were on edge. It was a fragile situation, made all the more dangerous by its complexity, with the hostages spread around the town and so many of them eager to act on their own initiative. The Germans were also sensitive to the presence of Italian partisans in the surrounding countryside and the risk of attack. Their fingers tapped on their triggers, waiting for any hint of danger or resistance.

Meanwhile, as the early hours wore away, the Prominenten settled down to an uneasy sleep. In the town hall, at the end of each row of beds sat a guard, cradling his machine pistol on his lap. Hermann Pünder lay on his straw mattress with his heart pounding with fear.[37] Every entrance and staircase was under surveillance, and German patrols roamed up and down the gloomy corridors. Outside, the truck with its load of grenades stood ominously in the town square. In the immediate vicinity yet more heavily armed Germans could be seen in the shadows. Barely a few hundred yards away, in the woods and hills, the partisans watched and waited for their moment of revenge.

Nobody had heard anything of Bonin and Thomas's attempt to negotiate with the German high command, the only hope of a bloodless resolution.

Nineteen
The Fatal Day

Sunday 29 April: Berlin

In the Führer bunker beneath the increasingly devastated capital city, the last days of the Third Reich were playing out with a lethal, farcical inevitability. It was a period of recrimination, betrayal, and execution.

A little after midnight, in a small civil ceremony, Hitler married his longtime mistress, Eva Braun. The haggard, exhausted Führer wore his habitual uniform, and his bride a long black taffeta gown—one of his favorites. Attending the wedding were the remaining handful of loyal and trusted people: Joseph Goebbels and his wife, Martin Bormann, and Hitler's secretaries, Gerda Christian and Traudl Junge.[1]

The previous day, Hitler had learned of Himmler's secret attempts to negotiate with the Allies, which had been announced on Swedish radio. Hitler was floored by the treachery of "loyal Heinrich." Himmler's deputy in Berlin, Hermann Fegelein, was interrogated and executed in the Chancellery garden, and an underling was dispatched to track the traitor down, punish him, and ensure that he did not succeed Hitler as Führer.[2]

With defeat clearly inevitable even to the most deranged fanatics, Hitler was contemplating his own end. Within thirty-six hours he would be dead. For SS officers Friedrich Bader and Edgar Stiller, there was no hope of orders or guidance from Berlin. They were entirely on their own, and their hostages solely at their mercy.

Sunday 29 April: Niederdorf

The early hours passed slowly. Those Prominenten who were fortunate enough to be accommodated in the Bachmann and Ebner hotels were not given the same close guard by Bader's and Stiller's night watch. They nevertheless felt uneasy and took turns standing watch over one another. The rumors of impending liquidation did not allow anyone to lower their vigilance or allay their fear.

Besides the British, the most at risk were the clergy and members of the Goerdeler and Stauffenberg families. Of all the hostages, Hitler had hated them the most intensely. Refuge had been found for the clergy in the presbytery of the Catholic church, which stood on a street off the square on the northern edge of the village. There, Father Josef Brugger, whom Karl Kunkel found "a warm-hearted person," was more than happy to open his doors to the distinguished visitors. Johann Neuhäusler would have preferred to stay with the other prisoners in the town hall, believing that it was only right that he should be with them in their hour of uncertainty. However, he was prevailed upon to move to the presbytery. "The SS are very excitable," two of the clerics told him. They had heard a rumor that Hitler had committed suicide; if it was true, they feared that Bader's men would be furious and seek vengeance.[3]

Canon Neuhäusler had gone to see Stiller and, with all the determination he could muster, told him, "We are going to the Presbytery now. Do not cause any difficulties." After a brief argument, Stiller relented. Neuhäusler had one final demand. The next day was Sunday and he was determined to hold Mass. "Do give your permission," he begged Stiller. "I will arrange everything with the pastor." Stiller resisted for a while but eventually agreed. At around midnight, twelve of the clergy and the members of the Stauffenberg and Goerdeler families made their way to the presbytery, where Brugger made them feel at home. Neuhäusler stayed up until 2:30

in the morning talking to the Stauffenbergs and Goerdelers. Kunkel made his bed in the pantry, wrapped in blankets and coats to ward off the cold. Few of them slept soundly that night.

At the Hotel Bachmann, it was about three o'clock in the morning when Payne Best, who had been waiting on tenterhooks, was roused from fitful dozing by the return of General Georg Thomas.[4]

Thomas explained that Bonin had managed to find a Wehrmacht command post in the village. In his colonel's uniform, Bonin had no difficulty in persuading the captain in charge to make a telephone call to Vietinghoff's headquarters.[5] With the army in retreat and communications typically fraught, Bonin had had to wait for hours before the call was put through. It was after midnight when he managed to talk to Vietinghoff's chief of staff, General Hans Röttiger. Bonin explained the situation the Prominenten were in and his hope that Vietinghoff could help. Röttiger told him that Vietinghoff wasn't there, but promised to speak to the general and have him call back.[6]

Bonin had then been kept waiting for two more hours. Finally, about two o'clock, Vietinghoff called.

He sympathized with the plight of the Prominenten and admitted that the war in Italy was effectively over. His orders were to conduct a fighting retreat into the Dolomite mountains, the region of the Alps in which the Prominenten now were, and defend it to the last. Meanwhile, he was attempting to negotiate with the Allies for an end to hostilities. (His envoy had flown to meet with Field Marshal Harold Alexander about thirty-six hours earlier.) He recognized that he would be responsible for any VIP prisoners murdered in his area of operations and promised to send a Wehrmacht officer with a company of infantry to take safe custody of the Prominenten. He also promised to notify the Americans that the area around Niederdorf was a neutral zone, and that he would take measures himself not to establish any defenses there.[7] It was a theoretically sound plan; a similar neutral zone had been set up two weeks earlier to facilitate the liberation of Bergen-Belsen concentration camp. But that had been on the western front, where the situation was far less chaotic, and where a typhus epidemic had helped keep people away.

Bonin had just put the receiver down when SS-Obersturmführer Stiller stormed into the room accompanied by several of his men, heavily armed. Stiller was furious, having spent much of the night looking for Bonin. As a senior officer, Bonin didn't take kindly to being spoken to like this by an SS lieutenant, and a heated argument followed in which Stiller threatened Bonin with immediate execution for having made an escape attempt. The captain of the command post was also angry with Bonin, who hadn't told him he was a prisoner.

In spite of himself, Bonin felt some sympathy for both of them. He was an officer after all. He had disobeyed Stiller's orders, and he had willfully misled the Wehrmacht captain. The confrontation cooled down, and Bonin was allowed to return to his quarters. Reunited with his fellow hostages, he was able to give them the glad news that the Wehrmacht had promised to liberate them as soon as possible.[8]

Payne Best felt a weight lifted from him and was able to sleep deeply and peacefully the rest of the night, although his snoring and "grunting like a warthog" kept General Falkenhausen awake.[9] The other Prominenten, scattered across Niederdorf and not privy to the news, spent most of the night in waking terror.

❧

Sunday morning came, cold and gray. Yet it was with a spring in his step that a well-rested Sigismund Payne Best walked out of the Hotel Bachmann accompanied by the former Abwehr officer Commander Franz Liedig and Colonel Bogislaw von Bonin.

The three men had already held a "council of war," at which they had decided that the most important preparation for a change of authority was to try to "put the wind up" Stiller themselves.[10] As luck had it, as they were walking out of the hotel they bumped into the man himself, standing in the little cobbled piazza in front of the building. Seizing the opportunity,

Payne Best told him that they would like to have a little chat with him indoors.

Stiller clearly didn't like the sound of this, but the three men looked very determined. Checking that there were none of his or Bader's men about, he followed them into the hotel and upstairs to Payne Best's room. He was nervous but scarcely guessed just how dangerous a trap he was walking into. Bonin was carrying his pistol under his jacket, and the three men had agreed that if Stiller proved intransigent "he would not leave the room alive."[11]

Payne Best, Bonin, Liedig, and Stiller sat around a table, and the British spy was the first up to bat.[12] Recalling their conversation in the Bunker at Dachau, he said, "Herr Obersturmführer, you told me that your orders were to ensure our safety until you were able to hand us over to our advancing troops. Now we have heard a lot of rumours which seem to indicate that you are either unwilling or unable to carry out this intention and that plans are afoot to liquidate the whole lot of us."

This was a somewhat biased summary of Stiller's unwilling promise, but he didn't argue. "No, Herr Best, really, I want to do the best for you—you have nothing to fear from me." Stiller reminded Payne Best that Richard Stevens had known him for a long time: "He can tell you that I have always treated prisoners well." Stiller blamed everything on Bader. "I had a big row with him last night when I told him that I would not allow any of you to be harmed and he threated to bump *me* off. . . . You can count on me to do anything I can to help, but I can't do anything with Bader."

Payne Best was unmoved. "Well, you say that you want to help but can't, so that's not much good to us," he said. "We most certainly are not going to allow you or anyone else to murder us. We have therefore decided that I shall take over command from you." Stiller was stunned by this incredible demand, but said nothing. "Do you agree?" said Payne Best. "Can I count on you for loyal cooperation?"

Stiller—caught between Bader on the one hand and these serious, determined officers on the other, and painfully aware that at this stage of the war he had no real choices left to make—recovered from his shock and gave his agreement. But he still insisted that there was nothing he could do about Bader or his SD troopers. "You will have to fix that yourself," he said. "Bader is a most dangerous man. He belongs to SS-Sturmbannführer Kurt Stawitzki's special detachment which does nothing but extermination."[13]

Kurt Stawitzki was one of the Gestapo's most feared killers, and Bader was one of his most brutal underlings. Stiller pointed out that Bader knew he was already doomed if he fell into Allied hands, and the blood of 139 VIP hostages wouldn't make his hanging any more inevitable than it already was.

Payne Best told Stiller about the promise from General Vietinghoff, that he was providing a company of Wehrmacht infantry who would soon take care of Bader if he proved difficult. He instructed Stiller to pass this information on to Bader and to organize a meeting of all the Prominenten for midday at the Hotel Bachmann, at which Stiller would formally surrender authority to Payne Best.

Backed into a corner and with no way of knowing just how weak Payne Best's hand was, Stiller agreed to both instructions. The meeting came to an end.

Satisfied that they were making good progress in a seemingly impossible situation, Bonin, Liedig, and Payne Best went downstairs again and out of the hotel. In the little piazza, they encountered Wings Day and John McGrath. Thoroughly pleased with himself, Payne Best informed them that he had everything in hand and would be taking charge later that day.

"Oh, you're hopelessly out of date, Best," said Day. "It's all fixed up." And he described to the astonished, horrified officers how Garibaldi had organized a rescue with his partisans. The Italians would kill the guards, occupy Niederdorf, and "take all of us up into the mountains." The attack would take place that very night.[14]

While Bonin, Liedig, and Payne Best had been busy strong-arming Stiller, Wings Day had been summoned from his billet in the town hall council chamber to Sante Garibaldi's headquarters on the top floor.

He and McGrath had gone up together and found a room packed with Italians, with Garibaldi presiding, resplendent in his blue uniform. Colonel Davide Ferrero had also managed to rustle up an appropriate outfit and was looking every inch the guerrilla leader in well-cut khaki with a Sam Browne belt. Day wondered how in the world they had acquired their paraphernalia and how they got away with wearing it under the noses of the SS men.[15]

Communication was difficult because Peter Churchill, who spoke Italian, was absent. However, Day could speak a little French and German, and both Garibaldi and Ferrero spoke good French.

The meeting centered on the attack planned for that night. Despite Garibaldi's concession the previous evening to postpone the attack because of Bonin's attempt to involve Vietinghoff, it was now back on.[16] Not only that, the plan had evolved in extremely alarming ways. Garibaldi and Ferrero now intended to massacre all the Germans in Niederdorf—not only the SS and SD guards but the German hostages as well. Only the women and children would be spared and taken up into the hills along with the rest of the Prominenten.

When Day translated this for McGrath's benefit, the Irishman "nearly had a fit."[17] Day, who was utterly horrified, immediately refused to have any part whatsoever in such a plan.

There was an acrimonious argument between Day and the Italians, with McGrath backing Day forcefully. Eventually, Garibaldi agreed to discard this part of the plan. Day considered him "a nice and kindly chap" at heart and believed he was swayed by the moral arguments; in any case, the plan stood little chance of success without the British playing their part.

Eventually the plan was hammered out. The British contingent's role would be to neutralize the SS guards in the town hall as soon as the Italian partisans launched their surprise attack. The guards elsewhere would have to be taken care of individually. Once the village was secure, the prisoners would be collected and taken to the hills. Ferrero would lead the attack in person. Day had every confidence in Ferrero's abilities, regarding him as a natural leader with a "strong personality, good brain and a great deal of soldiering experience."[18]

Day had no illusions about the dangers of the operation and feared that there might be casualties among the women and children from stray bullets. He could imagine their terror, caught in the middle of a gun battle. However, he concluded that "the war was on—so too bad. Men were killing and being killed. It was better to go this way than against a wall." He didn't feel happy about it but believed that he and McGrath were making the right decision in aligning themselves with the Italians. "We would have looked a pair of bloody cowards if we had not," Day reflected later. "I did not want a bad opinion from Ferrero."[19]

When Payne Best was told about the plan, he was utterly appalled, shocked out of his complacent belief that he had the whole situation in hand. He had seen some of Garibaldi's "so-called partisans," who looked to him like nothing more than "a lot of village youths" with red scarves around their necks.[20] He had no confidence at all in their ability to take on a substantial force of SS and crack SD killers while also keeping safe a scattered group of over a hundred men, women, and children, many of whom would be terrified and panicky. It was vital that Bader be defanged before any attempt to seize control could be made, whether peaceful or violent.

Payne Best could feel the situation slipping away from him. With Bader not yet neutralized, Stiller's promise to yield up authority couldn't be relied on. It was now about 10 a.m., and with the general meeting arranged for noon, Payne Best had two hours to resolve the crisis and "scotch this idea of an armed uprising."[21] Insisting on meeting Garibaldi, he set off for the town hall with Day and McGrath following. He told them diplomatically that he didn't want to force his views on anyone; instead an international committee should be formed to decide the best course of action.

The three men found Garibaldi in his headquarters with Ferrero. Payne Best—who was multilingual and had no difficulty at all with communication—told them in no uncertain terms that their plan could not be countenanced. Invoking democracy and overriding angry objections from Ferrero, he persuaded Garibaldi to agree to hold a meeting at eleven o'clock, including the five men present, plus Bonin, Liedig, Canon Neuhäusler, Major Jan Stanek, General Aleksandros Papagos, and General Pyotr Privalov.[22]

At eleven, the meeting commenced. Payne Best ended up dominating it, due to the language barriers; aside from their native languages, for example, Privalov spoke only German and Papagos only French. Payne Best focused most of his energy on Garibaldi, who was the most important person to win over; his say-so would halt or green-light the partisan operation.

Arguing his case in the face of strident, impassioned resistance from Ferrero, Payne Best appealed to Garibaldi's political sensibilities and his patriotism, pointing out that the South Tyrol had once been Austrian territory and still had a majority of ethnic Germans in its population. There was a risk of it being given back to Austria after the war, and that risk would be increased if, for example, a violent attack by Italian partisans resulted in the deaths of high-profile statesmen like Blum and Schuschnigg.[23]

Garibaldi thought this over. "I am a man of peace," he said, and admitted that he would prefer a nonviolent resolution.

Ferrero reacted furiously. He stormed out of the room, yelling that *he* would go ahead with the attack, regardless of what this committee arranged.

With Garibaldi on his side, Payne Best asked for other opinions. McGrath and Day both said they didn't trust promises from the Germans, but admitted that Payne Best was in a better position to judge whether the German officers concerned were trustworthy. Nobody else raised any objections. At Papagos's suggestion, Payne Best agreed to try to contact the International Red Cross and ask them to intervene.

❧

While the leading military Prominenten were debating and scheming, Hitler's other hostages were spending Sunday morning in as normal a manner as they could.

There were many observant Christians among them, including a number of Catholics. Today, 29 April, was the fourth Sunday after Easter, and Mass would be a great comfort for them that morning. During the night, Stiller had agreed with Canon Neuhäusler that the service could be held, as long as no members of the local community were in attendance. Thus, at ten o'clock—while Payne Best was learning about the partisan attack and rushing to see Garibaldi—the religious and many of the not-so-religious, including Catholics and non-Catholics, gathered at Niederdorf's Church of Saint Stephen.

Standing a short way from the square on the edge of the village, the church was a magnificent baroque edifice with bright white walls and twin terra-cotta cupolas. Gabriel Piguet, the Roman Catholic bishop of Clermont-Ferrand, read Mass assisted by Father Karl Kunkel. Canon Neuhäusler gave the sermon. He spoke of trust in God's leadership and brotherly love for one another.

Many of the Catholics and Greek Orthodox present received Holy Communion, among them young Flight Lieutenant Jimmy James. Later many attended confession. The sacred occasion produced a feeling of peace and serenity in the minds of those who attended, albeit overcast with uncertainty.[24] Beyond the walls of the church, events were unfolding in Niederdorf that would decide their future—and whether they would live or die during the coming twenty-four hours.

Payne Best, Bonin, and Garibaldi were not the only ones working to resolve the crisis. Anton Ducia, the Italian quartermaster and secret partisan leader, was playing his part.

An engineer by profession, Ducia had also worked as a ski instructor at a French club and spoke good English and French. He was, in Wings Day's opinion, "a very nice chap."[25] Ducia had traveled to Bolzano and returned with his assistant, Dr. Herbert Thalhammer. Arriving in the town square on this gray Sunday morning, they were greeted by the extraordinary sight of a mass of about a hundred men, women, and children in a panoply of garments, surrounded by a circle of SS and SD guards who were using their vehicles to try and cordon the prisoners off from the other people in Niederdorf. During the morning, the SS had grown concerned about security and had gathered all the Prominenten they could find in order to keep them under guard in one place.[26]

Recognizing how precarious the situation was becoming, Ducia sought out Stiller, who explained that, because the prisoners were being held in a variety of separate, insecure locations, there was a danger they might be liberated by partisans. He also knew the Prominenten had heard about plans to liquidate them and was worried they might try to escape. If any such attempt was made, Stiller added, his instructions were to shoot without asking questions.

Ducia was conscious of the delicacy of his task. Had he known about Garibaldi's attack plan, Payne Best's deal with Stiller, or Bonin's contacts with Vietinghoff's headquarters, he would have been even more anxious. The situation bore all the hallmarks of an approaching catastrophe. With the Allies possibly weeks away, he needed to calm the prisoners and prevent rash actions on the part of their guards.[27]

His immediate concern was to ease the SS's jitters by getting all the hostages accommodated under one roof. They needed to be moved to the place originally intended for them—the Pragser Wildsee hotel. Although he had little idea how he could accomplish it with the hotel occupied by the Luftwaffe generals, Ducia promised Stiller the hostages would be moved there by the following day at the latest.

With Stiller's permission, Ducia spoke to the prisoners present, assuring them that they would be safe and pleading with them not to do anything rash. He then located Payne Best and Bonin—fresh from their successful negotiation with Garibaldi—who invited Ducia to the big meeting taking place at the Hotel Bachmann at midday.[28]

In the meantime, Ducia drove out to the Pragser Wildsee, which was just seven miles away, a fifteen-minute drive.

With magnificent snowcapped mountains as its backdrop and set on the shore of the serene blue lake from which it took its name, the Pragser

Wildsee hotel was one of the best in the region. Ducia soon located the owner-manager, Emma Heiss-Hellenstainer, and told her that the three Luftwaffe generals would have to be ejected. When he told her that her replacement guests would be a large party of international VIP prisoners, Mrs. Heiss-Hellenstainer, a short and somewhat dour-looking lady with swept-back silver hair, was so excited she jumped up from her chair in delight.[29]

Mrs. Heiss-Hellenstainer immediately arranged a meeting between Ducia and the most senior of the Luftwaffe officers, the highly decorated General Hans Schlemmer, who agreed to consult his colleagues, generals Alfred Bülowius and Hans Jordan. They were swayed by Ducia's account of the dangerous situation in Niederdorf, and agreed in principle to evacuate the hotel; however, they insisted on being provided with a written or telephone order from commander in chief Vietinghoff.

Ducia promised to deliver it by the end of the day, and with that he set off back to Niederdorf to attend the big meeting.[30]

❧

As the clocks of Niederdorf struck noon, the Prominenten were gathered in the Bachmann's restaurant. All 139 were present, a remarkable assembly of generals, statesmen, clergymen, soldiers, airmen, spies, scholars, entertainers, wives, and children. Ducia arrived to find the room crammed to bursting and a buzz of excited anticipation in the air.

When the prisoners were settled, SS-Obersturmführer Edgar Stiller, dour-faced and defeated, announced that he would no longer be in charge of them. He added ominously that he would also therefore no longer be responsible for their safety; he was handing over authority to the Wehrmacht, personified for the time being by Colonel Bogislaw von Bonin. "Herr Best will tell you more," he concluded.[31]

It had been agreed that Bonin and Payne Best would take joint charge. Payne Best had become the de facto senior representative of the Allied prisoners, and Bonin, although not the most senior German officer among them, was the only one who was an honor prisoner and technically still serving. Of the two, Payne Best would take the lead. Both of them climbed onto a table and addressed their companions—Bonin in German and Payne Best in English and French. From this moment they should all consider themselves free, they said; the Prominenten were now guests rather than prisoners. However, they should remember that they were still in a war zone.

Anton Ducia underlined Payne Best's words, telling the gathering that they must think of themselves as guests of the Tyrolean community, whose intention it was to help them in any way possible. He asked for their trust and pleaded with them not to undertake any "romantic" actions that might endanger the safety of their fellows. Arrangements were in hand to have them moved to safer accommodations, where they would be under Wehrmacht protection.

In the meantime, Payne Best's leadership would be supported by a committee that included Colonel Bonin, Commander Liedig, and Canon Neuhäusler. There was a burst of applause at this, and for a few moments Payne Best and Bonin basked in the praise of their fellow prisoners.

After the meeting, while the Prominenten were given lunch, Ducia left for Army Group C headquarters at Bolzano. Despite all the reassuring words, the Prominenten were a long way from safety. With Bader excluded from the arrangement and the SS and SD men still at hand and growing ever more unruly, and without a Wehrmacht detachment in place to guard the VIPs, murder could break out at any moment.

Italian partisans were still a potential threat, although Ducia had taken precautions against the Garibaldi plot. Having learned of its existence, he had prepared to mobilize units of the local Standschützen, the underground Tyrolean militia, a relic of the old Austro-Hungarian Empire. He could call on several hundred militiamen, whereas he believed that Garibaldi, despite his grandiose words, had fewer than eighty partisans at hand. If Garibaldi's attack was launched, the militiamen would surround Niederdorf and prevent him from taking the prisoners to the mountains.[32]

The danger of a local civil war erupting—with the Wehrmacht, SS, and SD joining in and the Prominenten a target in the middle—was a real threat, although the prisoners were too busy enjoying their supposed freedom to be aware of it.

After enduring so much uncertainty for so long, the atmosphere was one of quiet celebration. Lunch for Neuhäusler was a repast of thick soup in the kitchen of the Bachmann with Josef Müller, Georg Thomas, the Schachts, and the Schuschniggs. The other clergy retired to the presbytery for Tyrolean dumplings and ham with all the trimmings. Afterward Karl Kunkel and Gabriel Piguet went for a walk and admired the splendor of the Dolomites, then went to pray in the chancel of the church.[33]

That evening the Prominenten disregarded Payne Best's and Ducia's warnings not to stray far from their rooms, and they walked around the streets of Niederdorf quite freely. Some dined in local restaurants, while Isa Vermehren was invited out for a glass of wine by one of the SS guards. That night Richard Schmitz, former mayor of Vienna, was gratified to sleep in a real bed for the first time in seven years. After a supper at the Bachmann with wine and good company, Pastor Niemöller retired to a comfortable bed at two o'clock in the morning.

Anton Ducia's ever-vigilant subordinate Dr. Herbert Thalhammer organized the "Niederdorf shooters"—a group of armed militiamen from the Standschützen—to keep an eye on the prisoners. They remained alert throughout the night.[34]

The night didn't pass without incident. Bonin entertained several guests in his room, including some generals, Payne Best, and Vera von Schuschnigg, and as they sat quietly speculating about the future, the door burst open and one of the SS guards staggered into the room in a drunken rage, brandishing a pistol. Bonin immediately rose to his feet, pulling out the pistol he had been concealing since his arrest. With icy disdain, he pointed the weapon at the interloper, who instantly capitulated and disappeared into the night.

Twenty

Showdown with the SS

Monday 30 April: Sexten, South Tyrol

With dawn rising over the Dolomites, spreading its first rays on the pretty little Tyrolean village of Sexten,* Captain Wichard von Alvensleben left his headquarters and climbed into his staff car, accompanied by his driver and one of his noncommissioned officers.[1] The car pulled out of the village and set off along the main highway toward Niederdorf.

The journey was the culmination of a long night's activity for Captain Alvensleben, which would transform his role in the war from that of a diligent but obscure Wehrmacht staff officer into that of a hero to both sides. This would be his second journey to Niederdorf in the space of a few hours and would bring the crisis there to a head.

It had all begun the previous evening. Following the momentous Sunday noon meeting of all the Prominenten, Anton Ducia had immediately taken the long drive to his office in the city of Bolzano, over sixty miles away on winding mountain roads choked with traffic. On arriving, he went straight to the headquarters of Army Group C, where Vietinghoff's liaison officer, a Major Reichel, told him that the commander in chief was aware of the situation in Niederdorf, thanks to Colonel Bonin. Assured that he could speak frankly with the general, Ducia was ushered into the

* Italian: Sesto

presence of Colonel General Heinrich von Vietinghoff. His chief of staff General Röttiger was also present. Over the course of three hours, Ducia briefed them on the situation of the Prominenten, and the three men discussed the best course of action. Vietinghoff agreed to order the Luftwaffe generals to evacuate the Pragser Wildsee and promised to send food and supplies to the hotel. He furthermore repeated his promise to send a Wehrmacht infantry detachment from Army Group C to disarm Bader's and Stiller's men.

Shortly after eleven o'clock that night, Captain Alvensleben was telephoned by Röttiger and instructed to take charge of the operation. Alvensleben was at his post in Sexten at the time, ten miles east of Niederdorf. As the commander of the staff company that guarded Army Group C's HQ, Alvensleben was in Sexten to oversee the imminent transfer of Vietinghoff's headquarters from Bolzano, which would soon come under threat from American forces advancing from Lake Garda.[2]

Alvensleben had had a tough war. Descended from Prussian aristocracy with a distinguished history of military service, he had served in Poland, France, the Soviet Union, Africa, and Italy. After being severely wounded on the eastern front, he was awarded the Iron Cross and a place in Vietinghoff's staff.[3] The collapse of Hitler's Reich had brought him personal tragedy when, in January 1945, his wife shot herself after Red Army troops arrived in the Tankow-Seegenfelde region, pillaging the family estate and burning down their castle. But Alvensleben, a Christian and member of the ancient chivalric Order of Saint John, had tremendous faith in God. He believed that the hand of fate was upon him when Röttiger called him that Sunday evening.[4] He was ordered to investigate the situation in Niederdorf, take over responsibility for the prisoners, feed them, and find accommodations for them.[5]

On that first exploratory trip on Sunday evening, Captain Alvensleben had arrived sometime after ten o'clock to find the village in pitch darkness. Almost immediately, and quite by chance, he had bumped into an SS-Obersturmführer who was taking a stroll in the fresh air. Alvensleben had immediately realized that the SS officer must have something to do with the hostages and introduced himself without revealing the reason he was in Niederdorf. The SS officer was Edgar Stiller, and within moments, with a characteristic lack of self-control, he began pouring out his feelings, describing the woeful predicament he was in.[6] The two men retired to a small restaurant together, and over cups of coffee Stiller told Alvensleben the full story of the hostages and his situation as guard commander. He confessed that he didn't get on well with the leader of the SD men, who had created anxiety and panic among the prisoners by telling them they would all be shot. Stiller also claimed that this had led to an escape attempt that was "only prevented with difficulty." Despite the agreement reached at the noon meeting that day, the possibility of a massacre was high, because Bader did not recognize the transfer of authority and would not hesitate to execute all the prisoners in cold blood.

Alvensleben was appalled by what he heard but disguised his feelings, not wanting to alert Stiller to his true reason for being in Niederdorf. He excused himself and left. It was too late to take any action that day, so he returned to his post in Sexten, intending to return to Niederdorf in the morning.[7]

The situation posed a major dilemma for Alvensleben, because Röttiger, contrary to Vietinghoff's promise to Ducia, had not given him authority to act against the SS. To do so without the highest authority would be a serious breach of the protocol between the Wehrmacht and the SS.

At dawn on Monday, Alvensleben set off on the return trip to Niederdorf with his driver, Hans Schäfer, and one of his subordinates, Special Officer Emil Langeling. Like Alvensleben, Langeling was a devoutly religious man, having been ordained a Catholic priest shortly before starting his military service.[8] They would both need divine guidance to cope with the perilous waters into which they were about to wade.

It took an hour or so to cover the ten miles from Alvensleben's headquarters to Niederdorf, negotiating a constant flow of military traffic threading its way along the narrow main road, and it was eight o'clock in the morning when they reached the town. Within moments, the small Wehrmacht party encountered the menacing figure of an SS-Untersturmführer standing in the main square in the company of several women.[9]

Guessing that this officer must be Stiller's second in command, Captain Alvensleben struck up a conversation with him, again without revealing his purpose. Although the SS officer did not introduce himself, it was clear that he was indeed the SD man Stiller had described so chillingly. SS-Untersturmführer Bader made an extremely unpleasant impression on Alvensleben, who was reminded of the notorious Roland Freisler, the bullying, brutal, and heartless Nazi judge who presided over the People's Court—a figure loathed and feared by most Germans.

In a subtle, roundabout way, Alvensleben endeavored to get Bader to talk about the prisoners, but the man was taciturn to the point of blankness. In the end, Alvensleben was forced to ask outright about them. Bader was reluctant to talk, revealing only that they were to be taken to the Pragser Wildsee. When Alvensleben pressed further, Bader said that his orders would only be fulfilled once the Prominenten were dead.[10]

Alvensleben's fears were confirmed. He had to take immediate action. He informed Bader that he was an emissary of the commander in chief of Army Group C and told him that he should consider his orders already fulfilled and his mission over. Alvensleben was acutely conscious that he was exceeding his authority. He had not been given the power to issue any such instruction to an SS officer, but he felt he had no alternative. He added that Bader should consider himself relieved of all his duties and demanded that he remain in the town at Alvensleben's disposal.[11] It was bold talk, and a man like Bader was hardly likely to respond well to it from a young Wehrmacht officer, even one who outranked him. Bader bristled and contemptuously refused Alvensleben's instructions.

Alvensleben was in deep water, and he knew it, alone with only a military priest and a driver to face dozens of well-armed, aggressive, and volatile SS troops. He needed reinforcements at once. Leaving Bader to simmer, Alvensleben withdrew and immediately radioed his battalion headquarters at Sexten to request the dispatch of a battle group.

Forty-five tense minutes later, a tiny detachment of fifteen sergeants and corporals, armed with machine pistols, reached Niederdorf. Alvensleben ordered them to position themselves in the square in front of the town hall, where the SS had their headquarters in the mayor's office and the SS and SD troops were gathered. It was a start, but not sufficient, and could easily prove more provocative than protective. Alvensleben decided to call for more reinforcements. Rather than wait for men from Sexten, he called on the force currently at the village of Dobbiaco,* only two and a half miles down the road from Niederdorf.[12] While he waited for the troops to arrive, he embarked on a goodwill mission to pacify the anxious Prominenten in their various inns and hotels.

Because of Alvensleben's discreet, circumspect approach, Payne Best and Bonin had been unaware of his presence and had begun to grow impatient. Bonin had telephoned Vietinghoff's headquarters several times early that morning, only to be told that a combat infantry company was on its way, with instructions to place itself under his orders. But so far all that had arrived from Army Group C were two cases of Italian brandy and another of Asti sparkling wine.[13] Nonetheless, Payne Best believed that the morale of the Prominenten was generally good.

When he began meeting the prisoners, Alvensleben did not share Payne Best's complacent assessment of their mood. Despite the change of authority, many remained nervous and in fear for their lives. He tried to persuade them that they were now under his protection and that they were safe from Bader's and Stiller's men.[14] It did little good; they knew Bader well. Once they understood just how small Alvensleben's force was, it was clear that the odds of the young Wehrmacht officer winning a fight against the dozens of SD and SS men were not good.

When Bonin finally met Alvensleben, he shared this view. He was not at all impressed by the captain, who admitted he had no authority to overrule the SS. More worryingly, to Bonin's rather harsh eye, Alvensleben

---

* German: Toblach

seemed a weak character who would stand no chance in a confrontation with Bader.[15]

It took two nerve-racking hours for the detachment from Dobbiaco to arrive; it comprised 150 men from an infantry training battalion. They weren't exactly battle-hardened combat troops, but they had numbers and brought with them two heavy machine guns. Alvensleben positioned them around the square with their weapons trained on the town hall. Now that he was in a militarily superior position at last, he felt confident enough to confront Bader and Stiller. He ordered them to stay in the mayor's office. Under no circumstances were any SD or SS personnel to leave the town hall environs.[16]

Witnessing this impressive display of military force, the mood of the Prominenten finally lifted, and they felt free to stroll around the streets, mingling with one another and with the locals. In the meantime, Alvensleben resumed introducing himself to the prisoners, meeting the Blums, the Schuschniggs, Maria von Hammerstein, Pastor Martin Niemöller, Prince Friedrich Leopold of Prussia, and Commander Franz Liedig.

Believing complacently (and wrongly) that he had taken care of the SS, Alvensleben was wholly unaware that trouble was brewing within the ranks of the Prominenten as well. He was not the only person to visit the Schuschniggs that day. At around noon, Colonel Davide Ferrero called upon the former chancellor and his wife in their room at the Bachmann, offering a proposition.

After his rage over the suspension of the partisan attack, Ferrero had accepted the force of the argument that keeping Schuschnigg safe was vital for the future of the Italian South Tyrol. He therefore urged Schuschnigg to put himself and his family under the protection of his partisan comrades. Their headquarters were in the mountain ski resort of Cortina d'Ampezzo, about twenty miles south of Niederdorf. Ferrero had procured transport to take the Schuschnigg family there. He pointed out that the situation in Niederdorf was still far from certain and that Schuschnigg needed to make his mind up quickly. Schuschnigg declined the offer, citing the solidarity pact shared by all the Prominenten. An escape of individuals, he said, could have unfortunate consequences for the rest of the group.

Meanwhile, Captain Alvensleben knew he could not rest easy until Bader's and Stiller's men were completely neutralized. That could only be achieved by removing them from Niederdorf, which would require authorization from his superiors in Bolzano. He entered the town hall and telephoned General Röttiger to make the request. By a stroke of good fortune, SS-Obergruppenführer Karl Wolff—the very man who had the direct authority to call off the SS officers—happened to be standing next to Röttiger when the call came through. For the young Alvensleben, it was an extraordinary and intimidating moment when Röttiger passed the telephone over to Wolff. Alvensleben explained the tense situation in Niederdorf, Wolff listening intently. To Alvensleben's relief, Wolff agreed wholeheartedly to withdraw Bader's and Stiller's detachment, adding, "Send the lads to me at Bolzano!"[17]

What Alvensleben did not know was that Wolff's position was every bit as tricky as that of the Prominenten. A surrender of German forces in Italy—not authorized by Berlin—had already been agreed by Wolff and Vietinghoff. Signed the previous day, the suspension of hostilities would come into effect two days from now, on 2 May, with surrender to follow. At the same time, Heinrich Himmler was playing his own dangerous game of negotiation with the Allies, jockeying to take control of the Reich. His position was critical; he had been found out by the Führer and was unaware of Wolff and Vietinghoff's surrender deal, but he did know about Wolff's trips to Switzerland and had Wolff's wife and children under the "protective custody" of the SS. That same day, Wolff's emissaries were returning from a frantic trip across the lines to the Allied headquarters in Caserta, where they had formally agreed the surrender. To Wolff's chagrin, however, his authority was undermined by the officials in Berlin, who were determined to head off any precipitate armistice. Vietinghoff and Röttiger had been relieved of their commands. That left Wolff's own fate in the hands of Kaltenbrunner. It remained to be seen, therefore, how far and for how long Wolff's—or Vietinghoff's—writ would run.

Unaware of these momentous developments, Alvensleben found himself facing a crisis. Bader and Stiller had suddenly found common cause now that they had both been deprived of their power and corralled in the town hall. While Alvensleben was on the phone, they had escaped from their confinement. Taking a car, they roared off at speed, only to screech to a halt at one of the barriers manned by Alvensleben's men. They were forced to turn back and returned to the town hall seething with anger. They burst into the room where Alvensleben was still on the phone with Wolff, confronting him in the middle of the conversation.

Both of them—even the usually weak-willed Stiller—were menacing. If Alvensleben's men dared to used their weapons, they warned, then the SS and SD would respond in kind.

It would only take the smallest mistake for the whole situation to spiral violently out of control. Alvensleben had to defuse the threat quickly, otherwise the citizens of Niederdorf as well as the Prominenten would be in grave danger. He assured Bader and Stiller that everything could be resolved without bloodshed if they would only let him finish his telephone call. It was clear that the removal of the SS men had to be accelerated.[18]

How that would be achieved was uncertain. He had force at his disposal, but little in the way of bargaining power.

A hasty meeting was convened with Alvensleben, Bonin, Liedig, and Payne Best. It was inconclusive. Payne Best's impression of the young Wehrmacht captain was less than encouraging; he was "a very charming, correctly behaved young officer," but seemed nervous and "disinclined to take any definite action."[19] There was an argument over what should be done, Alvensleben showing little enthusiasm for any of their suggestions. As the senior German officer, Bonin said he would take full responsibility for whatever occurred. Alvensleben was relieved—with the backing of SS-Obergruppenführer Wolff and a Wehrmacht colonel on hand, he returned to his men ready to face up to any eventuality.

A tense standoff had developed in the town square. The Wehrmacht company had cordoned off the area and mounted their machine guns. Their weapons were trained on the SD guards, who had gathered, fully armed, around their truck in front of the town hall and were holding their own heated discussion about what to do. Payne Best, accompanied by Bonin (now openly carrying his pistol), approached the SD troopers.

At the edge of the square, Wings Day and some of the other Allied prisoners watched breathlessly as the confrontation unfolded. They could sense that this was the critical moment, when there would either be peace or an explosion of gunfire.[20]

Payne Best drew the SD men's attention to the dozens of machine guns, rifles, and machine pistols pointing at them. "Throw down your arms," he demanded, "or those guns will go off."

The SD took a good look and for the first time seemed to recognize the size of the force ranged against them. They were executioners, not fighting troops, and when it came to it they had little desire to make a heroic, suicidal last stand. Quietly, and to Payne Best's considerable surprise, they began laying down their weapons. Machine pistols, sidearms, ammunition, and hand grenades were laid on the ground by the truck.

Bader, his claws drawn at last, suddenly lost all of his arrogant, belligerent demeanor. Humbly, he begged Payne Best and Bonin to use their influence to obtain fuel so that he and his men could leave town.[21] Bonin was outraged by this unbelievable show of effrontery. Furious, he began threatening to have Bader and all the SS and SD men shot on the spot. His anger—and everyone else's—grew when the truck was searched and 120 International Red Cross POW parcels were discovered inside, hidden under benches covered by blankets. While the Prominenten had starved during the journey, this bounty had been held back for the SS men's own use.[22]

It took time and a great deal of pressure to persuade Bonin not to execute Bader and his men. But he refused point blank to let them have any fuel.

Later, Bader managed to forage some fuel, and most of the former guards drove off in a bus and a truck in the direction of the Brenner Pass. Eleven of them remained, Stiller included, preferring the company of the Wehrmacht and the Prominenten to their erstwhile comrades.[23] Some others lingered in the area on their own account. According to stories that emerged later, those who stayed made the right choice. It was rumored that the fleeing SS and SD men were ambushed by a group of partisans some distance from Niederdorf and were captured and strung up from roadside telegraph poles. Whether Bader was among them was unrecorded.

In the meantime, although one danger had been largely, though not completely, dealt with, the Prominenten were still at risk scattered around Niederdorf. They needed to be moved immediately.

Twenty-One

Danger in Paradise

Monday 30 April: Pragser Wildsee

On the south side of the Puster valley, the Dolomite mountains rear up, forming a great massif eighteen miles broad. Among its peaks is the vast, shovel-shaped blade of the Seekofel, towering at the head of a deep, green glacial vale. At the foot of the mountain, lying long and oval like a jagged flint blade, is the Pragser Wildsee, which the Italians call the Lago di Braies, a glassy green-blue lake. Known as the pearl of the Dolomite lakes, the Pragser Wildsee is a central feature in local folklore, which holds that where the southern shore meets the foot of the Seekofel there is a door into the underworld.

On the northwestern shoreline, where the pine-cloaked rocky slopes roll down into gentler green hills, stands the Pragser Wildsee hotel, a magnificent piece of Alpine architecture created at the height of the Austro-Hungarian Empire. Four stories high, its three gable ends look out under deep eaves across the lake toward the Seekofel.

The Pragser Wildsee had been a popular resort for wealthy and titled Europeans for a long time—Archduke Franz Ferdinand himself stayed at the hotel in its early days, before his fateful assassination.

On this Monday afternoon at the end of April 1945, just after lunchtime, a single car drove up the winding forest road leading from the Niederdorf highway, passed under the pines, and came to a halt outside the hotel. In the car was Commander Franz Liedig, who had come on behalf of the Prominenten to ensure that the hotel was ready to receive 139 new guests.

Liedig was accompanied by two of the women kin prisoners who were considered best qualified to judge the suitability of the accommodations.[1] One was Miss Elisabeth Kaiser. Her father, Jakob Kaiser, was a socialist politician who had been involved in the conspiracy against Hitler; since his arrest, Elisabeth had been held prisoner along with her mother, Therese, and her uncle and aunt, Josef and Käte Mohr.[2] The other woman accompanying Liedig was Mrs. Käthe Gudzent, whose husband had been condemned as a member of the so-called League of German Officers, prisoners of war in Soviet hands who had been persuaded to turn traitor and fight for Russia. Like several other women prisoners, Mrs. Gudzent had been separated from her children after her arrest and had endured months without knowing their fate.[3]

The Luftwaffe generals had finally packed their bags and departed from the hotel, much to the satisfaction of proprietor Emma Heiss-Hellenstainer.[4] However, the hotel had been closed to the public and understaffed for so long that it had deteriorated considerably. The heating plant had been allowed to freeze during the winter and was now a mess of burst, leaking pipes. There was also an insufficient supply of fuel. Although it was now the middle of spring, they were high in the Alps and the temperature was wintry. Miss Kaiser and Mrs. Gudzent began making arrangements to ensure that at least the elderly Prominenten would have warmth in their rooms; over the next few days these two women would form the backbone of the establishment.[5]

Mrs. Heiss-Hellenstainer identified the warmest rooms and, with the information provided by Miss Kaiser and Mrs. Gudzent, set aside the first floor for the elderly Thyssens, Goerdelers, and Stauffenbergs, along with the Schachts and the Greek generals. The Heberleins and Schuschniggs were allocated the second floor with Martin Niemöller, most of the Irishmen, and the Englishmen. The third floor she allotted to the Blums, the remaining Austrians, the Czechs, the Danes, and the Hungarians. A man from the village arrived to turn on the water supply, and Mrs. Heiss-Hellenstainer fired up the ovens and began preparing a thick semolina soup for the guests, who were expected to arrive imminently.[6]

In Niederdorf there was still danger. Although Payne Best was quite satisfied with his own management of the situation and the disarmament of the SS, others—including Wings Day—felt differently. The town hall had now been entirely taken over by Garibaldi and was decked in Italian flags. Ferrero, still seething with frustration over his canceled attack, had led a band of partisans east of the town, in the direction of Sexten and San Candido,* where they harried retreating German columns, taking prisoners and bringing back great hauls of captured weapons to the town hall for distribution to other partisans.[7]

Although the Prominenten had been liberated from the SS, they were still in danger from deserters and fanatical Nazis carrying on the fight. The German Prominenten in particular were at risk from the various marauding bands of partisans—including Ferrero's—who were handing out summary justice to anybody they thought deserved it. Of the original SS guard detachment, eleven had remained in Niederdorf, some of them joining their former prisoners on the promise that the Prominenten would put in a good word for them when the Allies came. SS-Obersturmführer Edgar Stiller was not among them; he desperately wanted to come to the Pragser Wildsee but was too scared of retribution from the Allies if he was captured—and from the Gestapo if he was seen to have sided with the enemy.[8] Bonin, Ducia, and Payne Best all tried to persuade him that he was perfectly welcome to come with them, but he didn't dare. One of Stiller's men had been joined by his wife and daughter in Niederdorf and was similarly torn.[9]

Despite the dangers, the villagers and the Prominenten walked about freely, feeling a false sense of safety. Jimmy James and Sydney Dowse went for a stroll along the Puster valley with Isa Vermehren and Countess Gisela von Plettenberg, accompanied by the former Hungarian interior

* German: Innichen

minister Baron Péter Schell—a strangely assorted group of acquaintances who would never have been brought together in normal circumstances.[10]

Later that afternoon, the Prominenten boarded their transports for what they hoped would be the last journey of their captivity. Although they were technically no longer prisoners, they were still hostages to the changeable and volatile forces sweeping around them. And although Alvensleben's Wehrmacht infantrymen were ostensibly their protectors, in the present turmoil they couldn't be guaranteed not to become their murderers.

It took most of the afternoon to ferry all the Prominenten in relays. Boarding the trucks outside the town hall wasn't a comfortable experience for some of them, as they were subjected to taunts and insults from the hostile remnants of Bader's and Stiller's men who had lingered in Niederdorf. Some of the former guards were furious about what had happened, and as far as they were concerned the German Prominenten were traitors who bore the responsibility for Hitler's defeat and their own predicament. "Hitler would have succeeded were it not for these people," said one SS man, "and now they are being driven by car to big hotels and we have to fear for our lives."[11]

The journey to the Pragser Wildsee was typically fraught. Although most of the transports got there without incident, one of the buses broke down halfway up the steep, winding road. Jimmy James was among the passengers who had to walk the rest of the way. He marked the change in altitude; during his stroll with the ladies in the lower valley the weather had been sunny and pleasantly springlike, but as they ascended the narrow Pragser vale it grew colder and began to snow. However, as they rounded the bend that brought the Seekofel into view, the clouds broke and the sun shone on the pines, revealing "a fairyland of dazzling white snow crystals enhancing the beauty of this silent amphitheatre in the mountains. After my years of viewing barbed wire, guard towers and cells walls, it seemed like a wonderful dream."[12]

They arrived to find rooms arranged for them, but a deep chill permeated the building. Mrs. Heiss-Hellenstainer welcomed them at the door and apologized that the hotel was not presently equipped for a cold climate.

Despite the temperature, Fey Pirzio-Biroli rejoiced. She had her own room for the first time in months, and after the horrors of Buchenwald and Dachau, the Pragser Wildsee was a paradise on earth; she would spend hours at the window, gazing at the mountains.[13] It wasn't only the gorgeous view that drew her, however. She knew that beyond those peaks, less than sixty miles away, was Brazzà, the idyllic country villa near Udine where she and her little boys had lived before her arrest. She knew they were no longer there, but she felt Brazzà calling to her. It was seven months now since she had last seen Corrado and Roberto at Innsbruck; her head was still filled with the sound of Corrado's cries as he was taken away, the memory returning whenever she tried to sleep. Fey longed to strike out and find her own way home but couldn't make herself do it: "I felt too weak and unsure of myself. When one has been held in a group where everything is decided by others, one loses the courage to act alone."[14]

On that first evening the only rooms that could be heated were the kitchen and the large room next to it, which was temporarily converted into a social and dining area. Payne Best felt the building was "literally like being in a refrigerator."[15] It also looked as if there was more snow to come.

Security was not neglected. There were now two officers in charge of the Wehrmacht company, both of them from the Alvensleben family. During the standoff in Niederdorf, a solitary motorcyclist had ridden into town. In the general confusion, no one at first took any notice of Captain Gebhard von Alvensleben, a cousin of Wichard. Gebhard's sudden arrival was purely coincidental; he had been heading for Milan, where his wife was working on the staff of Army Group South West. With the fighting around Lake Garda, he had been unable to get through to her and had been forced to turn back. When Wichard realized his cousin was in Niederdorf, he press-ganged him into helping with the Prominenten, asking Gebhard to take charge of a detachment of eighty of his men and attend to the defense of the Pragser Wildsee, while Wichard remained with a second detachment in Niederdorf. It was necessary to secure both, because the village was the sole communication nexus between the Pragser Wildsee and the outside world. Gebhard agreed and was appointed support officer, liaising between Wichard and the former prisoners.

The hotel wasn't difficult to protect. Halfway up the snowy mountains and accessible only by one narrow, winding road, it was a natural fortress. Gebhard placed four heavy machine guns at key points around the hotel grounds and a fifth on the roof.[16] The sight of them might have reassured the Prominenten, but the situation outside their defensive ring was dangerous. Besides the threat of the partisans, there was the possibility that the embittered SS and SD men might come looking for blood.

In fact, on the very first evening Stiller and at least two dozen troopers did turn up at the hotel, but not to exact revenge. Stiller had changed his mind and hoped to take up the offer of accommodation extended to them by Bonin, Ducia, and Payne Best. Mrs. Heiss-Hellenstainer was taken aback by the sight of such a large force.

Liedig counseled caution, and the SS and SD men were held outdoors, in a repeat of the earlier standoff; this time, however, they were unarmed. The two sides glowered at one another for three hours, but eventually the renegades, refused entry to the building, melted away into the darkness.[17] There was no way of telling whether they would be back.

Tuesday 1 May: Pragser Wildsee

Among the many charms of the secluded, majestic setting was a private chapel on the hotel grounds. On this cold May morning it was the venue for a special Mass.

Our Lady of Sorrows was a tiny stone-built structure, standing in a picturesque spot by the lake's edge a few hundred yards from the hotel. The clergy among the prisoners had heard of it from the priest at Niederdorf, but when they set eyes on the chapel its serene beauty exceeded anything he had described. They had been supplied with hosts and wine for the service, and as soon as they arrived at the hotel they had immediately begun to prepare. Emma Heiss-Hellenstainer helped them carry cloths, a goblet, a ciborium, candles, and linen along the snowy path leading to the chapel, and that night the prelates drew up a notice with details of four Masses to be held there the following day.[18]

These sacred rites were among the few moments of peace and harmony. Many of the Prominenten, now that they weren't officially prisoners anymore, began to assert their rights. Feeling—quite wrongly—that their pleasant setting, isolated from the traffic and violence of war, was safe, many of them fell to bickering, complaining, and even pilfering. Accommodations had been allotted according to need, and this didn't please everyone. A few of the Allied military men, who were quartered on the third floor in the servants' rooms, grumbled about their situation, complaining that quarters should be allotted according to who had won the war. The Germans had started it and had been defeated; therefore the Allies should get the best rooms and the German Prominenten should sleep in the servants' attic. The complaints and arguments grew heated, and, as senior officer among the British contingent, Wings Day was called on to arbitrate. He dismissed the Allied prisoners' claims as petty and ruled that the arrangements should stay as they were.[19]

Another source of disgruntlement was Soviet lieutenant colonel Viktor Brodnikov. He claimed that he had lost everything during his captivity and all he now possessed was the uniform he stood up in. He began drawing up a list of demands: "A pair of shoes, a shirt with a collar, a pair of underpants, a pair of socks, a handkerchief, a razor with blades, a shaving brush, a sponge or flannel, a piece of soap and a toothbrush."[20]

Emma Heiss-Hellenstainer, having been delighted to welcome such august guests, quickly found that some of them were quite avaricious. On the first night she discovered that virtually all the soft pillows and eiderdowns from the third floor had disappeared—adding to the Allied men's grievances. It turned out they had been hoarded by the Greek general staff. At the first evening's meal she noticed that, despite being served generous portions, many of the diners smuggled extra rations back to their bedrooms. She put it down to "the prisoner mentality" whereby inmates were always looking to hide things away for harder times. She was less charitable, however, when fifteen gallons of wine disappeared from her cellars, which she had generously opened up for all to enjoy.[21]

After so many months—and in some cases years—of imprisonment and deprivation, it was hardly surprising that gluttony should break out. But the abuse of their hostess's hospitality by a few meant that from that day onward all food and wine would have to be strictly rationed.[22] It was back to the regimen of prisoner life.

Each person tried to cope with the new, rudderless situation in his or her own way. A few tried to assert their natural authority. Colonel John McGrath believed that a sense of military discipline was required. Putting on his full British Army uniform—which he had managed to keep in immaculate condition—topped off by his scarlet-banded Royal Artillery cap, he didn't actually try to take control, but he did lend "an air of military tone" to all goings-on, which didn't please everyone. Payne Best, who liked McGrath very much, "found his attempts to introduce a martial element in our pleasant casual life slightly trying."[23]

A prison-camp atmosphere lingered for some—and certainly surrounded the acquisition of a wireless set by Hugh Falconer, SOE agent and radio expert. The set he obtained was old and took some tinkering to get working, but it was soon picking up broadcasts from the BBC and the Allied Forces Network. Most of the ex-prisoners were hungry for news of the world outside, and what they heard was encouraging. But some of the SS men who had accompanied the Prominenten couldn't let go of their old rules and attitudes. One of them, discovering Falconer listening to the BBC, was furious. He berated Falconer, insisting that radios were verboten for prisoners and listening to foreign broadcasts was an offense. He refused to see sense and started threatening to turn violent. It was only when Bonin appeared and ordered him to behave himself that the situation calmed down.[24]

For a group of high-profile former prisoners in such a delicate situation, events in the outside world were not all good. German troops were flooding the roads toward the Brenner Pass in a disorderly retreat, and ugly incidents were not uncommon. There were rumors that a powerful force of Waffen-SS had been formed by Gauleiter Franz Hofer and was active around Bolzano; another rumor said that he had created his own Tyrolean partisan movement and was advancing south from the Brenner Pass.[25] There were also bands of German deserters and stragglers in the forests who, according to Jimmy James, would "slit a throat for a suit of clothes or some food."[26] Some of these renegades were foreign troops in the service of the Wehrmacht and Waffen-SS—the majority former Red Army troops who had chosen service to Germany over slow starvation in a POW camp. They would do anything to obtain civilian clothing to hide the evidence of their treason.[27]

Besides the threat of rogue groups of Waffen-SS or even the Wehrmacht, various partisan factions were increasingly terrorizing areas of northern Italy. Now that the Germans were all but finished, territorial and political claims were being staked, often violently. On this day—1 May—Yugoslavian partisans entered the Italian city of Trieste, causing terror among the local population.[28] Similar confrontations occurred in Tyrol, whose German-Italian history made it a hotbed of factionalism. Competing groups of heavily armed, undisciplined, and trigger-happy fighters—including Communists, Italian nationalists, and pro-Austrians—were all determined to make South Tyrol theirs, hating one another even more than they did the Nazis. The international and highly political Prominenten included individuals who would be hated by one side and feted by another; once discovered, they might be seized as trophies or figureheads.

All the various factions had armed themselves from the enormous stockpile of weapons left behind by the retreating army. To make matters even more perilous for the Prominenten, the Wehrmacht reinforcements that Captain Wichard von Alvensleben had been promised by Vietinghoff and Röttiger showed no sign of arriving.[29]

Partisans, deserters, and SS death squads weren't the only ones roaming the countryside. A few Prominenten, each with their own motives, had taken off into the blue. Garibaldi and Ferrero were leading their partisans around Niederdorf. They had set up an outpost in a house belonging to two German-Italian sisters, Emma and Theresa Wassermann. In the reigning chaos, the sisters would subsequently open their doors to a contingent of SS who briefly occupied their kitchen, and later to two American officers who had advanced far ahead of their units.[30]

Within the first hours after arriving at the Pragser Wildsee, Heidel Nowakowski, who had commanded the affections of some of the male prisoners and aroused the suspicions of many others, disappeared with Raymond van Wymeersch, who was apparently set on making one more Great Escape. The lovestruck couple found an abandoned car and set off into the snowy landscape for a romantic adventure. Heidel was never seen again by any of the Prominenten. It might have been her elopement that prompted another of her lovelorn suitors, Vassily Kokorin, to take up an offer from local Communist partisans to join them in their mountain hideout.[31]

Other Russians faced their liberation with varying degrees of dread. General Ivan Georgievich Bessonov procured a German pistol from Garibaldi's partisans and took off into the mountains alone. He was convinced that if he waited for liberation, he would be handed over to the Soviets and executed. "The Russians do not recognise prisoners," he said. "There is no return from captivity. We know the slick methods of the Americans. They'll say, 'Who is this?,' and when I am identified as a Russian, they'll stick a twenty-five-cent stamp on my backside and send me off to be hanged."[32]

He was right, and his compatriots Major General Pyotr Privalov and Lieutenant Colonel Viktor Brodnikov knew it, yet they seemed to have lost their nerve and their desire to live. They stayed put in the Pragser Wildsee and awaited their fate.

All but a few of their fellow Prominenten heeded Alvensleben's pleas to stay safely within the hotel grounds.[33] Their sense of security was rapidly evaporating. Aside from outside threats, their food supply was dwindling. The townsfolk of Niederdorf had showered the Prominenten with food, wine, and hospitality, but those splendid meals had only been possible thanks to years of squirreling away supplies. The cupboards of Niederdorf were almost bare, and there was no sign of any replenishment in sight.[34]

The most sinister threat to the Prominenten was entirely unknown and unguessed by any of them. On Tuesday 1 May, barely twelve miles away in the little Austrian village of Sillian, not far from the Italian border towns of San Candido and Sexten, the local Gestapo chief, Hans Philipp, had received an urgent telex from Gestapo headquarters in Klagenfurt. It ordered him to proceed to the Pragser Wildsee and seize the Prominenten. He was to take them immediately to the Austrian side of the border, where a transport of several buses would be waiting. The order went on to state in no uncertain terms that the intention was to execute them all.[35] Venturing into the inferno of northern Italy wasn't a prospect Philipp relished, and he sat on the order while he considered how to go about it.

On the same day, Anton Ducia arrived at the Pragser Wildsee to see how the former prisoners were settling in. He brought two pieces of news—one encouraging, the other extremely worrying. He arrived at lunchtime and found the Prominenten in the hotel dining room. He sat next to Wings Day at the end of one of the long tables near the doorway and told him the good news: the Americans were about to reach Bolzano at last, only sixty miles away by road. The less welcome news was that Italian partisans were operating in advance of the Americans. When they clashed with their South Tyrolean Austrian counterparts, there would be trouble. Ducia drew a bleak picture of untrammeled violence: murder, rape, arson, and looting. Soon the wave would reach the Pragser Wildsee, and the Wehrmacht company would not be strong enough to stop it. In Ducia's opinion, the only way to save the Prominenten was to make a direct appeal to Allied headquarters explaining the predicament, in the hope that a rescue operation could be launched. And since all radio communications were in a state of total confusion, the only way to get through to the Allies was by taking a personal message.

Three days had passed since Mad Jack Churchill's escape from Niederdorf. He might already have succeeded in reaching Allied lines, and, if he had, help might already be on the way. But without knowing that for certain, it was imperative to make another attempt.

Ducia was prepared to make the hazardous journey through enemy lines. Day felt a thrill at the thought. For him, sitting on the sidelines in a holiday hotel with a party of old men, women, and children while the greatest war in history reached its denouement was frustrating beyond endurance. He regretted not going with Mad Jack and had been thinking of joining Ferrero in Niederdorf, but now he could see a more palpable way of contributing to the victory that was to come.

He immediately volunteered to accompany Ducia. "I'm your man, Tony," he said. "Take me to the front. I'll get across somehow and you come with me."[36]

There wasn't a moment to lose; they would leave within the hour.

Twenty-Two

Running the Gauntlet

Thursday 3 May: Northwest of Bolzano, South Tyrol

With pleasant evening sunshine on his face, Lieutenant Colonel John "Mad Jack" Churchill strode contentedly along a secluded rural track in the tree-covered Tyrolean hills. His bright, hard eyes scanned the horizon for hazards and for signs of Allied troops. He had hoped to encounter them by now, but so far he'd seen nothing but Germans.[1]

Five days had passed since he had parted from Wings Day by the railway tracks in Niederdorf. He had struck out south, trekking through forests and climbing hills, and by daybreak he was well away into the Dolomites south of the Puster valley. The hills and mountain ridges stretched on into the distance without interval. In almost every valley the resourceful commando found farms, swift-flowing streams, and usually a road. The streams were essential for refreshment and the farms provided vegetables with which he replenished the food he carried in a bag, but the main roads were dangerous, with Wehrmacht traffic constantly crawling along them.

Churchill had decided to follow the roads but keep a distance from them, sticking to the footpaths that zigzagged along the hillsides, out of sight among the trees. From a distance he wouldn't attract attention. He wore an RAF service uniform, scavenged during his imprisonment; its color and cut made it the least military-looking type of Allied uniform, and he'd had it adjusted to make it look more civilian. Nonetheless, if he came into direct contact with Germans he would be in trouble.

His plans were vague. He'd acquired a map before setting out and had decided to head in the general direction of Trento and Verona, guessing correctly that Lake Garda and the valley leading to the Brenner Pass would be a main route of advance for Allied forces.

Day after day he walked, taking short rests, eating from his small stock of vegetables, the sun shining down pleasantly and alleviating the cold. His spirits were uplifted by the sights, sounds, and smells of the countryside, and he was urged on constantly by the thought that at any moment he would encounter British or American troops and his long ordeal would be over. His determination to stick to mountain paths while following the roads at a distance had carried him in a more westerly direction than he'd originally intended. Now, on the fifth day of his journey, with the early evening light fading to dusk, he was traversing a steep hillside above a broad river valley patched with fields, northwest of Bolzano.[2]

As he strode along beneath the trees about a third of a mile above the main road, he heard the roaring of a military convoy passing below. Peering down through the forest eaves, he could see tanks, tank destroyers, and troop-carrying trucks. He could just make out that at least some of them seemed to bear the white star of the US Army.

"Good heavens," he said to himself. "Have I got to the Yanks already?"

It occurred to him that they might be captured vehicles. He ran down the slope as fast as he could, trying to get a clearer view. Were the soldiers wearing American helmets or the distinctive coal-scuttle shape of the Germans? At this distance in the failing light it was difficult to tell. Slipping and sliding in his haste, he was within two hundred yards of the road before he felt sure that they were American helmets.

Dropping his bag of food in his excitement, Mad Jack ran wildly down the slope to the road. The convoy had almost passed. Its head was roaring away up the valley, and all that remained to pass was a single truck and then another three tanks. Churchill sprinted across the last stretch of ground and hurtled out onto the road just as the truck went past, waving and yelling. "Stop! I'm English! I'm an escaped English officer!"

The truck and the tanks behind it shuddered to a halt. The commander of the nearest tank leaned down from his turret hatch and shouted, "You're an escaped English officer?"

"Yes!" Churchill shouted back. "I've been heading down south."

"We're moving as fast as we can," said the tank commander, impatient at the interruption of his mission.

"Can I come up and join you?" Churchill asked.

"Sure, sure," said the commander. "Come and sit up on the tank."

Mad Jack found a foothold and pulled himself up onto the armor plating. The engine rumbled and the vehicles set off. He clung on, breathless from running but grinning happily. He'd made it to Allied lines.

Or so he believed. He didn't know it then, but what he had actually found was Task Force Thompson, a small, heavily armored unit that had penetrated deep into German-held territory. They were part of the 3rd Battalion, 86th Mountain Infantry Regiment of the 10th Mountain Division. The previous day, the battalion had been with the rest of the regiment at Torbole on Lake Garda when they received word that a cease-fire had begun. The war in Italy was officially over. This morning, the battalion had been ordered to assemble a fast-moving task force and send it with all speed up the road to guard the pass at Resia, where the borders of Italy, Austria, and Switzerland met. Resia and Brenner were the main passes through the high Alps—where Allied forces in Italy would link up with spearheads of the US Seventh Army coming south from Germany—and they had to be secured.[3]

Although the war in Italy was at an end, elsewhere it was not, and the German troops encountered thus far by Task Force Thompson, while letting them pass unmolested, had sometimes looked extremely unfriendly. The Americans weren't at all convinced that the Germans would respect the cease-fire, or even that they would all know about it.

As they roared along the highway, the tank commander shouted something to Churchill. He leaned closer. "You eaten lately?"

"No, I damned well haven't!" Churchill shouted back. "In fact, I dropped my bag of vegetables to run this last two hundred yards."

"Well, would you like some spaghetti and meatballs, or orange juice? We'll open up a box."

"Don't open one specially. Haven't you got an open box or a tin of some sort? I'll eat anything."

The American laughed at the Englishman's politeness, so incongruous in a starving escapee balancing on the front of a tank. "Aw, we'll open a box. We got plenty of stuff." He passed down a can and Mad Jack tucked in, overwhelmed by the American's generosity. He thought it was the most marvelous food he'd eaten for more than a year.

With darkness falling, the vehicles in the column turned on their headlights—the first time they had done so during any tactical operation. Churchill, who had no idea there was a cease-fire, was astonished. Holding on to the tank, he watched the night shadows flit by in the lights.

He was tired. His trek had carried him nearly one hundred miles in five days on winding mountain tracks; he was unshaven, half-starved, and indifferent to the fact that the Americans were carrying him right back the way he had come. All he cared about was that he was with his own side, even if they were heading deep into German-occupied territory.

The danger was underlined when the task force was brought to halt on a stretch of road blocked by a German antitank unit, whose 88 mm guns were trained on the American vehicles. They were here to defend against the US Seventh Army coming from the north and were not happy about having an enemy threat to their rear. It would take some delicate negotiation to get the task force past them.[4]

This was a dire complication for the situation in South Tyrol: the fighting still raging north and east of the border threatened to spill into Italy, reigniting the war there.

As Mad Jack Churchill rode on into the night, it never occurred to him to mention to the Americans that he had left behind more than 130 men, women, and children in German hands who would appreciate a prompt rescue from the dangers closing in on them. As far as he was concerned, he had seized his chance to escape; they had not. It was now up to them to look out for themselves.

❧

Tuesday 1 May: Pragser Wildsee

While Mad Jack was still tramping the Dolomites alone somewhere south of the Puster valley, at least some of his former companions were more concerned for the welfare of the women, children, and elderly than they were about taking their own chances.

Having decided on their plan, Wings Day and Anton Ducia quickly made their preparations to cross German territory to American lines. According to Ducia's information, the Americans were about to take Bolzano, which the Germans would not bother to defend.

The plan was simple enough. They would travel in Ducia's Volkswagen, a rare and distinctive but rather battered and weary vehicle. In his capacity as the regional billeting officer for the Germans, Ducia had every right to travel. Bearing papers with the stamp of the South Tyrolean Gauleiter, he should be safe in any German-held territory. Likewise, his position in the underground militia should ensure his safety if they met partisans—so long as they were a friendly faction. If they encountered hostile partisans, Ducia—who spoke good English—would pretend to be Peter Churchill, escaped SOE agent.

It was a more dangerous plan than either man knew. Not only was the cease-fire not in place yet, but Ducia's information was wrong. Allied troops were nowhere near Bolzano. Indeed, the contrary rumor—that Gauleiter Hofer was there with a large force of Waffen-SS—might turn out to be correct.[5]

Payne Best regretted that his health was too poor to go on the mission. He helped Day with his disguise, lending him a "rather dressy" black overcoat to wear over his threadbare RAF tunic and trousers, topping off his disguise with a trilby donated by Prince Philipp von Hessen.[6] By the time he was ready to leave, Day—a proud Royal Air Force officer, decorated naval hero of World War I, and veteran of many daredevil escape attempts—resembled a "second rate town clerk of the Third Reich."[7]

By about one o'clock in the afternoon, the two men were ready to depart. The sun was shining out of a blue sky, but there was still a frosty chill in the air. Day squeezed into the passenger seat of the small car and Ducia gunned its thrumming little air-cooled engine. They drove down the vale through the snow-covered forest and reached the highway at the point near the railway tracks where the transports had made their long and uncomfortable stop three days earlier. Ducia turned left. They drove west, passing through villages Day remembered seeing on the journey to Niederdorf.[8]

Day had few regrets about leaving the Pragser Wildsee. He'd been dismayed by the selfish behavior of some of the Prominenten—the pilfering and squabbling—which marred the courageous and honorable conduct of the majority. Above all, he was excited at the prospect of another escape, this time with real hope of reaching Allied lines.

They met little traffic on the Puster valley road; then after thirty-five miles, at Brixen,* they reached the main north-south highway connecting Bolzano with the Brenner Pass. It was jammed in both directions. Heading south were thousands of returning Italian forced laborers. Gaunt and starving, long lines of men, women, and children filled the road, a seemingly endless chain of human misery and suffering. Intermittently, the chain wavered and bent, forced to the sides of the road to make way for German military vehicles heading north to the pass. The Germans were starved of fuel, and each vehicle rumbling up the road had at least one other in tow. Dozens of cars, trucks, and armored vehicles lay abandoned by the roadside, either broken down or out of fuel.[9]

Crawling along through the tide of humanity, the little Volkswagen took three more hours to cover the remaining thirty miles to Bolzano, and it was around five o'clock in the afternoon when Day and Ducia entered the outskirts.

The "gateway to the Dolomites" was a large town cradled in a broad, verdant bowl where several mountain valleys met, cupped in the

* Italian: Bressanone

confluence of two rivers. Driving cautiously through the medieval streets, Day and Ducia noticed people reading newspapers with bold banner headlines. When Day stopped to picked one up, he discovered that Adolf Hitler was dead.[10] The impact of this news on people whose lives had been turned upside down was profound.

It was quickly apparent that the Germans had all but given up on Bolzano. They were clearly holding it only for its position as a central communication point. There were just enough troops to deter a partisan attack, but no preparations to withstand an Allied assault.[11] On the other hand, there was no sign that any Allied assault was imminent.

They would need to push farther south toward Trento, and that would require official sanction. Ducia led Day to the office of the prefect of Bolzano, a somber room with a large desk. Karl Tinzl was a local man rather than a German appointee and a leading member of the Tyrolean resistance; also present was the local resistance leader, a man named Erich Amonn. Ducia briefed them on his and Day's mission, and they agreed to help. Next he took Day to another building where they met with Dr. Andreas Fritz, the mayor of Bolzano, who promised to arrange their credentials.

While they waited, the two men retired to Ducia's apartment in a modern block on the outskirts of town. Ducia's wife was in Innsbruck, so the men scratched together an improvised dinner with whatever they could find. By the time they had eaten, information came through that the Americans were actually well south of Trento, at least another thirty or forty miles away. They decided to press on as soon as possible.[12]

The Volkswagen didn't have enough fuel to reach Trento, so Ducia went in search of more. The light was failing by the time he'd managed to forage enough. He poured the precious liquid into the tank and the trusty little car started up.

Leaving Bolzano on the southward road, they followed the winding river Adige, which clung to the foot of the precipitous, craggy west wall of the wide farmland valley. The going was slow, steering cautiously along a dimly lit road jammed with military traffic and soldiers and littered with abandoned vehicles. Darkness fell and the journey seemed to drag on painfully for hours.

Ducia was convinced they must be approaching Trento when they ran into a solid traffic jam. They both got out of the car and stood on the road among the groups of German soldiers. They could hear rifle fire and explosions somewhere ahead. The bang and thump of mortars were clearly discernible, while from a greater distance there came the concussion of much bigger artillery. Could that be the front line? It sounded very close—so close, in fact, that occasional overshot artillery shells were whining overhead and exploding unnervingly close to the road. The German soldiers seemed unconcerned, treating the whole situation as if it were a joke. Ducia asked them what was going on. They explained that it was just the partisans fighting each other in Trento. The Germans were simply waiting for them to run out of ammunition or for one side to wipe out their opponents.

After an hour or so of fruitless and perilous waiting, Ducia suggested it would be more sensible to return to Bolzano and spend the night in his apartment. It was frustrating in the extreme, but Day had to agree; it would be impossible to get through this jam. They climbed into the Volkswagen, turned around, and headed back the way they had come.[13]

Wednesday 2 May: Bolzano

Day and Ducia were up with the dawn the following morning, eager to get going as quickly as possible. Since there was nothing else to eat or drink in the apartment, they breakfasted on schnapps, then set off.

Viewing it for the first time in full daylight, Day saw that the valley south of Bolzano had suffered very little bomb damage. He also noticed that the Germans appeared to be digging defensive positions along it. This was the day the cease-fire was supposed to come into effect, but one wouldn't guess it from the level of military activity.

A few miles south of Bolzano, where there was a turning for the village of Auer,* the Volkswagen was brought to a halt at a heavily defended checkpoint. An aggressive German noncommissioned officer demanded that they hand over the car—he was commandeering it. Ducia refused to let him to lay a finger on his precious vehicle and began arguing angrily with him.[14] Day sat in the passenger seat trying to look inconspicuous, with the brim of Prince Philipp's trilby pulled down low. He watched as an idle group of German soldiers entertained themselves by firing handheld Panzerfaust antitank rockets along the road. It was a great game: each rocket flashed out of its flimsy handle with a *swoosh*, arcing out with a trail of smoke and exploding in the road a few hundred yards away with an enormous bang, sending a spiral of dust and smoke into the sky. The Germans seemed to have limitless supplies of these weapons.

After a while, it appeared that Ducia had managed to outwit or wear down the ill-tempered German, who brusquely waved them on their way. There was an extremely nervous interlude as the car puttered away from the checkpoint, an ideal target for the Germans and their lethal missiles. Day and Ducia expected at any moment to hear the fizz of a launch and be wiped instantaneously off the face of the earth. Eventually the Volkswagen passed out of the Panzerfausts' range. Day quietly gave thanks to the Almighty.[15]

They were about three and a half miles short of Trento when the little car—which had been sturdily reliable through years of service in spite of the privations of war—began to lose power. It lurched along weakly, then shuddered to a halt. Opening the rear cover, Ducia found the engine hot and fuming with burned oil, completely seized up.

It seemed as if some malign force was trying to prevent them from reaching their goal. Regretfully they pushed the Volkswagen off the road and begin walking. "I will not see that car again," said Ducia sadly. "It will be stolen."

---

* Italian: Ora

As they approached the outskirts of Trento, they were surprised that no one challenged them. The streets were almost deserted, the silence broken occasionally by the pop of distant gunshots. The two men found themselves in a pleasant, secluded little piazza, not far from the center, and sat down on a bench to rest and consider their next move. Two civilians came hurrying through the square, and Ducia called out to them, asking what was going on. The whole town was under partisan control, they said, except for the main street, which was still in German hands. The gunshots they could hear came from bands of partisans settling scores with their enemies and dealing out justice to known collaborators.[16]

Neither Day nor Ducia fancied the idea of getting swept up. The risk of being mistaken for Germans or collaborators now seemed worse than that of falling into the hands of the Wehrmacht or the SS. Day discarded his overcoat, revealing his RAF tunic, and replaced the trilby with his own forage cap, marking him clearly as an escaped Allied POW. From now on, Ducia would play the role of Peter Churchill.

Their transformation was not a moment too soon; the next people they saw were two partisans in armbands and red scarves. Day stopped them, explained who he was, and asked to be taken to their leaders. If they were going to avoid getting entangled with Germans, they would need help.

Partisan HQ was a two-story house in its own grounds well off the main street, with stables and outhouses. Until the day before, it had been the local Gestapo headquarters; the former occupants had decamped during the night. Day and Ducia were ushered into a room full of excitable Italians, all armed to the teeth. Their chief was a youngish man who bore a passing resemblance to Mussolini. Ducia did the talking, introducing himself as Peter Churchill and telling the story he and Day had cooked up between them. They had escaped from a Gestapo camp near Innsbruck, they said, and had been on the run for a week. They had vital intelligence that they were duty bound to convey to the Americans with all speed. They'd stolen a car but had been forced to abandon it outside the town. Could the partisans help them reach the American lines?[17]

It was a credible enough story, and Day's uniform and obvious Englishness clinched the matter. After a brief discussion, the partisans agreed to help. The Americans were believed to be a further fifty miles south of Trento. (In fact they were only half that distance away, on a line running northeast from the north end of Lake Garda.) The Germans controlled only the main roads, whereas the partisans controlled the mountains. By sticking to side roads, they could bypass German forces.

The partisans were not merely willing to help—they were positively thrilled by the idea of a dash through danger carrying vital news to the Allies. A dozen of them volunteered on the spot to accompany Wing Commander Day and "Agent Churchill" on their mission.

Within an hour a car had been provided, a rather elderly vehicle that to Day's eye looked even smaller than the Volkswagen. The partisans were not deterred and proceeded to cram into the vehicle along with Day and Ducia, poking one another in the back and face with their gun barrels and dropping hand grenades, which rolled about loose on the floor. Day was surprised no one was wounded or killed before they'd even started the engine.

With partisans jammed inside or riding on the running boards, French Maquis style, the little car revved its tiny engine and set off, limping and struggling a hundred yards down the street before juddering and grinding to a halt with its engine seized up. No amount of cranking would start it again. The partisans extricated themselves and hurried back to headquarters, demanding that another car be found for the *inglesi* officers.

Another hour passed while a replacement was located—whether stolen, requisitioned, or bartered for, Day did not know—and filled with fuel. It was larger than the other, but not by much. Once again the partisans squeezed inside, and the journey recommenced. This time they made it over half a mile to the outskirts of town before the car died with a broken axle. Day and Ducia and their increasingly frustrated escorts walked back into town to try again.

Day was impressed by the Mussolini lookalike's patience as they waited for a third car to be found. By this time, the two travelers had become honorary members of the unit, provided with scarlet armbands. Eventually another car was produced. It proved to be much larger than the others and was in such good condition that Day suspected it had been kept in storage for some time. This time he was firm; only four partisans—one of whom was the owner of the car—could come with them. The leader agreed.[18]

With only six men and their weapons in the car, they set off without a hitch, heading northeast out of Trento and climbing into the mountains. They intended to sweep round in a southeasterly arc, avoiding German forces and aiming for the main American lines. Considering the strain the car was under on the steep, poorly surfaced roads, it did remarkably well, running for nearly two hours before the clutch burned out.

Leaving the car in the care of its owner, Day and Ducia and the remaining three partisans set off on foot. During the ordeal that followed, Day would become close to all three. Even so, they would remain almost mythic figures in his memory: all Day knew of their regular lives was that one, Ezio Caneppele, was a chauffeur. The partisans were an oddly assorted band of idealistic fighting men, devoted to the mountain country of their home. Mario dell'Elmo was the oldest, aged about fifty, with the manner of a lawyer and "dressed for the boulevard rather than the mountains," although he kept pace with the younger men easily enough. Michele Mucci knew the countryside best and was their guide.[19] The Italians had high hopes for this mission, imagining themselves, having delivered Wing Commander Day to the Allies, returning in triumph to liberate Trento, riding aboard the first wave of American tanks.

They slogged for hours along rough mountain paths, up and down steep inclines, through forest and snow, following the shoulder of a valley that curved east before turning southeast toward the town of Pergine Valsugana and Lake Caldonazzo. Then they began to climb, winding ever upward through forest. The temperature was freezing and the going arduous, and Day soon began to suffer badly. Ducia was a fit young man who had worked as a ski instructor for ten years before the war, and the three partisans, though not all young, had enjoyed well-fed lives during the war years. Wings Day, although only forty-six, had spent years as an under-nourished prisoner and felt like an old, exhausted man. The journey was hell for him. As they scrambled along precarious mountain paths, through forest undergrowth and across rocky ravines, he struggled to keep up. After a few hours, he no longer cared where they were heading—he only wanted the torment to stop. But still he kept going.

Ducia had brought his schnapps with him and offered Day a nip to keep off the chill. Day felt exhausted, not chilled, but accepted anyway. Ducia frequently sipped at his flask, and Day wondered at his stamina. If Day had taken that much booze on board he'd have been plastered in no time.[20]

At last, when they'd been walking for about six hours and dusk was descending, they came to a large building with broad Alpine eaves, surrounded by a few smaller chalets, all nestled in the folds of the mountains. They had reached the mountaintop resort of Vetriolo, and the large building was the Hotel Trento. It was closed and shuttered, but the proprietor came out and greeted them. He appeared acquainted with the partisans and invited the party to stay the night, opening up the bar and serving Italian schnapps.

His name was Giovanni Oss, and for Wings Day he was a lifesaver. Oss was kindness personified, providing his guests with comfortable rooms and a dinner of roast kid with local wine, one of the best meals Day had ever eaten in his life. He was feeling the chill now that they had stopped, and he relished the warmth and rest. The five men spent a convivial evening with their host, and eventually Day sank into a large bed with a soft mattress, sliding in between heavenly linen sheets.[21]

He had no way of knowing that, only thirty or so miles to the north, Mad Jack Churchill was at that moment making his way on foot westward toward Bolzano, hoping to encounter American units at any moment. Day was also unaware that a fragile cease-fire had begun that day.

It was without doubt the most comfortable night's sleep Wings Day had enjoyed since leaving England. But unlike Mad Jack's conscience, Day's dreams were clouded by anxiety for the other Prominenten. It was his second night away from the Pragser Wildsee. Time was ticking remorselessly by.

Thursday 3 May: East of Trento

It was before dawn and still pitch dark when Wings Day was roused from sleep by Ducia. It was time to go. They were given a little breakfast by Signor Oss, and then the band of travelers set off just as the eastern sky was beginning to lighten.

Thankfully the first leg of the journey was downhill, heading southeast around the mountain, sticking to the northern slopes of the Brenta valley and gradually descending toward the valley bottom, which was a broad patchwork of farm fields and villages on either side of the meandering river. They had been walking for two or three hours when they reached the flat land and stopped for a bite to eat at a small town—possibly Levico Terme on the east shore of Lake Levico. There they were joined by a fourth partisan, heavily armed and dressed in a German paratrooper's smock with a bullet hole in the back; he proudly described how he had shot its former owner.[22]

This was the first evidence—though Day didn't realize it at the time—that this valley marked the front line, which on the German side was held by the elite paratroopers of the Luftwaffe's 1st Fallschirmjäger Division. These troops were not keen to honor the cease-fire with the Allies and were inclined to shoot at anything they didn't like the look of. All Day knew at the time was that as soon as they ventured into the valley the partisans grew more alert to the risk of encountering German patrols.

Coming to a main road, the partisans ordered Ducia and Day to take cover. This road—which was visible for about half a mile in each direction—was regularly patrolled by Germans, and they must get over it without being seen. "Do as we do," the partisans instructed. They began crossing the open ground in short rushes, throwing themselves into cover behind rocks and bushes. As an RAF officer, Day had never trained to do such things and felt like an utter fool as he dodged from one piece of cover to the next like a commando; he felt even sillier "rushing madly bent double across a road with nothing in sight."[23]

With that hazard behind them, they were back in deep country and relatively safe. Following the valley east, they stopped off occasionally at farms where friendly farmers shared a glass of grappa with them. It was about eleven o'clock in the morning and they had been walking for seven or eight hours when they reached one of the many tiny hamlets along the northern valley slopes that were in partisan hands. Feeling in need of rest and refreshment, they went into the inn and ordered wine.

Day, Ducia, and their four friends were relaxing and enjoying their wine when the inn door suddenly burst open and two local men entered. They wore scarlet armbands and were armed as if they'd just come from battle: both carried submachine guns, with revolvers in their holsters, grenades clipped to their bandoliers, and binoculars hanging around their necks. They glared with open hostility at the newcomers and demanded to know what they were doing there. A vehement argument broke out between the six armed men, with Ducia joining in. Day watched in bewilderment, unable to understand a word.[24]

The argument blazed for about ten minutes. Then, with a final insult, the two men stormed out and slammed the door behind them.

"What was that?" Day asked.

Ducia explained that the two men were the commander and adjutant of the local partisan group and were furious that partisans from Trento had entered their territory without permission. Although they'd been persuaded to accept the urgency of the mission and would probably offer no further trouble, it was a small taste of the hostility between groups—even those that were politically aligned. The fighters in this region were part of the same Catholic republican anti-fascist resistance as Sante Garibaldi and the Trento men. Partisans from rival political tendencies were apt to come in shooting.

The same thing happened again when they rested at the next hamlet. This time the angry anti-fascists insisted that they were the only "official" partisans in this area and should be obeyed; any other so-called partisans the travelers might happen to meet were "phonies." The explanation for this came ten minutes later when Day and his party met another aggressive pair who bore the insignia of the Garibaldi Communists (named after Giuseppe Garibaldi, the nineteenth-century revolutionary general). Naturally they claimed that *they* were the true partisans and that any others were false. Wings Day was growing weary of this and decided to leave "before a third lot could come along."[25]

Around noon the travelers reached Roncegno, a pretty little town of brightly painted Tyrolean houses and narrow lanes perched on the hills above the valley bottom. One of Day's companions had a friend here, a butcher named Andrea Hofer, who provided the hungry party with a "right royal" lunch of spaghetti, which Day found delicious. For him, this quest for deliverance was becoming quite a culinary odyssey. More important than the spaghetti was the welcome news that the American lines were only two or three miles away, somewhere in the vicinity of Borgo Valsugana, a similar little town on the opposite side of the valley.[26]

Day and Ducia were excited but were warned to be cautious. To get to the Americans, they would have to pass through the German lines, which were extremely dangerous. They were provided with several local men to act as guides. Day would have preferred to keep the numbers down to be less conspicuous, but of course the men were keen to take part in this intriguing adventure. They set out right away.

Roncegno and its surroundings had been battered by fighting the previous day, when the German parachute regiment occupying the area, ignoring the cease-fire, had savagely resisted a push by the US 351st Infantry Regiment attempting to advance toward Trento; 88 mm guns had been fired at the Americans, who replied by pouring five hundred artillery rounds into the hills behind Roncegno, where the German guns were believed to be. Since then, the Americans had stayed in their positions and peace had descended. The cease-fire was being observed, but it was fragile. The commanding officer of the 1st Fallschirmjäger Regiment had crossed the valley under a white flag and offered to cease hostilities, but he warned that his men had orders to shoot if the Americans pressed ahead with their advance. An uneasy truce had settled over the Brenta valley. The 1st Fallschirmjäger Division and the US 351st Infantry had met in battle twice the previous year—in May 1944 at Monte Grande and in October at Vedriano—and the Americans had been hit hard. Now they were keeping their eyes open and their weapons ready.[27]

The guides claimed it was easy to get across the lines so long as one kept to the right path, hugging the line of the hill along the north side of the valley. After walking for several miles, the guides stopped at a high point on the hillside and pointed out to Day where the military lines were.

Before them, the Brenta valley sat spectacularly like a vast, long bowl walled in by distant jagged peaks. Away to the right, the light flecks of the houses of Roncegno could be picked out on the forested slopes, and below them the fields in the valley bottom spread across the vista to the river and main road. Borgo Valsugana was a large cluster of red-roofed buildings straddling the river beneath the precipitous green slopes of the south side of the valley. The guide pointed to some farm buildings near the village, where he said the Americans had their advanced positions. The German regiment was now to Day's right, in the direction of Roncegno, a little over half a mile from the Americans.

Day could see no signs of movement, so they walked on without making any attempt to hide, allowing any American observers to get a clear view of him and his uniform. They were about a hundred yards from the farm buildings when Day spotted an American GI crouched behind a bush, leaning on his rifle and watching the approaching party with interest.

Hesitating, Day called out, "I'm a British officer. Can we come over?"

The GI studied the strange assortment of men: the Englishman, with his crisp accent and threadbare old uniform with the incongruous red partisan armband; the smooth-looking Italian civilian; the partisans, including the dapper middle-aged Dell'Elmo and the group of guides from

Roncegno. The American saw no obvious signs of danger. "Sure," he said. "You can all come over."

As the group filed past him, the GI directed Day to his company HQ, which was in the farmyard. Day found the company commander, a young captain from Chicago named Johnson, and introduced himself as Wing Commander Harry Day of the Royal Air Force, an escaped prisoner of war tasked with an extremely important and sensitive mission. While Captain Johnson's men hospitably offered cigarettes and chocolate to their visitors, Day told his story as succinctly as he could, underlining the danger his fellow hostages were in. It was vital that a force be sent as quickly as possible to rescue them.

Johnson was doubtful; he appreciated the hostages' plight, but the situation here was precarious. He expected the cease-fire to be temporary and to receive orders at any moment to resume hostilities. He knew well what fanatical fighters the paratroopers were and wasn't relishing the prospect. The likelihood of there being troops to spare for long-range rescue missions was slim. However, Wing Commander Day was welcome to go up the chain of command to regimental headquarters, and Johnson would be happy to provide transport.

As Day and Ducia boarded the jeep, they bade farewell and thanks to their partisan companions. Day had grown attached to them, and he took down their names and addresses so that he could remain in touch. As they parted, he told them he hoped they fulfilled their often-expressed wish to return to Trento aboard an American tank.[28] The jeep roared away down the road. Day could only hope for a more positive response from the regimental commander.

They arrived at regimental HQ just as the commanding officer, Colonel Franklin P. Miller, was beginning a press interview, and they were forced to wait. Eventually they were introduced. Miller, a small, wiry man, was as full of kindness as Captain Johnson had been—and just as pessimistic. Just that morning he had sent two of his officers to parley with General Karl-Lothar Schulz, the German division's commander, who was only willing to maintain the cease-fire if directly ordered by his superiors at Fourteenth Army HQ. Schulz was concerned about partisan attacks and would not stand down. The situation was extremely tense, and, like Johnson, Miller believed his regiment would be fighting again very soon.[29] Nonetheless, Day was welcome to go still further up the chain to the headquarters of the 88th Infantry Division.

Setting off again in the jeep, heading south toward Vicenza, farther and farther away from the Pragser Wildsee, Day could only wonder what was going on at the hotel, hoping that help could be sent in time to prevent disaster. Fortunately for his nerves, he was completely unaware of German plans for the Prominenten, plans that were contradictory in their aims but equally terrifying.

On the one hand, there was the order issued to local Gestapo chief Hans Philipp on 1 May—while Day and Ducia were setting out on their mission—to snatch the Prominenten and take them across the border into Austria for execution.[30]

On the other hand, on the very same day, SS-Obergruppenführer Karl Wolff, having told Captain Alvensleben to send Stiller's and Bader's men to him in Bolzano, had cooked up a scheme to curry favor with the Allies by seizing the Prominenten himself. As the regional SS leader, he had been aware of the presence of VIP hostages on his turf, but only when he spoke to Alvensleben did he realize their identities and status. This was a golden opportunity. He would assemble a small detachment of SS and SD troopers and dispatch them to the Pragser Wildsee to guard the hostages, displacing Alvensleben's company. Assuming the hostages survived the inevitable violent confrontation, Wolff would join them there in person and surrender to the Allies in the guise of a savior rather than an enemy.[31]

That night, while Day and Ducia were being forced to turn back to Bolzano because of the partisan fighting in Trento, Wolff had prepared for the operation by sending a radio message to Field Marshal Harold Alexander, supreme commander of Allied forces in the Mediterranean, advising him of the dangers still faced by the hostages. His message suggested that Alexander should use airborne troops to take custody of the hostages and accept Wolff's surrender.[32]

Wings Day was already anxious enough. Had he known that the Gestapo, SS, and SD might be converging simultaneously on the lakeside refuge with desperate and conflicting objectives, with the woods full of partisans itching for German blood, the Prominenten caught in the middle, and only Alvensleben's little Wehrmacht force for protection, his worries would have been redoubled.

Twenty-Three
Dash for Deliverance

Thursday 3 May: Pragser Wildsee

It was morning, and Sigismund Payne Best was taking the air outside the hotel when he heard the distant droning of aircraft. A single plane flew over the Pragser vale and from it came a little snowstorm of paper. He and several other Prominenten watched as the little slips came fluttering down over the trees and the lake. A few people ran after them to find out what they were.

One was handed to Payne Best. It was a communiqué from the headquarters of the Allied supreme commander, Field Marshal Alexander, intended for German troops; it informed them that General Vietinghoff had surrendered and instructed them to cease all hostile actions, remain where they were, and await further orders.[1]

The announcement couldn't have come at a better time for the Polish Prominenten. Today was their national Constitution Day, an annual occasion for revelry. Jørgen Mogensen, who had been the last foreign diplomat to leave Warsaw in late 1939, was counted as an honorary Pole and had promised Count Aleksander Zamoyski that he would help collect food from Niederdorf to make a decent celebratory dinner. He was returning through thick snow with Polish RAF officer Jan Izycki when he managed to grab one of the falling leaflets. He and Izycki ran the rest of the way to the hotel and burst into the hallway, full of the wonderful news.[2]

It spread rapidly throughout the hotel, and the Prominenten rejoiced. Had they known more about the situation outside their little enclave, they would have received the glad tidings with rather more moderate optimism. If they'd known the full facts, they'd have been too terrified to celebrate.

Some had become dangerously complacent almost from the moment Bader and his men departed Niederdorf. Fey Pirzio-Biroli and Alex von Stauffenberg were among them. Ever since Schönberg, they had found an ever-deeper consolation in each other's company: Fey over the separation from her children and Alex over the death of his beloved wife, the aviatrix Melitta. Together they took long walks from the hotel through the forest trails all the way to Niederdorf, stopping off at peasant cabins and farms to talk to the locals. Fey, as a German with ties to Italy, was fascinated by the local people, who were officially Italian but considered themselves Austrian.[3]

A few Prominenten were at least partially aware of the dangers beyond the perimeter formed by the Wehrmacht company. Peter Churchill shared Bonin's view that nobody should stray outside the small zone immediately around the hotel, but he didn't think it applied to him. His presence had been requested by Sante Garibaldi, who had need of his language skills in Niederdorf. His fellow SOE agent Hugh Falconer was also restless; he felt he had "a few accounts to settle" with the Germans over the way he'd been treated since his capture in 1943.[4]

Falconer and his two-man team had been seized in Tunis as they attempted to locate their safe house. The Germans had subsequently used Falconer's transmitter in a deception that led to the capture of another ten SOE agents sent to reinforce Falconer's unit.[5] Delivered to the Berlin Gestapo, Falconer was interrogated harshly, constantly threatened with execution. Eventually he was transferred to Sachsenhausen. Like Jack and Peter Churchill, Falconer's life was saved by the German belief that he was related to "somebody important," although in his case it was never revealed who that somebody was supposed to be. Now that he was free, he seized the opportunity to go looking for some action and, if possible, payback.

He and Peter Churchill had discovered a dilapidated old two-seater sports car in the hotel garage. Falconer used his technical skills to get it running, and they took off at speed down the snowbound road toward Niederdorf, Churchill clinging on anxiously as the car swerved and skidded on the steep, icy track. Driving into Niederdorf, they found the square in front of the town hall crowded with partisans. Operating under Ferrero's leadership, the Tyroleans had collected such a vast armory of German weapons that many of the men in red scarves had two MP40 machine pistols apiece slung over their shoulders.

Most of the weapons had been surrendered by the retreating Germans without any fuss—like people in line handing over tickets so that they could pass through—but there had been occasional resistance. One company of infantry had refused to comply and had opened fire on Ferrero's partisans. The Tyroleans won the ensuing firefight. Afterward, the bloodthirsty Ferrero personally gunned down the German survivors. He also rounded up a dozen officers and marched them back to the town hall for summary court martials, condemning every one of them to death. Garibaldi, discovering what was going on, intervened and ordered Ferrero to rescind the death sentences. "None of you will be executed," he said to one of the Germans. "We shall not repay you in the coin of some of your SS."[6]

Falconer and Churchill explored the town hall, finding two rooms stuffed almost from floor to ceiling with captured weapons. They chose for themselves a "couple of shining Lugers" complete with holsters.[7] While Falconer elected to stay with Ferrero and join his band of fighting men, Churchill went off to perform the task he'd been requested for. Word had been received that there were American troops at the next town to the east, and Garibaldi needed Churchill to act as interpreter.

With a small retinue of fighters, the two men drove out of town. All along the road they passed little groups of partisans who waved and whooped excitedly when they recognized the great Garibaldi. Eventually, after a ten-mile drive, they met up with a heavily armored battalion of the

US Army 339th Infantry Regiment—or at least its lead company.[8] They were directed to the command post and Garibaldi introduced himself, with his typical air of importance, to the American captain, who was visibly stressed and fatigued.

Garibaldi announced that he was in overall control of this whole district and was therefore the man to talk to on all military and civil matters. Oblivious to the American captain's irritation—which was acutely obvious to Churchill—Garibaldi recited a detailed list of requests for supplies, support, administrative organization, and military liaison arrangements.

The captain shook his head firmly at each request. Other than the most basic agreement to liaise with Garibaldi, he had no power to authorize any of this. His unit was a small task force sent a very long way ahead of its parent division to secure specific objectives. It was not an occupation force. Since dawn that morning, they had traveled over fifty miles, much of it through snowbound mountain passes; all the way the captain had been subjected to "endless chatter" from partisans who bombarded the Americans with requests for assistance. He and his men were too exhausted to focus on anything other than their objective.[9]

Peter Churchill, playing his limited part in the discussion, sympathized with the captain. He understood the use of small-unit task forces operating far from the safety of the armies they belonged to. It was clear to Churchill that there would be no point in trying to persuade this officer to come and liberate the Prominenten, even though such a plea might have carried more weight with him than Garibaldi's imperious demands.

When he and Garibaldi returned to Niederdorf, Churchill decided to go back to the Pragser Wildsee. It was, after all, the closest thing he had to a home. But things were starting to fray even there.

The fractiousness of the local partisans was spinning out of control. A group of them had appeared at the hotel in a wild and noisy display of triumph. Some of the Prominenten detected a threatening undertone to the celebratory mood and found their presence uncomfortable and intimidating. Meanwhile in Niederdorf the atmosphere was becoming ugly. Youths in red scarves, brandishing machine guns and waving the Italian flag, drove up and down the main thoroughfare, shooting indiscriminately. Others were going from door to door, searching for collaborators and shooting suspects at random.[10]

In the afternoon a car screeched to a halt outside the hotel and four young partisans piled out, waving submachine guns. They demanded to see Léon Blum and the young Soviet officer Vassily Kokorin. These young men were not part of Garibaldi's faction but came from a Communist group based in the mountain resort of Cortina d'Ampezzo, twenty miles to the south. The leader of the group claimed to be a French officer, a Captain Lussac, who told Sigismund Payne Best that he was under instructions to remove both Blum and Kokorin to a place of safety. Payne Best refused to be intimidated and told them that the guests were under the protection of a Wehrmacht detachment and that as the appointed leader of the group he could not permit anyone to be taken away against their will. This seemed to have a sobering effect on the interlopers. Nonetheless, Payne Best allowed them to meet with the Blums and Kokorin. Neither Janot nor Léon Blum had any wish to depart with the partisans, but Vassily Kokorin agreed to go.[11]

Kokorin told Payne Best he was worried about his fate at the hands of the American and British armies. "I don't want to be slaughtered," he said. Payne Best tried to reassure him that as Molotov's nephew he would be perfectly all right, but he had worked himself into a state of panic, and nothing short of physical force would restrain him. Like most of his fellow Russians, he believed that Stalin would execute all returning prisoners of war. They were not far wrong.

Before Kokorin left the hotel, he went to say goodbye to Dr. Josef Müller, whose friendship had meant a lot to him. There were tears in his eyes as he embraced Müller and kissed him on both cheeks.

"Vassily, what's wrong with you today?" Müller asked him.

"I have to say goodbye to you."

"You are leaving? Why don't you stay with us? We're going to be liberated very soon."

Kokorin reminded Müller that he had formerly fought with a special Soviet unit behind enemy lines. "I'm an officer of the partisans and it is my duty to make it back to my unit. I will go with the freedom fighters to Cortina." Müller pleaded, but Kokorin was adamant. "My uncle and the Marshal," he said, meaning Stalin, "would never forgive me if I was liberated by the English whore."[12]

Captain Gebhard von Alvensleben also tried to dissuade Kokorin. He was so concerned about breaching his code of care for the prisoners that he asked two witnesses to confirm that he had tried his best to warn Kokorin of the dangers. Soviet major general Pyotr Privalov and the Czech major Jan Stanek signed the written affirmation.[13]

It was with a heavy heart that Payne Best watched the likeable but melancholy youth disappear down the road with the partisans. Payne Best tried to find out more about the group through Garibaldi, but it was impossible; the Communists were rivals, bitterly hostile to Garibaldi's democratic anti-fascists.[14]

None of the Prominenten ever saw Vassily Kokorin again. Müller later learned that he suffered badly during his time with the partisans in the snowbound mountains; his feet were so frostbitten that gangrene set in. He was said to have died before anything could be done for him.[15]

Thursday 3 May: Between Borgo Valsugana and Vicenza

Holding on to his hat as the jeep sped along the highway leading south, Wings Day was amazed at the buildup of US Army traffic. On and on it went as the road wound through the southern fringe of the Tyrolean Alps then out onto the plain of Veneto: trucks, jeeps, armored personnel carriers, tanks, artillery, and more trucks, nose to tail as far as the eye could see. He was struck not just by the scale but by the orderliness and the smooth-running efficiency of this vast military machine, compared with the rank chaos and malfunction he'd witnessed among the retreating German forces along the road from Munich to the Brenner Pass and on the highway down to Bolzano.

Somewhere near Vicenza, the jeep turned in at the entrance to a large camp of tents and military trailers, signposted 88th Infantry Division HQ. The jeep pulled up outside the commanding officer's trailer, and Day was shown in.

Major General Paul W. Kendall, the divisional commander, was a heavyset, square-jawed man from Wyoming who'd commanded the 88th Infantry Division throughout the northern Italian campaign.[16] Kendall had his G-2 (intelligence) officer, Colonel Walker, take Day's report. Walker thought perhaps an armored column might be sent forward to relieve the hostages. This was encouraging, but there was still no immediate sign of action. The Puster valley and the Pragser Wildsee were a very long way ahead of any of the 88th Division's units, with a lot of mountain roads and German forces in between. From the 351st Regiment's position at Borgo Valsugana, for example, it was about 125 miles to the Pragser Wildsee via Trento. The officers of the 88th shook their heads. This task needed to be referred upward.

Back to the jeep again. From Vicenza, Day and Ducia were conveyed up the chain of command again, this time to the headquarters of II Corps at Padua. They drove through dusk, arriving at around nine o'clock in the evening. Day was dizzy with fatigue and beginning to become disoriented from repeatedly recounting his mission and describing the plight of the Prominenten to a succession of commanding officers and G-2 staff. This time it was the staff of Major General Geoffrey Keyes, corps commander.

Again there were suggestions of an armored column. Ducia, who was the expert on the situation in the region around the Pragser Wildsee, was taken aside for a special interview. Before they parted, Ducia shook his friend's hand. "I can't thank you enough, Wings," he said. "I could never have got so far without you. I shall be very lost and alone."[17]

Day felt the same way about Anton Ducia; they had come through so much together and had developed a close bond of comradeship. Exhausted and already missing his friend, Day headed for the headquarters mess, where he'd been invited to stay the night. He found he still had Ducia's briefcase, which the Italian had carried across the Dolomites with his precious bottle of schnapps inside. Wings took it out and silently sipped a warming toast to the mission and a good night's sleep.

Meanwhile, the II Corps staff got to grips with the problem of the VIP hostages, unaware that the Gestapo and the regional SS commander also had plans for them. The 88th Division was in no position to help, but the corps' other infantry formation, the 85th "Custer" Division, might be. One of their regiments had been dispatched ahead just that day and should be in exactly the right spot to mount a rescue.

4:45 a.m., Wednesday 4 May 1945: San Candido

Lieutenant Melvin G. Asche looked up and down the line of trucks and jeeps as they coughed and roared to life, filling the village street with noise and fumes. The pretty fronts of the chalet houses were dim and lifeless in the early morning gloom; the light of sunrise gleamed on the mountain peaks but was only just beginning to slant down and spill into the green valley.[18] Lieutenant Asche was tired. His men were tired. The regiment had been advancing at breakneck speed, eating up sixty-five miles of enemy territory in a single day—and now, just when they thought the war was over, they'd been assigned this risky new mission.[19]

Asche was acting commanding officer of G Company, 2nd Battalion, 339th Infantry Regiment, having taken over for the day from Captain John Atwell, who'd been delayed during the advance.[20]

The men of the 339th—nicknamed the "Polar Bears" due to the regiment's service in Russia in World War I—were a long way from their fellow Americans. The previous morning they'd been at the town of Belluno in the Piave valley, on the same east-west front of II Corps that ran through Borgo Valsugana. When the cease-fire began on 2 May, most of the Allied forces had been on that line, occupying the southern edge of the Dolomite mountains or the Veneto plain—the high-water mark of their rapid fighting advance from the Apennines and across the river Po. Later that same day, an order had come down from 85th Infantry Division HQ to dispatch a force to block the roads into northeast Italy at the Austrian border, to help contain the surrendering German forces in Italy and prevent enemy forces who were not subject to the cease-fire from causing trouble. It was essentially part of the same mission that was being carried out on the same day by the 10th Mountain Division task force encountered by Mad Jack Churchill north of Bolzano. The main aim of the 339th was to secure Highway 49, the road that passed along the Puster valley through Niederdorf and crossed the Austrian border east of San Candido. As it was also a main route from northeast Italy to the Brenner Pass, Highway 49 was doubly important.

Before dawn on 3 May, the task force had set out north from the division start line. It was well equipped and capable of operating as a self-contained unit. The 339th Infantry Regiment was the core of Regimental Combat Team 9, a formation composed of the regiment plus an artillery battalion, a company of engineers, and a medical battalion. The whole combat team was engaged for the mission.

Throughout that day, the combat team dashed north from Belluno along Highway 51. Halfway, they split, with one battalion going northwest to cut off Highway 49 at Dobbiaco, near Niederdorf (it was probably the leading element of this force that Peter Churchill and Sante Garibaldi met), while the other two kept heading north for San Candido. It was an arduous advance. The company of engineers performed Herculean feats, improvising river crossings where bridges had been blown and clearing snow-blocked mountain passes.[21] Half an hour after midnight, approximately twenty-one hours after setting out from Belluno, the 2nd Battalion task force reached their checkpoint at San Candido, an advance of sixty-five miles—farther than any other unit in Fifth Army.[22]

The men of G Company, 2nd Battalion had barely had a chance to set up their roadblock and find billets for the night when a new order came down from regimental commander Colonel John English, relayed from II Corps. It said that General Keyes had been informed by an escaped prisoner that the Germans were holding over 130 VIPs and prisoners of war hostage at a hotel on the Pragser Wildsee lake. Colonel English ordered Lieutenant Colonel John Hesse, commander of 2nd Battalion, to organize and dispatch a "strong combat patrol" immediately to rescue them.

Hesse picked G Company for the job, augmented by the battalion's intelligence and reconnaissance platoon and a radio truck. In the absence of Captain John Atwell, the patrol would be led by Lieutenant Melvin Asche. They assembled in sleepy San Candido in the darkness before dawn, ready to leave at first light.[23]

Under Asche's supervision, and with platoon sergeants barking orders up and down the line, Private Arthur Ferdinand and his squad buddies, bleary from lack of sleep, climbed up to the truck bed of their vehicle. Just nineteen years old, Ferdinand was a combat veteran toughened by a year on the front line. A native of New Jersey, he had been drafted into the army in September 1943, just two months after his eighteenth birthday. After basic training he'd been meant to proceed to a one-year college program, but the need for front-line troops took precedence, and in March 1944 he'd been posted to Italy as a replacement combat infantryman.[24] Even before yesterday's breakneck rush north, for the past four days the 339th had been relentlessly pursuing the remnants of Germany's forces. Already at the limits of fatigue, Ferdinand and his buddies had managed to snatch only a couple of hours' sleep before being rousted out by their sergeant for this special mission.

On hearing the briefing, the men had felt a sense of foreboding. There might be an official cease-fire, but the countryside ahead and around was crawling with die-hard German units. They were also right by the border with Austria—indeed, it was part of the regiment's mission to guard it. Southeast of here, in the British Eighth Army's sector, there had been fatal clashes between British troops and German forces who were part of Army Group South East, which was not under Vietinghoff's command and not subject to his surrender.[25] Besides that, the danger of being caught in the cross fire between rival partisan groups was significant. Finally, there was the SS detachment said to be holding the hostages.

"We were quite disturbed about this entire thing," Ferdinand recalled, "because we knew the end of the war was on hand and we were facing possibly another battle."[26] Nobody wanted to be the last man killed when the war was as good as over, especially in a unit that had already had its full share of hard fighting.

But there was no alternative—up ahead were over 130 hostages, including civilians, women, and children, whose lives hung in the balance. The patrol had been briefed that "before the Germans fled they would eliminate all the prisoners."[27] At 0450 hours, just as light was breaking over the mountains, Lieutenant Asche gave the signal and the task force revved up and rolled out onto Highway 49, heading west.

The mission, thrown together on short notice, was based on intelligence that was not only insufficient but flat wrong. Wing Commander Day's report—given only a few hours earlier at corps headquarters—had become garbled. The volatile SS and SD guards were no longer there; instead there was a much larger and more heavily armed detachment of Wehrmacht infantry. And although the Germans were there to protect the prisoners until liberation, they were not expecting the Allies to come suddenly at dawn, without the slightest advance warning and ready to fight. In the half-light of sunrise—which would come later to the deep vale of the Pragser Wildsee—it would be easy for a sleepy German machine gunner or sentry to mistake the American combat patrol for an SS or Gestapo force coming to seize or execute the Prominenten.

Unaware that their mission was even more dangerous than they feared, G Company passed through Niederdorf and reached the junction just over half a mile beyond. There the convoy of trucks, jeeps, and armored carriers turned left, thumping over the railway crossing and driving past the railwayman's cottage.

In high summer, the climb through the vale would have been picturesque and green; in early May, it was a journey into winter's last refuge. The narrow, icy road ascended in long straights and winding curves, through isolated hamlets, open fields, and forests, past lone churches and farms hugging the roadside or perched on snow-covered hilltops. The vale alternately closed in and opened up, its sides rising ever more steeply until the rocky crests of mountains began to loom over the treetops. This last leg of the journey was the most dangerous, and the task force followed the trail to their objective cautiously.

Some distance short of the hotel, Lieutenant Asche ordered the convoy to halt. He selected a single platoon, ordering them to dismount from their vehicles and follow him. They were all getting more nervous by the minute—not least Private Arthur Ferdinand, whose platoon was the one chosen. Leaving the rest of the company behind, they advanced stealthily along the road on foot, weapons at the ready, safety catches off. At last, through the gloom of the trees, the hotel could be made out, framed against the backdrop of the colossal rock face of the Seekofel. The hotel looked asleep, with only a few lights glowing behind curtained windows. The men on point suddenly spotted a German machine-gun post beside the road up ahead. They took cover, ready to fire.

There was a tense silence as the German machine gunners and the American infantrymen watched one another, fingers on triggers, each waiting for the other to make a move. Every man on both sides was tired, nervous, and uncertain of what he could make out in the incipient dawn light under the trees. An instant's panic, one man with a jumpy trigger finger, and there would be a bloodbath.

After a few moments, the Wehrmacht sentries realized that the soldiers approaching their position were Americans. This was what they had been waiting for. Laying down their weapons, they offered their surrender. Lieutenant Asche and his men emerged from cover and, leaving a man to guard the Germans, moved on toward the hotel.

One by one, the German sentry positions were discovered and taken. Within a few minutes, all eighty of Gebhard von Alvensleben's men had surrendered and been disarmed. Company G had achieved its objective without one drop of blood being shed. The Pragser Wildsee was in American hands, and the hostages were safe.

While Lieutenant Asche sent word for the rest of the company to advance to the hotel, Private Ferdinand met the first of the freed prisoners, who greeted him and his comrades with open arms. All he could think of was sleep, and he asked if there was anywhere he could take a short nap. "Why not use my room?" said one gentleman, and he led Ferdinand and his buddy there. Crashing out on the bed, they fell asleep. They didn't wake for twelve hours.[28]

G Company's final approach and capture of the Pragser Wildsee had been so stealthy that some Prominenten were only aware that salvation was at hand when, taking an early breakfast in the hotel dining room, they saw mud-splattered military vehicles drawing up outside bearing the unmistakable white star of the US Army.

Sigismund Payne Best was just finishing dressing in his room when Corporal Andy Walsh, his self-appointed personal servant, came in and announced that the whole hotel was "full of Italians," who were going into bedrooms and threatening the women prisoners with guns.

Believing that the long-feared partisan assault on the German kin prisoners had begun, Payne Best hurried downstairs. In the hallway, he found half-a-dozen American GIs standing by while Sante Garibaldi talked with their officer. Jubilant partisans were everywhere, making noise and barging into rooms. Bewildered, Payne Best informed the American officer that he was in charge here and asked what was going on. The officer introduced himself as Lieutenant Melvin Asche of G Company, 339th Infantry Regiment; his unit had made a forced march through the night to come to the hostages' rescue.[29]

If Lieutenant Asche was expecting joyful thanks from this stiff-backed Englishman, he was to be disappointed. Payne Best took all this in and explained that the Prominenten had been "getting on quite all right" until now. "I would be much obliged if you would get rid of these partisans. They are upsetting all our arrangements and disturbing the women and children in our party."

Payne Best apparently thought the Americans had brought the Italians with them. Somehow the partisans had heard about the operation—presumably when the convoy passed through Niederdorf—and had followed. Lieutenant Asche saw Payne Best's point and began ordering his men to remove the unwelcome intruders.

Jimmy James and some of the other Catholics were at Mass in the little lakeside chapel while all this was going on and returned to the hotel to find a positive field day going on, with US Army vehicles parked at the front and soldiers mingling with the Prominenten. G Company had been joined by more men from the battalion, accompanied by the company commander, Captain John Atwell.[30]

Isa Vermehren was among the worshippers returning from Mass. She was fascinated by the sight of weary, battle-stained American soldiers swarming through the hotel. Tired out, they draped their lanky forms on chairs and sofas, their long legs stretched out in front of them or propped up on the tops of coffee tables. Some had their hands dug casually in their pockets; others had cigarettes dangling between their lips. She was struck by the relaxed behavior they had brought from the New World. "The only movement some of them made was to move their jaws up and down energetically as they chewed gum," she observed. "They didn't shout and they didn't scream. If they talked to each other at all, it was in fragments of sentences, grunts and brief comments that were hard for a foreigner to understand."[31]

Fey Pirzio-Biroli and Alex von Stauffenberg had been on one of their "excursions"—apparently overnight—and arrived back at the hotel as the GIs were trying to clear out the partisans. The Italians were insisting preposterously that the whole area was under their control, and the Americans were rapidly losing patience with them.[32]

Payne Best, keen to display his authority and play the host, introduced Captain Atwell to some of the Wehrmacht officers, including the two Alvenslebens, who were now prisoners of war. Payne Best gave them a glowing report and suggested to Atwell that they be treated well.

With introductions out of the way, Payne Best decided to treat the tired, hungry Americans to breakfast. Red Cross parcels were opened, and the astonished GIs—who had expected to find the prisoners starving and desperate—were given a "magnificent breakfast" served by the hotel staff of "pretty and very charming girls." Payne Best was immensely proud that he and his companions could "provide our rescuers with three square meals, and even with cigarettes."[33]

Despite his initially somewhat spiky welcome, Payne Best felt profoundly thankful for the Americans' arrival. It relieved him of a responsibility which, "in my poor state of health, was almost more than I could cope with." He normally drank very little, but since arriving at the Pragser Wildsee he had been consuming nearly a bottle a day of Vietinghoff's brandy. Thinking back on this day a few years later, he recalled:

> The American Army did us proud. It is simply astounding what trouble they took to promote our comfort and security, and what nice fellows they were too. There was a spontaneous, almost childlike kindliness shown to us by all of them. . . . They thought everything wonderful, said so, and obviously enjoyed being with us. They seemed to be entirely devoid of national hatred. . . . There seemed to be amongst them men of all nationalities, men who spoke German, French, and even Russian, and yet, all bore the stamp of being citizens of the USA and showed that they were proud of it.[34]

Kurt von Schuschnigg felt much the same. That day he wrote in his diary, "The Americans! . . . We are free!":

> I cannot write about it. I cannot begin to express our feelings. Who can describe Freedom?
>
> The American troops make a deep impression on us. Apart from their equipment and supplies, which to us seem utterly unbelievable, the perfect discipline in the ranks and the relation of officers to men is exemplary. They do what they can for us; they are helpful, sympathetic, understanding, unobtrusive—in short, they are human.

> So that is America. This is the unsoldierly, utterly mechanized and decadent nation of which we read in the Nazi papers. Well, it is easy to understand now why they have won the war.[35]

Later that day, a Pathé camera team arrived at the hotel and shot footage and photographs of the Americans mingling with the Prominenten on the hotel's lakeside terrace. By then, the American senior officers—including Colonel John T. English, commanding officer of the 339th Regiment, and even Major General John B. Coulter, the division commander—had arrived to shine the light of their countenances on the liberated VIPs and participate in the photo lineups.[36]

One person who was not there was the one who had made it all happen, whose initiative and arduous ordeal had brought the news of the plight of the Prominenten to the Allied lines. That morning, while Anton Ducia was being shuttled back to the Pragser Wildsee, Wing Commander Harry "Wings" Day had been taken to the headquarters of US Fifth Army at Bologna, where he had been interviewed by senior intelligence officers—a veritable "galaxy of Brass." In the afternoon he was flown by light aircraft to Florence, where he was interviewed once more. That night he was accommodated in a gorgeous villa. "It was a marvellous experience," he recalled later, "sitting on a terrace in a warm evening, talking to people whose language was the same as yours and having a civilised meal."[37]

A long and strange journey had brought him here from England. From the moment he'd been shot down, only a few weeks into the war, he'd spent years in POW camps; played a leading role in the Great Escape; been incarcerated in concentration camps, held hostage by the SS and SD, and subjected to threats of execution; and finally endured an exhausting trek through the Alps. Every one of the Prominenten had been on a unique journey—some betrayed by fellow secret agents, some captured in battle, some caught in conspiracies against Hitler, some taken unexpectedly from their homes by the Gestapo—and each had a unique view of the trials they had shared since the order had come down from Berlin to round up the VIPs and use them as hostages, to be bargained for or murdered.

For all but a few, the journey ended on the hotel terrace overlooking the glassy green waters of the Pragser Wildsee, smiling into the newsreel cameras and chatting casually with the GIs as if it were the most natural thing in the world. Or at least the ordeal had ended there; the journey would not be complete until they were home again and reunited with those family members who had survived the war.

The journey could have ended very differently if Gestapo chief Hans Philipp, who had been ordered to round up the hostages and take them to Austria for execution, had carried out his mission. He did not, and three days later, while the Prominenten were celebrating their deliverance, he committed suicide.[38] SS-Obergruppenführer Karl Wolff's SS and SD unit never materialized, and by the time his message about the hostages reached Field Marshal Alexander, the Prominenten had already been freed.

Celebrations at the Pragser Wildsee continued for several days. On 8 May the evacuation began. With a large escort of armored cars and an umbrella of aircraft flying overhead, the liberated hostages were transported south to Verona and then to the island of Capri, where they gave official interviews about their experiences. After that, they went their separate ways—some back to the devastation of Germany, others to their liberated homelands, some to pick up the vestiges of their former lives, and a few to Allied prisons. For many there was little or nothing to celebrate. A few—including some of the Soviet prisoners and other collaborators—were destined for execution when they reached home.

Parts of Europe were still not free. Kurt and Vera von Schuschnigg and their little daughter Sissy spent the last weeks of May on Capri. It was idyllic, and their American hosts were as generous and caring as ever, but for the Schuschniggs there would be no joyful homecoming. Eastern Austria, including Vienna, was under Soviet occupation and would remain so for many years. The former chancellor and his family were now just three displaced persons among millions of others. "We would give our last penny to know how things are at home," he wrote in his diary, "which of our friends are still alive; who has not survived these terrible years." Occasionally he and Vera would meet an Allied officer who had been in Austria. "At such times an overpowering longing for home grips us."[39]

Former Great Escapers Jimmy James and Sydney Dowse were reunited with their old friend and leader Wings Day and flew home together in an RAF transport on 13 May. For Day, as they crossed the English coastline on a bright, clear day, it seemed as if the ordeal had all been a bad dream: "I might have only left it a few hours ago; not six years previously." The arrival brought him down to earth in more ways than one. Moved to a rehabilitation camp for returning POWs at RAF Cosford in Shropshire, he was in no mood for poetic reflection: "Phoned my wife. My Mother dead. So got plastered."[40]

Jimmy James felt more reflective when they landed. "We stepped out on to the soil of our native land and with tremendous relief and joy breathed in the air of freedom," he recalled later. "Many times over the past years we had doubted whether this moment would ever come. Whatever the peace might bring, we could face it. We had passed through a nightmare experience of what can happen, in any country, when the forces of totalitarianism prevail."[41]

Hitler was dead. The Third Reich was a smoking ruin. But the journeys of the Prominenten—such a diverse body of men and women brought together by Hitler's hatred and despair, united by a shared endurance of fear and hardship—went on into the future, diverging.

For the rest of his life Jimmy James would recall three lines from a letter he wrote to his Aunt Florence on 6 May 1945 from the Pragser Wildsee: "I hardly know where to begin, the great thing is that the Americans are here and we are free. I can hardly realise it after five years of waiting, it all seems like a dream. I thought it would never end." As he left Blackbushe Airport on 13 May, Jimmy carried in the pocket of his battered old

RAF greatcoat two pages of crumpled paper filled with the signatures of the strange collection of men and women with whom he had spent the penultimate leg of his long journey through the corridor of death. Looking at those names, he knew that, although it all seemed beyond the realms of imagination, it had not been a dream.

Epilogue

Despite all the odds, 139 of Hitler's hostages—some of them hated by the Führer more than any other living souls—survived the Nazis' last desperate gamble.

Isa Vermehren returned to her family in Hamburg in June 1945 and published an account of her experiences, which became a best seller. She studied to become a teacher, supporting her education with the odd cabaret appearance and minor film role. In 1951 she took holy orders, joined a convent, and embarked on a successful career as teacher, public speaker, school director, and TV host. She died in 2009 at the age of ninety-one.

After a heartbreaking separation from Alex von Stauffenberg in Capri, Fey Pirzio-Biroli drove back to Rome with her husband, Detalmo, to resume their interrupted lives. Their sons were eventually traced to an SS children's home near Innsbruck and were finally reunited with their parents in October 1945. Fey continued to correspond with some of her fellow kin prisoners, especially Alex. The romance of their forced interlude had gone forever, although Alex had wanted to continue their relationship. Their last meeting was in Rome in the early 1960s. Alex died at the age of fifty-eight in 1964. Fey died in 2010, aged ninety-one.

Kurt von Schuschnigg published his memoirs, and in 1947 was invited to conduct a lecture tour in the United States. In 1948 he was appointed a professor of political science at Saint Louis University. Vera and Sissy accompanied him to live in America. Vera kept in touch with some of the Prominenten after their release, especially former Colonel Bogislaw von

Bonin, to whom she had become close. Sigismund Payne Best acted as the conduit for this clandestine correspondence, possibly encouraged by a certain disdain he harbored for Kurt. (In a postwar letter, Payne Best referred to him as "an indeterminable quantity" in whom he couldn't summon up any interest.) Vera von Schuschnigg lost her battle with lung cancer in September 1959 at the age of fifty-five. Kurt von Schuschnigg took US citizenship in 1954, but following his retirement in 1968 he returned to Austria, where he lived at his maternal grandparents' home near Innsbruck until he too died of lung cancer in 1977. Sissy, who had graduated from Saint Louis University, traveled to Europe and in 1966 married French nobleman Aubrey de Kergariou. In 1989, at the age of only forty-eight, Sissy fell victim to the same disease that had claimed both her parents.

After his repatriation to France, Léon Blum went back into politics and served briefly as prime minister in the transitional postwar coalition government. He corresponded with several of the Prominenten, including Payne Best. Blum later undertook a mission to the United States, where he secured a loan for postwar reconstruction and then acted as head of the French mission to UNESCO. He finally retired in January 1947 but briefly served again as vice premier in August 1948. He continued writing for the socialist newspaper *Le Populaire* until his death in 1950. His wife, Janot, continued to live on the family estate at Jouy-en-Josas until her death in 1982.

Of the five Greek generals, only Aleksandros Papagos rejoined the Greek army. In 1949 he was appointed commander in chief, finally defeating the Communists in the Greek civil war that had been raging since 1946. In 1951 Papagos entered politics, becoming prime minister in 1952. He died in office in 1955.

How many of the ten Hungarian Prominenten were repatriated after the war is not known. Hungary had become a satellite state of the Soviet Union. A return for some of the former hostages would have been a death sentence. Former regent Miklós Horthy's son Nicky went into exile with his father in Portugal. He died in 1993. Former prime minister Miklós Kállay became another exile, finally settling in the United States in 1951.

Baron Péter Schell did likewise, emigrating to the United States with his family in 1947.

Resistance leader General Sante Garibaldi moved to the French city of Bordeaux, where he died in 1946 as a result of the treatment he had received at the hands of the Nazis. He was sixty years old.

Of the twenty-three German Prominenten, nine were identified by the Allied authorities as either being in an arrestable category or as potential war criminals. Despite his involvement in resistance activities, General Georg Thomas was still in US custody when he died in 1946 at the age of fifty-six. Hitler's former army chief of staff, Colonel General Franz Halder, was finally released in 1947 and was employed by the US Army as a war historian. He was also responsible for advising on the redevelopment of the postwar West German army. He died in 1972.

General Alexander von Falkenhausen, former Nazi governor of Belgium, was not so lucky. He remained in custody until March 1951, when he was tried in Brussels for his role in the deportation of thirty thousand Jews from Belgium to Auschwitz. Despite much lobbying on his behalf—including testimonials from Léon Blum, Hugh Falconer, and Sigismund Payne Best—he was sentenced to twelve years hard labor. However, having already served one third of his sentence, he was released and returned to West Germany. In July 1951 he was pardoned by Chancellor Konrad Adenauer. He died in 1966 at the age of eighty-seven.

Former intelligence officer and anti-Nazi resister Commander Franz Liedig was kept in custody because of his Abwehr connection. By August 1945 the decision was made to use Liedig as a deep penetration agent on behalf of the US Army's special counterintelligence units, a joint operation of Britain's MI5 and the OSS. The intention was apparently to insert him into the German manufacturer IG Farben.[1] When Dr. Josef Müller founded a new political party, the Christian Social Union, Liedig was one of the founding members. He then resumed his career as a lawyer. Payne Best, who met him in 1950, believed that Liedig "had lost all powers of concentration" and was living "in a sort of mental fog." During their time at Buchenwald and on the road, "he had been a tower of strength," and seeing him now "depressed me greatly."[2] Liedig died in 1967.

Prince Philipp von Hessen was detained as a result of his governorship of Hesse-Nassau during the Nazi regime. Complicit in a euthanasia program, Prince Philipp was charged with murder, but the charges were eventually dropped. He became an interior designer while remaining as the head of the House of Hesse until his death in Rome in 1980.

Hitler's former financial backer Fritz Thyssen was tried for his support of the Nazi Party and the mistreatment of Jews employed by his companies. He agreed to pay compensation and was acquitted on other charges. In 1950 he and his wife, Amélie, who had accompanied her husband during his captivity, emigrated to Buenos Aires, where he died the following year. Amélie died in 1965.

Dr. Hjalmar Schacht, former president of the Reichsbank and Hitler's minister of economics, was classified as a "major offender" and was one of twenty-two Nazi leaders tried at Nuremberg. He was not charged with war crimes but with "crimes against peace." He was acquitted, but a West German denazification court later sentenced him to a term of hard labor, which was overturned on appeal in 1948. He was finally cleared of all charges in 1950. In 1953 he founded a private bank in Düsseldorf. He died in 1970.

Colonel Bogislaw von Bonin was held as a prisoner of war until 1947. Captivity had taken its toll. The debonair, handsome colonel who had played such a decisive role in saving the Prominenten from the clutches of the SS in Niederdorf was now a shadow of his former self. Payne Best met him in January 1950 and was shocked by his frail, aged appearance. Following his release, Bonin worked briefly as a manual laborer. With the influence of Léon Blum, he was able to find a house in Reutlingen and settle there. He subsequently took a position with Daimler Benz, then in 1952 joined the West German government, with a role in military planning for the new armed forces. His ideas brought him into conflict with the Adenauer government. Dismissed from his post in 1955, Bonin became a journalist. He died in 1980.

Most of the German Prominenten were not detained in Allied custody following their initial interrogations in Capri in May 1945. Landowner and agriculturist Wilhelm von Flügge vanished back into obscurity and died in 1953.

Lawyer and resistance hero Josef Müller—as a founding member of the first German political party to bring both Catholics and Protestants together, the Christian Social Union—served as party chairman from 1946 to 1949. In 1947 he became the minister of justice for Bavaria, then deputy prime minister. He died in 1979.

Joseph Joos, the Catholic political activist and journalist, returned to West Germany in 1949 but did not regain the citizenship revoked by the Nazis in 1938. He worked as a consultant for a Catholic men's organization in Fulda. After becoming ill he moved to Switzerland, where he died in 1965 at the age of eighty-six.

Diplomat Dr. Erich Heberlein and his wife Margot returned to their Spanish farm in Toledo. Margot kept up a correspondence with a number of Prominenten until at least the mid-1950s. Erich had retired from public life but in 1954 accepted a position with the Foreign Office under a 1951 law passed to ensure that anti-Nazi public servants were not discriminated against. Erich and Margot Heberlein both died in 1980.

Resistance fighter and would-be Hitler assassin Fabian von Schlabrendorff was thoroughly interrogated by the US Counterintelligence Corps. He was also visited by Gero von Schulze-Gaevernitz, the German-born right-hand man of Allen Dulles, who had been assigned to question some of the German Prominenten during their custody on Capri. The OSS officer was so impressed with Schlabrendorff that he obtained permission to take him back to the Swiss office for a full debriefing on the history of the German resistance. As a result, Schulze-Gaevernitz published Schlabrendorff's account in 1947 under the title *They Almost Killed Hitler*. Having served as a judge in West Germany's Constitutional Court, Schlabrendorff died in 1980.

Canon Johann Neuhäusler's first job following his release was to write a book about the Catholic Church's struggle against the Nazi regime. He also testified in the Dachau war crimes trial. Despite all he had suffered, in 1949 Neuhäusler became cofounder of an organization providing aid to former members of the Nazi armed services, including the SS, and after the Nuremberg Trials he campaigned for clemency for convicted war criminals. In 1951 he helped found an organization assisting German ex-POWs that operated in secrecy and counted many SS war criminals among those it supported. In 1960 he was instrumental in establishing the first religious monument to be built on the grounds of the former Dachau concentration camp. Neuhäusler died in 1973 at the age of eighty-five.

In October 1945, Pastor Martin Niemöller was one of the initiators of the Stuttgart Declaration of Guilt. Signed by leading members of the Protestant church, it acknowledged that the churches had not taken sufficient action to resist the Nazis. In 1954 he became an ardent pacifist and antinuclear campaigner. During the Vietnam War, his visit to the North's communist leader, Ho Chi Minh, caused an international uproar. He became president of the World Council of Churches in 1961 and was awarded the Lenin Peace Prize in 1966. He died in 1984 at the age of ninety-two. His piece "First They Came for the Socialists . . ." is inscribed on the wall of the United States Holocaust Memorial Museum in Washington, DC, and stands as the universal warning against passive complicity in fascism.

Young clergyman Karl Kunkel was unable to return to his former homeland of East Prussia, which had been divided between the USSR and Soviet-controlled Poland, and in July 1945 he took up a position at Schlehdorf Abbey in Bavaria. After retirement in 1977 he continued to provide pastoral care and was active in providing information on the concentration camp system based on his own experiences. In 2008 he celebrated his seventieth anniversary as a priest. He died in 2012.

The "accidental" hostage, Russian-born British citizen Wadim Greenewich, rescued from certain death at Flossenbürg by Wings Day, Jimmy James, and Sydney Dowse, returned to London and contacted his wife to tell her he was safe. She had worked for SOE in Jerusalem during the war and was evacuated to Kenya in 1943. It is presumed that Greenewich continued working for SIS after the war. His wife died in 1954 and Greenewich passed away in 1982.

Of the six Russian Prominenten, none was keen to be repatriated, particularly those who had collaborated with the Nazis. Stalin had passed a law that any soldier captured by the Germans was a potential traitor. The penalty for treason was death. Under the terms of the Yalta Conference agreement of February 1945, Britain and America were required to repatriate all Soviet prisoners in their hands. Both governments made the decision to use force if necessary, well aware of what would probably happen to most of the two and a half million prisoners they returned to the USSR. The one million who had swapped sides and served in the German armed forces knew exactly what their fate would be.

At the Pragser Wildsee hotel in May 1945, all the Russian Prominenten had contemplated their futures. General Bessonov had disappeared into the mountains before the Americans arrived. Nevertheless, he was taken into Allied custody sometime in May 1945 and then repatriated to Russia. Upon arrival he was arrested and imprisoned. In October 1946 he was formally expelled from the Red Army and then imprisoned without trial until 1950, when he was sentenced to death and executed.

Major General Pyotr Privalov was repatriated and arrested; he was expelled from the Red Army in December 1946 and held in prison until his execution in 1951. Privalov was officially rehabilitated in 1968. Unfortunately, as he had been dead for over sixteen years, he was unable to benefit from the decision.

Vassily Vassilyevich Kokorin, who was believed to have died of frostbite with the Italian partisans in South Tyrol in May 1945, was subsequently found to have had hidden depths. Most published works and government documents described him as the nephew of Vyacheslav Mikhailovich Molotov, the Soviet foreign minister. In fact, Kokorin was not Molotov's nephew and did not die in South Tyrol in 1945. Vassily Kokorin was an impostor. His deception of the Nazis and his fellow prisoners was a breathtaking feat of cunning.

Far from having died in the mountains with his partisan comrades, later in May Kokorin was in a car en route to the Russian military mission in Rome. It has not been possible to establish whether he went voluntarily or not. Interviewed at the mission, Kokorin neglected to mention his alleged family connections. Instead he simply gave his name and stated what camps he had been held in. The authorities showed little interest in his case and he was sent for repatriation. Kokorin was immediately arrested on arrival at Odessa. Although this was standard procedure for repatriated prisoners, somebody must have discovered what Kokorin had been up to because he was then taken to the infamous Lubyanka prison in Moscow and interrogated personally by the head of SMERSH, the Soviet counterintelligence service. Kokorin was charged with treason and accused of masquerading as Molotov's nephew.

He was in fact the son of impoverished peasants and had been a sergeant in the 1st Soviet Airborne Brigade, which had infiltrated through German lines in 1942. The Germans spotted the infiltration and the Waffen-SS were waiting for them. Despite tremendous losses, one company of Russian paratroopers managed to engage the SS in hand-to-hand fighting. Kokorin was among the survivors. He had developed severe frostbite in his feet and, unable to evade pursuit, was captured.

Kokorin's deception began as a desperate bid to save his own life. Claiming to be Molotov's nephew, he was interrogated by a dozen German officers. Comparing a photo of him with one of Molotov, they concluded that the two men did look alike. As the cases of Jack and Peter Churchill showed, the Germans were very apt to believe that they had captured highly connected prisoners, and, despite obvious flaws in Kokorin's story, they fell for it. In January 1943 he was transferred to Sachsenhausen and assigned to Sonderlager A. Stalin's son, Yakov Dzhugashvili, was in the same block but had refused to cooperate with the Nazis and kept to himself as much as possible. Privately, the Germans were skeptical about Kokorin's claims but realized that he could still be extremely useful as an informant for the Gestapo. By April 1943, Dzhugashvili was sharing a bedroom with Kokorin. He subsequently committed suicide, and we shall never know if he knew that Kokorin was an impostor, or if Kokorin contributed in any way to his death. The Soviets later charged him with complicity. Vassily Kokorin was executed in March 1952.

Lieutenant Colonel John McGrath was exhaustively questioned about his activities while in charge of the Irish camp at Friesack. He described how he had endeavored to thwart German plans for the Irish prisoners, but his story could not be authenticated. Although the military was inclined to believe McGrath, they were more skeptical when it came to considering the position of the four other Irishmen from Friesack, who were labelled "British Renegades." Despite the absence of substantial evidence, the four were put under close arrest, but later released without charge. Meanwhile, McGrath returned to Dublin and went back to his old job as the manager of the Theatre Royal. He never fully recovered from the psychological trauma and physical privations he had suffered during his imprisonment, and he died in November 1946 at the age of forty-seven.

In 1964 the West German government agreed to the distribution of one million pounds to British nationals who had suffered as a result of Nazi persecution. Guidelines were drawn up and the thirteen British Prominenten submitted a claim. It was initially rejected on the basis that they had all been "special prisoners" and had not suffered greatly. Member of Parliament Airey Neave (himself a former Colditz POW and successful escaper) took up the case in 1966 but, despite personal approaches to Prime Minister Harold Wilson, he was unsuccessful. However, there was considerable public sympathy for the former Sachsenhausen prisoners, and the British government was obliged to pay twenty-five thousand pounds to the Sachsenhausen group. The Irishmen were each given a share, despite strong suspicions among some of the British Prominenten that Gunner John Spence and Corporal Andy Walsh were traitors.

Squadron Leader Hugh Falconer flew back to the United Kingdom with SOE colleague Peter Churchill. He was then assigned to the British Control Commission in West Germany. After leaving the RAF, he trained as an engineer and traveled to India in 1954 with his wife and child. In 1968 Falconer received 2,293 pounds from the Sachsenhausen fund. He eventually settled in Rhodesia, where in 1980 he died from inoperable brain cancer.

Peter Churchill was reunited with his wartime SOE courier and lover, Odette Sansom, and they were married in 1947. Odette had been cruelly treated at Ravensbrück but survived, mainly due to her adopting the surname Churchill and pretending to be a relative of the prime minister. Her memoirs were published in 1949 and a film, *Odette*, was made shortly afterward, starring Anna Neagle in the lead role and Trevor Howard as Peter Churchill. The couple divorced in 1955, and Churchill married again in 1956. In the late 1950s he settled on the French Riviera and acted as a real estate agent. In 1968 he received 1,284 pounds from the Sachsenhausen fund. He died at the age of sixty-three in 1972.

After the war, Colonel John "Mad Jack" Churchill was circumspect about the question of his escape from Niederdorf. Postwar articles, including his obituary in the *Daily Telegraph*, implied that he had escaped from an Austrian POW camp rather than a loosely guarded village. Immediately after his return to the UK, he was posted to a commando brigade and sent to India in preparation for the invasion of Japan. The war ended without an invasion being necessary, so he took a parachute course, making his first drop on his fortieth birthday. He assumed command of a battalion of the Parachute Regiment and became the only officer to command both commando and parachute battalions. In 1948 he saw action in Jerusalem before returning to Britain and serving in various army training establishments. After his retirement in 1959, he devoted himself to buying and refurbishing steamboats on the river Thames. He was one of the prime movers in the Sachsenhausen compensation case and received 1,009 pounds, and was active in Sachsenhausen reunions during the 1970s and 1980s. He died in 1996 at the age of eighty-nine.

After a brief hospitalization, Sigismund Payne Best returned to England in late May 1945. His slight frame accentuated his drastic loss of weight during his imprisonment. He met with his old boss at SIS, Sir Claude Dansey, who informed him that he would receive his normal salary of sixty pounds per month until August, at which time his employment was to be terminated, supposedly on health grounds. He would receive a further payment of 1,200 pounds, representing accrued pay while he was a prisoner. At the same time, after taking issue over Payne Best having spoken to the press in Italy, Dansey half-heartedly suggested that he write a brief account of the events leading up to his capture. Eventually Payne Best wrote a whole book, published in 1950 as *The Venlo Incident: A True Story of Double-Dealing, Captivity, and a Murderous Nazi Plot.*

Payne Best was not a man to forget details. When Wings Day and Anton Ducia had set out on their mission to find the American lines, Payne Best had donated a rather smart overcoat to conceal Day's uniform. Best had not forgotten and now wanted his coat back; obtaining Day's address from Dansey, he wrote to request its return. Whether he subsequently got it back, or compensation in lieu, is not known.

According to his wife, Payne Best received five hundred pounds for his book and a further five hundred pounds from a newspaper serialization. Mrs. Payne Best also revealed, following their highly acrimonious split in December 1953, that he had been feted by the West German government in Bonn in the summer of 1952, with the result that he had been given a Mercedes-Benz as compensation for his wartime treatment. She also claimed that he had been appointed to the board of a British company and fired eight months later "because he had done something wrong." He had talked about shooting himself, and, on the advice of a doctor, she removed his gun from the house.

In January 1958 Payne Best was the subject of bankruptcy proceedings as a result of a debt that, again according to his wife, went back to 1931. In 1964, he was the first to make an application for compensation under the terms of the Anglo-German Agreement. Following the denial of compensation to the Sachsenhausen prisoners, Wings Day wrote to the German foreign minister, "I regret to understand that your opinion has been influenced by Captain Payne Best's book. He was never in a 'Sonderlager.' He is very pro-German and a fluent German speaker and made his own terms with his jailers." The misplaced overcoat was clearly not the only issue between the two men. In 1968 Payne Best received the highest (and maximum) award of the fourteen Sachsenhausen claimants, totaling four thousand pounds. Since he was in Sachsenhausen for far longer than most of the other British, and suffered worse privations in the cellblock, there was some justice in this. Bequeathing his papers to the Imperial War Museum, Sigismund Payne Best died at the age of ninety-three in 1978.

Wing Commander Harry Melville Arbuthnot "Wings" Day was forty-six years old when he returned to England. Within a few hours of landing, he learned that his mother had died and that his marriage was over. In December 1945 he received the Order of the British Empire for distinguished service while a prisoner of war and, at the same time, the Distinguished Service Order for his contribution to, and participation in, the Great Escape. In 1946 he was promoted to group captain. He retired from the RAF in 1950 and remarried in the same year. Without doubt, Wings was a hero and a genuine derring-do adventurer who received full credit for everything he accomplished during his career—except for one thing. He received scant recognition for the invaluable and dangerous part he and Anton Ducia had played in locating the American forces and bringing about the task force that finally liberated the hostages. This was due partly to the confusion and chaos reigning at the time and partly to Payne Best's determination to take credit for everything.

In 1956, Day acted as technical adviser on *Reach for the Sky*, a movie about the life of fighter ace Douglas Bader, starring Kenneth More. As one of Bader's flight commanders and a fellow acrobatic pilot with No. 23 Squadron, Day was played in the film by Michael Warre. In November 1961 Day was selected as the subject of the UK series *This Is Your Life*, in which he was reunited with Anton Ducia. In 1963 *The Great Escape* was screened in Britain, but as it was a fictionalized version, using composite characters (it starred Steve McQueen and James Garner, despite there having been no Americans involved in the real Great Escape), Wings Day was not identifiable in it.

In 1968 Day received compensation totaling 1,192 pounds from the Sachsenhausen fund. The same year, a biography by Sydney Smith, titled *Wings Day*, was published. It produced libel problems over the portrayal of some fellow prisoners. In 1969 Payne Best took it upon himself to contact the lawyer of former SS officer Kurt Eccarius, who was on trial for war crimes, suggesting that Smith had libeled his client.

Around the same time, Wings began to succumb to Parkinson's disease. He moved to Malta, where he stayed until his illness necessitated his return to the UK for treatment. By 1975 he had also begun to show symptoms of paranoia. Despite this, he managed to return to his beloved Malta where he passed away in December 1977.

Sydney Dowse was awarded the Military Cross for his conduct while a prisoner of war. After serving as an equerry to King George VI for a short period, he was discharged from the RAF in January 1946. Later he worked in British Malaya as a colonial administrator and rubber plantation manager. According to some sources, he divided his time between elegant residences in Monte Carlo and Chelsea. Having spent much time in the company of wealthy women, in old age he was able to indulge in driving Rolls-Royces and sports cars. In 1993 a rather acrimonious spat developed between Dowse and Jimmy James over arrangements for the fiftieth anniversary of the Great Escape. They later resolved their differences. By the early 2000s Dowse was displaying signs of Alzheimer's disease, and he was looked after by a married lady friend with whom he had been having an unconventional relationship for many years. He finally passed away in 2008. He was buried in a graveyard with plots on either side reserved for his lady friend and her husband.

The last Great Escaper, Bertram "Jimmy" James, took some leave after returning to England in 1945, then resumed duty with the RAF. While awaiting a refresher flying course, he was sent back to Germany, mainly due to his knowledge of the language, and posted to the headquarters of the British Air Force of Occupation. While there, in April 1946 he met his future wife Madge at a party. Madge was to remain the love of Jimmy's life until he died. He was awarded the Military Cross in recognition of his many escape attempts. In 1948 he joined No. 540 Squadron, flying Mosquitos on photo reconnaissance missions. In 1958 he left the RAF. He tried unsuccessfully to make a life in Canada with his wife and son, and they returned to England. In 1960 he became general secretary of the Great Britain-USSR Association, responsible for organizing cultural activities and exchanges. In 1964 he joined the Foreign Office, acting as a British vice consul in various countries.

After retirement in 1975, Jimmy James began recording his wartime activities. This eventually led to his election to the International Sachsenhausen Committee, a group of former prisoners whose aim was to educate current generations about the horrors of the concentration camp. He wrote his wartime memoirs, published as *Moonless Night* in 1981, and gave speeches and lectures on his escapades to ex-servicemen's associations and many schools, including the King's School at Canterbury, where he had been a pupil in the 1930s. He and his friend Sydney Dowse were the subject of intense media interest when the Imperial War Museum celebrated the sixtieth anniversary of the Great Escape in March 2004. Old age finally caught up with Jimmy James, and he passed away in January 2008, aged ninety-five.

Of the 139 Prominenten, there remains one particularly enigmatic character who was a mystery to all her fellow hostages. The femme fatale Heidel Nowakowski, suspected by some of the other prisoners of being a Gestapo spy, has continued to be a blank ever since 1945—no birth record, no background, and no subsequent life story. Until now. New research has uncovered some of the truth about her.

"Heidel" was born Johanna Nowakowski on 18 August 1914 in Brzeźnica, Poland. After the German conquest of Poland in World War II, Johanna applied for German naturalization through the Einwandererzentralstelle (Immigrant Control Center), which regulated the resettlement of ethnic Germans from occupied territories. In her application it was noted that she had lost some teeth. (This may be the truth behind the claim she made to Sigismund Payne Best about having been subjected to dental torture in Ravensbrück, which he doubted at the time.) She declared her occupation as factory worker.

Accurate information relating to Johanna's wartime activities prior to her first recorded appearance as "Heidel" at Buchenwald concentration camp in March 1945 has not yet been located. Following successive affairs with SS Dr. Sigmund Rascher, Russian imposter Vassily Kokorin, and finally the Belgian RAF officer Raymond van Wymeersch, she disappeared (accompanied by Van Wymeersch) just before the hostages were rescued.

Despite speculation among the hostages that Heidel Nowakowski was a Gestapo informant, there does not appear to be any evidence. It is possible that she became a VIP hostage through chance or smart maneuvering to escape the concentration camp, as Wadim Greenewich did at Flossenbürg. There is no evidence to suggest that she had committed treason against the Reich or that she would have qualified to be included in the kin prisoner group.

During their captivity, Heidel gave Payne Best two addresses where she could be contacted—both in the Essen area—along with a telephone number. She told Hugh Falconer that she was from Düsseldorf, which is close to Essen. As a result of inquiries in those areas, we now know that Johanna Nowakowski lived in Essen after the war and gave birth to a daughter in 1946. She was married in Rünthe in July 1953 to Harold Kaiser. They were divorced in June 1955, and she remarried, to Hans Gunther Liell, in Dortmund in April 1956. Johanna died in Dortmund in October 1956 at the age of forty-two. The following year, a report revealed that Johanna Liell, née Nowakowski, had been convicted eight times for fraud under the aliases "Heidel von der Marwitz," "Jensen," "Stauffenberg," and "Smith." A further report indicates that the Dortmund police had investigated Mrs. Liell for attempting to secure financial compensation from a fund established to assist individuals who had been arrested, imprisoned, or otherwise affected by their involvement in the attempted assassination of Adolf Hitler in July 1944. It was presumably in this act of fraud that she adopted the "Stauffenberg" alias.

Many accounts have suggested that both SS-Obersturmführer Edgar Stiller and SS-Untersturmführer Friedrich Bader, along with some or all of their men, came to a sticky end, possibly at the hands of Italian partisans. If such an event did take place, it certainly did not involve Edgar Stiller.

After being relieved of his command by the Wehrmacht in Niederdorf, Stiller and some of his remaining men hesitated over what to do next. He later acknowledged that there had been a move among certain Prominenten to execute him and his men, but that General Garibaldi had managed to prevent it. He said in a postwar statement that he and his men eventually left Niederdorf on foot and began walking north toward the Austrian border. On 12 May they were captured by an American unit and imprisoned at Bruck an der Grossglocknerstrasse. To avoid culpability, Stiller posed as a lowly noncommissioned officer and, despite having served in the police since 1926, gave his former occupation as farmer. He eventually found himself at the civilian internment enclosure at Moosburg in Bavaria, where he was detained until October 1945. Identified as a war crimes suspect, he was later required to testify in the August 1947 US military tribunal against a number of personnel from the Mauthausen-Gusen concentration camp. His file was marked "hostile witness." In October 1945 he returned to Dachau, where he ended up in a cell in the Bunker, the building he had formerly commanded.

In March 1947 Stiller and three others were arraigned before a US military tribunal on war crimes charges. He was accused of participating in the subjection of prisoners of war and civilians to cruelty and mistreatment and charged with involvement in the murder of General Charles Delestraint. He testified that he had been with the hostage convoy at Reichenau when he learned of Delestraint's death, which occurred on 19 April. Karl Kunkel confirmed that Stiller had not been in Dachau at the time. Despite a spirited and favorable testimony from Dr. Lothar Rohde, Stiller was found guilty on all charges and sentenced to seven years imprisonment, reduced to five on appeal. He was released from Landsberg Prison in 1949. He then worked as the private secretary to Princess Helene Elisabeth von Isenburg, a controversial character who was behind a covert organization established to help former SS men, including those imprisoned for war crimes, with financial and legal aid. Its assistance extended to arranging the escape and resettlement of Adolf Eichmann and Josef Mengele. In 1951 the operation was partly legitimized under the guise of becoming a nonprofit welfare organization and received support from the church. One notable promoter was Johann Neuhäusler.

After leaving Princess Helene Elisabeth's employ, Stiller took up a position as a vehicle controller with Rohde & Schwarz in Munich. Dr. Rohde still owed Stiller a favor, even after testifying in his defense at the war crimes tribunal—Stiller having been his protector for the last part of the war—irrespective of whether his motives were all charitable. Rohde, who died in 1985 at the age of seventy-five, never seems to have spoken or written about his wartime experiences. Stiller's employment with Rohde & Schwarz was short-lived; after only a couple of weeks he was arrested by the West German police and charged with complicity in the murder of Georg Elser, but was finally cleared. The murderer, Theodor Bongartz, had died of natural causes while a prisoner of the Americans in May 1945.

The investigating magistrate in the Elser case appeared to be more concerned with Stiller's role in commanding the hostage convoy. The magistrate was especially anxious to obtain more information concerning the identity of SS-Untersturmführer Bader and whether or not he and his men had been members of an SD unit. The general consensus of those questioned was that they had all been SD. Stiller, for his part, made absolutely no reference to Bader whatsoever. He was perhaps nervous that the subject might lead to more intensive and embarrassing questions concerning the exact nature of the convoy and the proposed final disposal of the Prominenten. According to the case records, Bader was never tracked down. What occupation Stiller followed after he was cleared is unknown. He died in 1978.

Friedrich Bader did not disappear. After he and his men left Niederdorf, if it is true that they were ambushed by partisans, then Bader definitely survived. He was in Merano, just short of the Austrian border, on 2 May, where he was arrested by the US Army as a member of the Gestapo, a fact he readily admitted to. He was taken to a US military prison at Bad Aibling in Bavaria before being transferred to the War Crimes Central Suspect and Witness Enclosure at Dachau, where he was formally charged in July 1946.

Bader duly completed the mandatory *Fragebogen*, a document containing 131 questions summarizing the subject's life and professional and political activities. Bader attempted to pass himself off as a fairly unimportant policeman. He admitted to membership in the Nazi Party from 1932 and provided his membership number. He described himself as a member of the Allgemeine (or general) SS, whose role in Nazi Germany was essentially to assist the police in maintaining order. He confirmed that he had attained the rank of Untersturmführer. He portrayed himself as a victim rather than a perpetrator, claiming that the Gestapo had arrested him in 1944 for anti-Nazi activities and that he was dismissed from both the SS and the Nazi Party. In reality, Bader had been the head of the local Gestapo counterintelligence unit known as Nachrichten-Referat. This ultrasecret department recruited indigenous informants who were assigned to infiltrate political or opposition groups. Funding was always a problem, but Bader overcame this by allowing his agents to engage in black-market dealing and currency smuggling. It was this that had led to his getting into trouble with his superiors.

In February 1947 Bader was released from US imprisonment, having applied successfully on the grounds that he was not guilty of any crime. However in July of that year he was required to complete another *Fragebogen*. This time there were some interesting discrepancies. He couldn't remember his party membership number and omitted being a member of the Allgemeine-SS. The other notable omission was in the "Travel or Residence Abroad" section. His trip to South Tyrol had disappeared. His case went before the German denazification committee, which judged Bader to be a category III case, a "lesser offender" who would have to suffer certain restrictions and two to three years' probation. However there would be no further internment. Finally, in November 1950 the Düsseldorf denazification board ruled that Bader could be downgraded to category V status. He was free at last. It is not known what occupation he subsequently followed but it is believed that he continued with his police career in Oberhausen. He died at the age of seventy-two in 1972.

The 139 Hostages

SURNAME	CHRISTIAN NAMES	NATIONALITY	YEAR OF BIRTH	YEAR OF DEATH
PROMINENTEN				
Praxmarer	Konrad	Austria	1895	1959
Schmitz	Richard	Austria	1885	1954
Schuschnigg	Kurt Alois Josef Johann	Austria	1897	1977
Burda	Josef	Czech	1893	1946
Rys-Rozsévač	Josef	Czech	1901	1946
Hansen	Hans Frederik	Denmark	1919	2009
Larsen	Adolf Theodor	Denmark	1906	1978
Lunding	Hans Mathiesen	Denmark	1899	1984
Mikkelsen	Max Johannes	Denmark	1911	1984
Mogensen	Jørgen Lønborg Friis	Denmark	1909	2000
Pedersen	Knud Erik	Denmark	1910	1984
Blum	(André) Léon	France	1892	1950
Mottet	Armand Jules	France	1895	
Piguet	Gabriel Emmanuel Joseph	France	1887	1952
Van Wymeersch	Raymond N.	France	1920	2000
Xavier	Prince of Bourbon-Parma	France	1889	1977
Bonin	Bogislaw	Germany	1908	1980
Cerrini	Baron Fritz	Germany	1894	1985
Engelke	Friedrich "Fritz"	Germany	1900	1981
Falkenhausen	Alexander Ernst Alfred Hermann	Germany	1878	1966

SURNAME	CHRISTIAN NAMES	NATIONALITY	YEAR OF BIRTH	YEAR OF DEATH
Flügge	Wilhelm Albert Edward	Germany	1887	1953
Franz Joseph Oskar Ernst Patrick Friedrich Leopold	Prince of Prussia	Germany	1895	1959
Halder	Franz	Germany	1884	1972
Hamm	Anton Johann	Germany	1909	1986
Heberlein	Erich Ernst	Germany	1889	1980
Joos	Joseph	Germany	1878	1965
Kunkel	Karl	Germany	1913	2012
Liedig	Franz Maria	Germany	1900	1967
Müller	Josef	Germany	1898	1979
Neuhäusler	Johann	Germany	1888	1973
Niemöller	Friedrich Gustav Emil Martin	Germany	1892	1984
Petersdorff	Horst	Germany	1892	1962
Philipp	Prince of Hesse	Germany	1896	1980
Pünder	Hermann	Germany	1888	1976
Schacht	Hjalmar Horace Greeley	Germany	1877	1970
Schlabrendorff	Fabian Ludwig Georg Adolf Kurt	Germany	1907	1980
Thomas	Georg	Germany	1890	1946
Thyssen	Friedrich "Fritz"	Germany	1873	1951
Churchill	John Malcolm Thorpe Fleming "Jack"	Great Britain	1906	1996
Churchill	Peter	Great Britain	1909	1972
Day	Harry Melville Arbuthnot	Great Britain	1898	1977
Dowse	Sydney Hastings	Great Britain	1918	2008
Falconer	Hugh Mallory	Great Britain	1910	1980
James	Bertram Arthur "Jimmy"	Great Britain	1915	2008
Payne Best	Sigismund	Great Britain	1885	1978
Stevens	Richard Henry	Great Britain	1893	1967
Bakopoulos	Konstantinos	Greece	1889	1950
Dedes	Panagiotis	Greece	1890	1972

SURNAME	CHRISTIAN NAMES	NATIONALITY	YEAR OF BIRTH	YEAR OF DEATH
Dimitriou	Vassilis	Greece	1910	
Grivas	Nicolas	Greece	1908	
Kosmas	Georgios	Greece	1886	1964
Papagos	Aleksandros	Greece	1883	1955
Pitsikas	Ioannis	Greece	1881	1975
Ginzery	Aleksander	Hungary	1895	
Hatz	Josef	Hungary	1894	
Hatz	Samuel	Hungary	1872	
Hlatky	Andreas	Hungary	1895	1957
Horthy	Miklós "Nicky"	Hungary	1907	1993
Igmándy-Hegyessy	Géza	Hungary	1882	1980
Kállay	Miklós	Hungary	1887	1967
Kiraly	Julius	Hungary	1893	1979
Onody	Desiderius	Hungary	1915	
Schell de Bauschlott	Baron Péter	Hungary	1898	1974
Cushing	Thomas Joseph	Ireland	1909	1981
McGrath	John	Ireland	1899	1946
O'Brien	Patrick	Ireland	1911	1963
Spence	John	Ireland	1912	1968
Walsh	Andrew	Ireland	1911	1969
Apollonio	Eugenio	Italy	1903	1985
Badoglio	Mario Ferdinando Antonio Luigi	Italy	1905	1953
Ferrero	Davide	Italy	1910	
Garibaldi	Sante	Italy	1885	1946
Tamburini	Tullio	Italy	1892	1957
Celmiņš	Gustavs	Latvia	1899	1968
Van Dijk	Jannes Johannes Cornelis	Netherlands	1871	1954
Daehli	Arne Simensøn	Norway	1897	1973
Izycki	Jan Piotr	Poland	1913	1958
Jensen	Stanislaw	Poland	1906	1984
Zamoyski	Aleksander	Poland	1898	1961
Bessonov	Ivan Georgievich	Soviet Union	1904	1950
Brodnikov (Brodnikoff)	Viktor Viktororovitch	Soviet Union	1901	1950

SURNAME	CHRISTIAN NAMES	NATIONALITY	YEAR OF BIRTH	YEAR OF DEATH
Ceredilin (Tcheredilin)	Fjodor Nikiforovitch	Soviet Union	1919	
Kokorin	Vassily Vassilyevich	Soviet Union	1923	1952
Privalov	Pyotr Frolovitch	Soviet Union	1898	1951
Rutchenko	Nikolaj Nikolaevitch	Soviet Union	1917	2013
Karvas	Imrich Anton	Slovakia	1903	1981
Stanek	Jan	Slovakia	1900	1996
Edquist	Carl Göran	Sweden	1915	1998
Dragic-Hauer	Hinko	Yugoslavia	1899	
Popovic	Novak D.	Yugoslavia	1898	
Tomalevsky	Dimitrije	Yugoslavia	1891	
KIN PRISONERS				
Gisevius	Annelise Ella Hedwig	Germany	1903	
Goerdeler	Anneliese Emilie	Germany	1888	1961
Goerdeler	Benigna	Germany	1929	
Goerdeler	Gustav Karl Franz	Germany	1875	1955
Goerdeler	Marianne	Germany	1919	2011
Goerdeler	Irma Anna Klara	Germany	1909	
Goerdeler	Jutta Juliana Ulriche (Tominski)	Germany	1928	2017
Goerdeler	Ulrich Karl Julius	Germany	1913	2000
Gudzent	Käthe	Germany	1915	
Halder	Gertrud Margarita Barbara	Germany	1886	1973
Hammerstein	Hildur	Germany	1923	2012
Hammerstein	Maria	Germany	1886	1970
Heberlein	Margot	Germany	1891	1980
Hoepner	Horst Albert	Germany	1889	
Hofacker	Anna-Luise	Germany	1929	2016
Hofacker	Eberhard	Germany	1928	2001
Hofacker	Ilse Lotte	Germany	1898	1974
Kaiser	Elisabeth Maria	Germany	1921	
Kaiser	Therese	Germany	1889*	1952
Kuhn	Arthur Julius	Germany	1883	

SURNAME	CHRISTIAN NAMES	NATIONALITY	YEAR OF BIRTH	YEAR OF DEATH
Lindemann	Lina Marie Eugenie Eleonore Margot	Germany	1898	1982
Mohr	Josef Hermann	Germany	1899	1976
Mohr	Käte	Germany	1905	2001
Pirzio-Biroli	Fey	Germany	1918	2010
Plettenberg	Gisela Maria Martha Ida Huberta	Germany	1915	2011
Plettenberg	Walther Clemens Augustinus	Germany	1881	1972
Schröder	Hans-Dietrich	Germany	1937	
Schröder	Harring	Germany	1935c	2006
Schröder	Ingeborg Elizabeth	Germany	1913	2006
Schröder	Sybille-Maria	Germany	1940	
Stauffenberg	Alexander Franz Clemens	Germany	1905	1964
Stauffenberg	Alexandra Leopoldine Olga Maria	Germany	1922	2016
Stauffenberg	Clemens Anton	Germany	1929	1987
Stauffenberg	Elisabeth Luise Marie	Germany	1891	1946
Stauffenberg	Maria	Germany	1900	1977
Stauffenberg	Marie Agnes	Germany	1920	1956
Stauffenberg	Marie-Gabriele Luise Sofie	Germany	1914	2018
Stauffenberg	Markwart Sebastian Ludwig Philipp Maria	Germany	1889	1975
Stauffenberg	Otto Philipp Franz Christof Maria	Germany	1926	2015
Thyssen	Amélie	Germany	1875	1965
Vermehren	Isa Beate	Germany	1918	2009
VOLUNTARY				
Schuschnigg	Maria Dolores Elisabeth “Sissy”	Austria	1941	1989
Schuschnigg	Vera	Austria	1904	1959
Blum	Jeanne Adèle “Janot”	France	1899	1982

SURNAME	CHRISTIAN NAMES	NATIONALITY	YEAR OF BIRTH	YEAR OF DEATH
ANCILLARY				
Wauer	Paul	Germany	1900	1979
Visintainer	Wilhelm	Germany	1897	

SURNAME	CHRISTIAN NAMES	NATIONALITY	YEAR OF BIRTH	YEAR OF DEATH
ACCIDENTAL				
Greenewich	Wadim	Great Britain	1899	1982
Nowakowski	Johanna (aka Heidel)	Germany	1914	1956

NB. Some hostages were of Irish nationality but were serving in the British armed forces on capture. Some prisoners mentioned in the text (e.g., Reinhard Goerdeler) are excluded from this list because they were not among the 139 hostages taken to the Tyrol.

Notes

Prologue

1. 351st Infantry Regiment, History for April 1945, p. 15.

2. 351st Infantry Regiment, History for May 1945, pp. 1–2.

3. 351st Infantry Regiment, History for May 1945, pp. 2–3.

4. Day (notes, no. 23, p. 32) describes this exchange.

5. Day (notes, no. 2, p. 7; no. 23, p.32) is vague about the precise number in his group; besides himself and his companion, Anton Ducia, he lists three partisans by name and remarks that the group was "rather augmented in numbers" by the addition of some partisan guides during the final leg from Roncegno to the American lines at Borgo Valsugana.

1. The Corridor of Death

1. Wachsmann, *KL*, p. 628.

2. The other senior SS figures included Ernst Kaltenbrunner, head of the RSHA. Although Hitler approved the roundup of the prisoners, his involvement in the conception of the plan to use them as hostages may have been slight—he continued to believe that Germany would win the war. However, he did accept that the VIP prisoners were of value to the enemy and could be useful. See Chapter 3 for more on this.

3. Middlebrook and Everitt, *Bomber Command*, pp. 689–690; Freeman, Crouchman, and Maslen, *Mighty Eighth*, p. 475.

4. Churchill, *Spirit*, p. 199; James, *Moonless Night*, p. 163; Smith, *Wings Day*, p. 209.

5. James, *Moonless Night*, p. 162.

6. James, *Moonless Night*, pp. 160, 199.

7. James, *Moonless Night*, p. 162.

8. Churchill, *Spirit*, pp. 127–141; James, *Moonless Night*, pp. 117–130; Smith, *Wings Day*, pp. 170–174.

9. Schuschnigg, *Austrian Requiem*, pp. 223–224.

10. Schuschnigg, *Austrian Requiem*, pp. 223–224.

11. *Time*, 16 December 1940.

12. Day, notes, no. 23, p. 1.

13. James, *Moonless Night*, p. 127.

14. Smith, *Wings Day*, p. 209.

15. James, *Moonless Night*, p. 163; Smith, *Wings Day*, p. 209.

16. Churchill, *Spirit*, pp. 145–157; James, *Moonless Night*, pp. 129–147; Smith, *Wings Day*, pp. 176–189. There were many escapes from concentration camps, usually in small numbers and involving disguises or overpowering guards on outside work details (Wachsmann, *KL*, pp. 532–533). A mass escape took place at Mauthausen concentration camp in February 1945, when over four hundred Soviet POWs seized machine guns and used wet blankets to short-circuit the electric fences (Wachsmann, *KL*, pp. 569–570). But there were no other recorded tunnels.

17. Mohr, letter to James, 20 December 1946, quoted in James, *Moonless Night*, p. 204.

18. Mohr, letter to James, 20 December 1946.

19. James, *Moonless Night*, p. 153.

20. Day, notes, no. 23, p. 1.

21. Day, notes, no. 23, p. 1; Smith, *Wings Day*, p. 209.

22. Van Wymeersch, statement.

23. This story was confirmed by historian and fellow commando Peter Young (Young, *Commando*, p. 78).

24. Reports differ on the course of the journey. Day (notes, no. 23, p.1) says that the first city reached was Leipzig, whereas James (*Moonless Night*, p. 167) recalls passing through Berlin. Day is possibly more reliable, since his memories were written down much earlier, but James's description is remarkably clear and vivid.

25. James, *Moonless Night*, p. 167.

26. James, *Moonless Night*, p. 168.

27. Parrish, *Sacrifice*, pp. 43–44.

28. Day, notes.

29. James, *Moonless Night*, p. 168.

30. Smith, *Wings Day*, p. 20; James, *Moonless Night*, p. 160.

2. Blood Guilt

1. Buchenwald was founded in 1937, a few years after Dachau (1933) and Sachsenhausen (1936).

2. Stein, *Buchenwald*, pp. 195–196; Hackett, *Buchenwald Report*, p. 70.

3. Payne Best, *Venlo*, p. 190; Hassell, *Mother's War*, pp. 158–160.

4. Hackett, *Buchenwald Report*, pp. 97–98.

5. Quoted in Birnbaum, *Léon Blum: Prime Minister*, p. 133; also Colton, *Léon Blum: Humanist*, p. 438.

6. Hackett, *Buchenwald Report*, p. 42.

7. Blum, quoted in Stein, *Buchenwald*, p. 196.

8. Colton, *Léon Blum: Humanist*, p. 436.

9. Colton, *Léon Blum: Humanist*, pp. 423–424.

10. Quoted in Colton, *Léon Blum: Humanist*, p. 440.

11. Hassell, *Mother's War*, p. 92.

12. Hassell, *Mother's War*, p. 116.

13. Hassell, *Mother's War*, p. 158.

14. Hassell, *Mother's War*, p. 158.

15. Hassell, *Mother's War*, p. 160.

16. Neveu, *Le Gestapo*, p. 94; Counterintelligence Corps, Dossier XE-123106, Karl Friedrich Bader. The question of Bader's rank is vexed. Some say he wore the insignia of an SS-Obersturmführer (first lieutenant), but there is no firm evidence that he was promoted to that rank other than his appearance as such on a 1943 list of personnel signed by an SS-Gruppenführer in command of the SS and police in Metz. Bader's SS file ceased in 1941, at which time he was an SS-Untersturmführer (second lieutenant). It is possible that he was promoted after that. But since the junior rank is the only one for which there is firm evidence, he is referred to here accordingly.

17. Vermehren, *Reise*, p. 160.

18. Payne Best, *Venlo*, pp. 173–175.

19. Payne Best, *Venlo*, p. 16ff.

20. Both men later claimed not to have revealed anything substantial to their German inquisitors, though it was widely intimated otherwise, and the two men became embroiled in mutual recrimination about their respective trustworthiness.

21. Payne Best, *Venlo*, p. 60ff.

22. The system—known as a *Holzbrenner* (wood burner)—worked by heating wood to the point where it would produce flammable gases, which were fed into the combustion engine.

23. Payne Best, *Venlo*, p. 190.

24. Wachsmann, *KL*, pp. 428–433.

25. Payne Best, *Venlo*, p. 190.

3. Alpine Fortress

1. Waller, "Reichsführer Himmler."

2. Marrus, *Nazi Holocaust*, p. 558; Cesarani, *Final Solution*, pp. 724, 761.

3. Smith, *Otto Skorzeny*, ch. 4.

4. Black, *Kaltenbrunner*, p. 243.

5. Black, *Kaltenbrunner*, p. 243, n. 45; Wolff, interrogation.

6. Smith and Agarossi, *Operation Sunrise*, pp. 125–126.

7. Black, *Kaltenbrunner*, p. 243.

8. Black, *Kaltenbrunner*, p. 235.

9. Black, *Kaltenbrunner*, p. 235.

10. Hofer in Stuhlpfarrer, *Die Operationszonen*.

11. Black, *Kaltenbrunner*, p. 236, n. 34; Hofer in Stuhlpfarrer, *Die Operationszonen*; on Hitler's orders see Hagen, *Unternehmen Bernhard*, pp. 231–232; Minott, *Fortress*, pp. 24–26.

12. Black, *Kaltenbrunner*, p. 236.

13. Lessner, *Collier's Weekly*, 27 January 1945.

14. *Weltwoche*, 2 February 1945.

15. Schiff, *New York Times*, 11 February 1945.

16. Schiff, *New York Times*, 11 February 1945.

17. The order was revealed after the war by SS general Walter Schellenberg, head of foreign intelligence in 1945. At his trial before the International Military Tribunal in Nuremberg, he related a conversation in the Reich Main Security Office between himself, Kaltenbrunner, and the chief of the Gestapo, Heinrich Müller. Schellenberg testified, "Müller said that on Kaltenbrunner's orders he had started to evacuate the most important prisoners from the respective camps. . . . Kaltenbrunner said: 'Yes, that is correct. It is an order that Hitler himself has issued and has been recently confirmed . . . therefore all VIP prisoners are to be transported South.'" According to Schellenberg's account of the timing, the order would have come from the Führer bunker in the first few days of April. See Schellenberg testimony in Nuremberg Tribunal, *Trial*, p. 382.

4. Journey South

1. Payne Best, *Venlo*, pp. 190–191.

2. Payne Best, *Venlo*, pp. 196–197; Vermehren, *Reise*.

3. Payne Best (*Venlo*, p. 192) refers to this as a "police station"; however, it must have been an SS or Gestapo office if it was the calling place for inquiries about the concentration camp.

4. Payne Best, *Venlo*, p. 192.

5. Payne Best, *Venlo*, p. 186.

6. Hassell, *Mother's War*, p. 161.

7. Hassell, *Mother's War*, p. 161.

8. Fey Pirzio-Biroli (Hassell, *Mother's War*, p. 162) identifies them as Gestapo, whereas Payne Best (*Venlo*, p. 192) describes them as uniformed police. If in uniform, they were almost certainly not Gestapo; presumably they were SS security police (an umbrella including the Gestapo and Kriminalpolizei, or Kripo, which prior to the formation of the RSHA had been the Sicherheitspolizei, or Sipo). Payne Best, inside the Grüne Minna, was unaware of the presence of the buses and the Blums' car and doesn't mention them in his memoir.

9. Payne Best, *Venlo*, p. 192.

10. Payne Best, *Venlo*, pp. 180–181.

11. Hassell, *Mother's War*, p. 162; Payne Best, *Venlo*, p. 192.

12. Payne Best, *Venlo*, p. 193.

13. Hassell, *Mother's War*, pp. 162–163.

14. Fey refers to this individual throughout her memoir (Hassell, *Mother's War*) as "Stiller," but this appears to be an error on the part of her editor. In fact, SS-Obersturmführer Stiller came into the story of the Prominenten at a later stage (see Chapter 10).

15. Colton, *Léon Blum: Humanist*, pp. 441–442.

16. Payne Best, *Venlo*, p. 193.

17. Payne Best, *Venlo*, p. 193.

18. Payne Best, *Venlo*, pp. 193–194.

19. Loeffel, *Family Punishment*, pp. 45–46.

20. Hassell, *Mother's War*, p. 164.

21. Vermehren, *Reise*.

22. Payne Best, *Venlo*, p. 194.

23. Fey Pirzio-Biroli (Hassell, *Mother's War*, p. 164) states that "for three hours Allied planes roared over Regensburg" but did not bomb it. The US Eighth Air Force flew several large daylight operations in southern Germany on 5 April, with three forces totaling over 1,300 heavy bombers hitting targets at Ingolstadt, Bayreuth, and around Nuremberg (Freeman, Crouchman, and Maslen, *Mighty Eighth*, p. 480).

5. Flossenbürg Concentration Camp

1. Narrative based on James, *Moonless Night*, p. 168ff; Smith, *Wings Day*, p. 210ff; Churchill, *Spirit*, p. 199ff; Day, notes, no. 23.

2. Churchill, *Spirit*, p. 63.

3. Day, notes, no. 23, p. 1.

4. James, *Moonless Night*, p. 168.

5. Day, notes, no. 22, p. 11.

6. Day, notes, no. 22, p. 11.

7. James, *Moonless Night*, p. 168.

8. Middlebrook and Everitt, *Bomber Command*, p. 691.

9. Day, notes, no. 23, p. 2.

10. Churchill, *Spirit*, pp. 199–200.

11. Huebner, "Flossenbürg," p. 563; Wachsmann, *KL*, pp. 568–569. These murders occurred on 29 March 1945, six days before the arrival of the Prominenten.

12. Churchill, *Spirit*, p. 200.

13. James (*Moonless Night*, p. 169) names the commandant as "Stavitsky"; in fact, Max Koegel was commandant from 1943 to the end of the war (Huebner, "Flossenbürg," p. 563).

14. Wachsmann, *KL*, p. 228.

15. Slightly varying versions of this dialogue are given by Jimmy James (*Moonless Night*, p. 169) and Wings Day (Smith, *Wings Day*, p. 211). It was presumably reported to them by a third party.

16. Slightly varying versions of this confrontation are given by Jimmy James (*Moonless Night*, p. 169), Wings Day (Smith, *Wings Day*, pp. 210–211), and Churchill (*Spirit*, p. 200).

17. Smith, *Wings Day*, p. 212.

18. James, *Moonless Night*, p. 170.

19. Schlabrendorff, *Secret War*, p. 329.

6. The Condemned

1. Höhne, *Canaris*, p. 591.

2. It is believed that a written order for the execution of Canaris and his associates was issued, but because it did not survive the war, we are largely dependent on the testimony of Colonel Walter Huppenkothen, the SS prosecutor selected to provide

legal justification, via a drumhead court-martial, for the proposed executions. However, there were no witnesses, no defense counsel, and no record of the proceedings. During one of his postwar trials, Huppenkothen indicated that, while Himmler may not have been involved, he believed that the order had been passed down the chain of command from Hitler to Kaltenbrunner to Gestapo chief Müller, who issued the written order that afternoon (Landgericht Augsburg, judgement).

3. Landgericht Augsburg, judgement.
4. "Müller Order."
5. "Müller Order."
6. Höhne, *Canaris*, p. 469.
7. Höhne, *Canaris*, p. 592.
8. Payne Best, *Venlo*, p. 169.
9. Landgericht Augsburg, judgement.

7. Bavarian Interlude

1. Payne Best, *Venlo*, p. 195.
2. Hassell, *Mother's War*, pp. 164–165.
3. Payne Best, *Venlo*, p. 195.
4. Payne Best, *Venlo*, p. 195.
5. Payne Best, *Venlo*, p. 195.
6. Hassell, *Mother's War*, p. 165.
7. Hassell, *Mother's War*, pp. 165–166.
8. Payne Best, *Venlo*, p. 196. Presumably the room was a dormitory for boarding pupils, though one can only speculate as to why a village school would take boarders.
9. Payne Best, *Venlo*, p. 196.
10. Payne Best, *Venlo*, p. 196.
11. Vermehren, *Reise*; Quoted in Payne Best, *Venlo*, p. 197.
12. Payne Best, *Venlo*, pp. 197, 199.
13. Hassell, *Mother's War*, p. 165.
14. Payne Best, *Venlo*, p. 180.
15. Payne Best, *Venlo*, p. 200.
16. Payne Best, *Venlo*, p. 200.
17. Hassell, *Mother's War*, p. 166.
18. Payne Best, *Venlo*, p. 200.
19. Payne Best, *Venlo*, p. 200.

8. Death of the Damned

1. Schlabrendorff, *Secret War*, p. 311.
2. Schlabrendorff, *Secret War*, p. 312.
3. Hoffmann, *German Resistance*, p. 527.
4. Schlabrendorff, *Secret War*, p. 330. The voices could not have been Wings Day and his companions, who were being held in the camp infirmary.
5. Richardi, *SS-Geiseln*, p. 148.
6. Richardi, *SS-Geiseln*, p. 148.

7. Höhne, *Canaris*, pp. 592–594.

8. Höhne, *Canaris*, p. 595.

9. Höhne, *Canaris*, p. 596.

10. James, *Moonless Night*, p. 170.

11. James, *Moonless Night*, p. 170. It isn't certain whether the bodies actually were some of the victims of the Huppenkothen/Thorbeck trials. If they were, then since they were hanged, the blood and gore on the blankets must have come from elsewhere. Possibly the blankets were reused; more likely the three bodies were other victims of SS brutality. Shooting prisoners "while attempting to escape" was a common method of murder in concentration camps.

12. Smith, *Wings Day*, p. 212.

13. Smith, *Wings Day*, p. 213; James, *Moonless Night*, pp. 171–172; Churchill, *Spirit*, pp. 201–202.

14. Churchill, *Spirit*, p. 201.

15. Churchill, *Spirit*, p. 201.

16. Somewhat different versions of (presumably) the same conversation are given by Churchill (*Spirit*, pp. 201–202), James (*Moonless Night*, p. 172), and Müller (*Bis zur letzten Konsequenz*, p. 252). The version recounted here is a mix of the three.

17. Höhne, *Canaris*, p. 597, n. 247.

18. Smith, *Wings Day*, p. 213.

19. James, *Moonless Night*, p. 171. According to James, the two "British" SOE agents were Brian Rafferty (who was actually Irish) and Flight Lieutenant Jack Agazarian.

20. Smith, *Wings Day*, pp. 213–214.

21. Schuschnigg, *Austrian Requiem*, pp. 189–220.

22. Schuschnigg, *Austrian Requiem*, pp. 221–225.

23. Schuschnigg, *Austrian Requiem*, p. 221.

24. Schuschnigg, *Austrian Requiem*, p. 224.

25. Quoted in Petropoulos, *Royals*, p. 4.

26. Petropoulos, *Royals*, pp. 287–288.

27. Petropoulos, *Royals*, pp. 295–297.

28. Petropoulos, *Royals*, pp. 299–300.

29. Petropoulos, *Royals*, pp. 301–304.

30. Schuschnigg, *Austrian Requiem*, p. 227.

31. Schuschnigg makes no mention of this in his diary (Schuschnigg, *Austrian Requiem*, p. 227). However, there is an unexplained missing day in his account, and he refers to an agonizingly long wait in the van at the other end of the journey (see Chapter 9), which is contradicted by other accounts.

32. Huppenkothen, Flossenbürg-Müller message.

33. Schacht, *Seventy-Six Years*, p. 439.

9. Murder at the Crematorium

1. Payne Best, *Venlo*, p. 200.

2. Payne Best, *Venlo*, p. 200.

3. Payne Best, *Venlo*, p. 200.

4. Hassell, *Mother's War*, p. 168.

5. Payne Best, *Venlo*, p. 168.

6. Payne Best, *Venlo*, pp. 200–201.

7. Schuschnigg, interview in *Daily Telegraph*, 3 March 1946, quoted in Payne Best, *Venlo*, p. 201.

8. Payne Best, *Venlo*, p. 202.

9. Payne Best, *Venlo*, p. 203.

10. Payne Best, *Venlo*, p. 202.

11. Payne Best, *Venlo*, p. 204.

12. Wachsmann, *KL*, chap. 1; Distel, "Dachau," p. 442.

13. Berben, *Dachau*, p. 211, plan.

14. Wachsmann, *KL*, p. 628. Like Buchenwald, Sachsenhausen, and Flossenbürg, Dachau did not double as a death camp. In Auschwitz, designed as both a concentration camp and a death camp, over a million were killed.

15. According to Schuschnigg (*Austrian Requiem*, p. 228), they were kept in the Grüne Minna during this time, whereas Payne Best (*Venlo*, p. 204) says they were taken out and put in "a sort of large hall" in the gatehouse. Schuschnigg may have been misremembering a long wait in the van prior to leaving Flossenbürg (see Chapter 8).

16. "Müller Order."

17. Freeman, Crouchman, and Maslen, *Mighty Eighth*, p. 484.

18. Richardi, *SS-Geiseln*, p. 116.

19. Brissaud, *Nazi Secret Service*, p. 287.

20. Lechner's testimony, cited in Brissaud, *Nazi Secret Service*, p. 287; Payne Best, *Venlo*, p. 212. It is possible that Fritz too was a musician. Payne Best mentions that Lechner had a fellow guard who was a musician but doesn't give his name.

21. Lechner's testimony, cited in Brissaud, *Nazi Secret Service*, pp. 287–288.

22. Brissaud, *Nazi Secret Service*, p. 288.

23. Payne Best, *Venlo*, p. 204.

24. Payne Best, *Venlo*, p. 205.

10. Traitors in Their Midst

1. Payne Best, *Venlo*, p. 205.

2. Payne Best, *Venlo*, p. 205. Like Bader's, Stiller's rank is a questionable quantity. His SS record shows that he was actually an Untersturmführer (second lieutenant) at this point and continued to be referred to in SS communications as such, but he was about to be promoted to Obersturmführer (first lieutenant), the promotion taking place ten days later, on 20 April 1945 (Judicial investigation of Stiller). For consistency he is referred to here by his effective rank.

3. Payne Best, letter to Munich District Court II, 7 September 1951, Sigismund Payne Best papers, Imperial War Museum; Judicial investigation of Stiller.

4. Payne Best, *Venlo*, p. 205. Payne Best describes it as being "at the eastern end" of the building. However, in the eastern wing only the rooms closest to the central

administrative block have the windows described in his narrative; the rest have typically small cell windows. (The cellblock still exists as part of the Dachau memorial museum.)

5. Schuschnigg, *Austrian Requiem*, p. 228.

6. Distel, "Dachau," p. 444. In 1942, Rascher directed pressure-chamber and cold-water experiments for the Luftwaffe at Dachau, which involved respectively subjecting prisoners to sudden drops in air pressure or to freezing water. Dozens died and hundreds experienced horrific suffering in Rascher's experiments.

7. Berben, *Dachau*, pp. 219–220; Distel, "Dachau," p. 445.

8. Schacht, *Seventy-Six Years*, p. 439.

9. Schuschnigg, *Austrian Requiem*, p. 228.

10. Payne Best, *Venlo*, p. 205; Wauer, statement.

11. Payne Best, *Venlo*, p. 205.

12. Payne Best, *Venlo*, p. 207.

13. Payne Best, *Venlo*, p. 209.

14. Payne Best, *Venlo*, p. 208.

15. Payne Best, *Venlo*, p. 212.

16. Payne Best, *Venlo*, p. 212.

17. Payne Best, *Venlo*, p. 212.

18. Payne Best, *Venlo*, p. 213.

19. Payne Best, *Venlo*, p. 213.

20. Payne Best, *Venlo*, p. 213; McGrath, letter to Payne Best, 14 April 1945.

21. McGrath, letter to Payne Best, 14 April 1945. Although Payne Best summarizes McGrath's letter in his published memoir (*Venlo*, p. 213), he entirely omits the information about Stevens, who was still alive at the time.

22. Payne Best later told Stevens he pitied him, believing that he simply wasn't mentally or physically equipped for such a torturous ordeal: "I had a much harder time than you, but I could stick it where you could not" (Payne Best, letter to Stevens, 3 April 1947, Payne Best papers).

23. Kállay, statement.

24. Kállay, *Hungarian Premier*, pp. 486–487.

25. Payne Best, *Venlo*, p. 213.

11. All in One Place

1. Smith, *Wings Day*, p. 214.

2. James, *Moonless Night*, p. 173.

3. Huebner, "Flossenbürg," p. 563.

4. There are slightly different versions of this exchange in Smith (*Wings Day*, p. 215) and James (*Moonless Night*, p. 173).

5. James, *Moonless Night*, p. 173.

6. Huebner, "Flossenbürg," p. 563.

7. Churchill, *Spirit*, p. 203.

8. James, *Moonless Night*, p. 174.

9. James, *Moonless Night*, p. 174.

10. James, *Moonless Night*, p. 174; Freeman, Crouchman, and Maslen, *Mighty Eighth*, p. 489.

11. James, *Moonless Night*, p. 174.

12. James, *Moonless Night*, p. 174.

13. Churchill, *Spirit*, p. 204.

14. Churchill, *Spirit*, p. 204.

15. Marcuse, *Legacies of Dachau*, p. 127; Berben, *Dachau*, p. 211.

16. Smith, *Dachau: The Harrowing of Hell*, p. 200.

17. Smith, *Wings Day*, p. 216.

18. Hassell, *Mother's War*, p. 166. Fey names Stiller as the officer who gave permission; this is clearly an error on the part of her editor.

19. Hassell, *Mother's War*, p. 166.

20. Mulley, *Women Who Flew*, p. 304ff.

21. Mulley, *Women Who Flew*, p. 311.

22. Hassell, *Mother's War*, p. 167.

23. James, *Moonless Night*, p. 174; Freeman, Crouchman, and Maslen, *Mighty Eighth*, p. 489; Hassell, *Mother's War*, p. 168.

24. Hassell, *Mother's War*, p. 168.

25. Hassell, *Mother's War*, p. 169.

26. Hassell, *Mother's War*, p. 169. According to Isa Vermehren (*Reise*, pp. 171–172), they arrived in the early hours of the morning. However, this does not fit the timescale of the journey and is contradicted by Payne Best (*Venlo*, p. 213), who says the newcomers arrived in the afternoon.

27. Vermehren, *Reise*, pp. 171–172.

28. Vermehren, *Reise*, pp. 171–172.

29. Hassell, *Mother's War*, p. 169.

30. Richardi, *SS-Geiseln*, 145.

31. Payne Best, *Venlo*, pp. 213–214.

32. Payne Best, *Venlo*, p. 214.

33. Hassell, *Mother's War*, p. 170.

12. The Exodus Begins

1. Payne Best, *Venlo*, p. 213.

2. Smith (*Wings Day*, p. 218) calls it a "very heavy air raid" (also James, *Moonless Night*, p. 175). In fact, there were two relatively small raids on Munich and Gablingen airfield (Middlebrook and Everitt, *Bomber Command*, p. 696).

3. James, *Moonless Night*, p. 175.

4. Churchill, *Spirit*, p. 205.

5. Davidson, *God's Man*, p. 130.

6. Smith, *Wings Day*, p. 223.

7. Smith, *Wings Day*, p. 218; Churchill, *Spirit*, p. 206.

8. There are slightly different versions of this conversation in James (*Moonless Night*, p. 176) and Churchill (*Spirit*, p. 206).

9. Churchill, *Spirit*, pp. 206–207; James, *Moonless Night*, p. 177.

10. Smith, *Wings Day*, p. 219.

11. "Statement of Ludwig Rottmaier," 3 October 1951, Judicial investigation of Stiller.

12. James, *Moonless Night*, p. 177.

13. Churchill, *Spirit*, p. 207.

14. Smith, *Wings Day*, p. 219.

15. Payne Best, *Venlo*, pp. 216–217.

16. Payne Best, *Venlo*, p. 216.

17. Payne Best, *Venlo*, p. 211.

18. Payne Best, *Venlo*, p. 212.

19. Hassell, *Mother's War*, p. 171.

20. Hassell, *Mother's War*, p. 172.

21. Hassell, *Mother's War*, p. 172.

22. Schuschnigg, *Austrian Requiem*, p. 229.

23. Schuschnigg, *Austrian Requiem*, p. 223.

24. Schuschnigg, *Austrian Requiem*, p. 229.

25. Schuschnigg, *Austrian Requiem*, p. 235.

26. Schuschnigg, *Austrian Requiem*, pp. 235–236.

27. "Statement of Ludwig Rottmaier."

28. Payne Best, *Venlo*, p. 215.

29. Kunkel, diary.

30. Kunkel, diary.

31. Payne Best, *Venlo*, p. 216.

32. Payne Best, *Venlo*, p. 216; Freeman, Crouchman, and Maslen, *Mighty Eighth*, p. 495.

33. Middlebrook and Everitt, *Bomber Command*, p. 697. Payne Best mistakenly says this was "the evening before," i.e., 20 April (*Venlo*, p. 216).

34. Payne Best, *Venlo*, p. 219.

35. Payne Best, *Venlo*, p. 219.

36. Payne Best, *Venlo*, p. 219.

37. Payne Best, *Venlo*, p. 219.

38. Payne Best, *Venlo*, p. 219.

13. Into the Redoubt

1. The following day, 25 April, the US Eighth Air Force flew its last bombing mission against an industrial target. Most of its heavy bombers by this point were dedicated to leaflet drops over liberated zones (Freeman, Crouchman, and Maslen, *Mighty Eighth*, pp. 496–497).

2. Vermehren, *Reise*, p. 175.

3. Payne Best, *Venlo*, p. 220.

4. Kunkel, diary.

5. Richardi, *SS-Geiseln*, p.174.

6. Payne Best, *Venlo*, p. 220.

7. Payne Best, *Venlo*, pp. 220–221.

8. Richard, *SS-Geiseln*, p. 168.

9. Niemöller, quoted in Richardi, *SS-Geiseln*, p. 171.

10. Joos, *Leben*, pp. 138–139.

11. Mogensen, *Die grosse Geiselnahme*, p. 85.

12. Payne Best, *Venlo*, p. 221.

13. Joos, *Leben*, pp. 139–140.

14. Counterintelligence Corps, Dossier XA-0244414, Richard Schmitz.

15. Richardi, *SS-Geiseln*, p. 169.

16. Payne Best, *Venlo*, p. 221.

17. Payne Best, *Venlo*, p. 221.

18. Payne Best, *Venlo*, p. 221. According to Josef Müller's own account (*Bis zur letzten Konsequenz*, p. 266), he sat on one of the buses, with Stiller sitting in front of him. Possibly the prisoners were moved around at some point.

19. Payne Best (*Venlo*, p. 222) mentions the luggage trucks, which are oddly absent in other sources.

20. Kunkel, diary. Fey Pirzio-Biroli (Hassell, *Mother's War*, p. 173) claims that Niemöller left Dachau by a later transport; possibly she mistook someone else for him or it was an error on the part of her editor.

21. Payne Best, *Venlo*, p. 222.

22. Payne Best, *Venlo*, p. 222.

23. Kunkel, diary; Schmitz, quoted in Richardi, *SS-Geiseln*, p. 176. From this point, there are differing accounts of the journey given by Kunkel, Schmitz, and Payne Best. This narrative reconciles the three.

24. Kunkel, diary; Payne Best, *Venlo*, p. 222. Kunkel says it was a blown bridge; according to Payne Best it was a blind alley.

25. Payne Best, *Venlo*, p. 222.

26. Payne Best, *Venlo*, p. 222.

27. Kunkel, diary.

28. Neuhäusler, diary, quoted in Richardi, *SS-Geiseln*, p. 176.

29. Schmitz, quoted in Richardi, *SS-Geiseln*, p. 176.

14. SS-Sonderlager Innsbruck

1. Zegenhagen, "Innsbruck (SS-Sonderlager)," p. 484. There was a second camp adjacent to it: Innsbruck I, a concentration camp that had been part of the Dachau system since 1942 and provided labor for local construction projects run by the Waffen-SS and the police (Zegenhagen, "Innsbruck I," p. 485).

2. Schwarz, "Rohde, Lothar."

3. Payne Best, *Venlo*, p. 223.

4. Payne Best, *Venlo*, pp. 223–225; James, *Moonless Night*, p. 178.

5. "Statement of Ludwig Rottmaier."

6. Churchill, *Spirit*, p. 208.

7. Smith, *Wings Day*, p. 220–221.

8. Payne Best, *Venlo*, p. 225.

9. Payne Best, *Venlo*, p. 225.

10. Payne Best, *Venlo*, p. 225.

11. See Drooz, *American Prisoners of War*, pp. 8–9, 197–199.

12. Each source gives a different date for the third and final transport of Prominenten leaving Dachau. Fey Pirzio-Biroli, who was on the transport but whose memoir was subject to editing and secondhand reworking says 25 April (Hassell, *Mother's War*, p. 172); Payne Best, who was not on the transport but is generally reliable, indicates 26 April (*Venlo*, pp. 220–227); the diary of Karl Kunkel (who wasn't on the transport) indicates 24 April, whereas his later statement gives the 26th; Kurt Schuschnigg, who was on it, gives 27 April (*Austrian Requiem*, p. 238). Surviving records of Reichenau also give varying dates for movements of Prominenten (Zegenhagen, "Innsbruck (SS-Sonderlager)," p. 484). Thursday 26 April, attested by two sources, agrees most consistently with the overall relative chronology.

13. Schuschnigg, *Austrian Requiem*, p. 237.

14. Schuschnigg, *Austrian Requiem*, p. 238. Schuschnigg gives the date here as 27 April, having apparently gotten ahead of himself (see note above).

15. Berben, *Dachau*, p. 192; Distel, "Dachau," p. 445; Hassell, *Mother's War*, p. 172.

16. Hassell, *Mother's War*, p. 172.

17. Hassell, *Mother's War*, pp. 172–173.

18. Schuschnigg, *Austrian Requiem*, p. 238.

19. Schuschnigg, *Austrian Requiem*, p. 238.

20. "Isa Vermehren statement," 15 July 1952, Judicial investigation of Stiller.

21. Hassell, *Mother's War*, p. 173.

22. Wachsmann, *KL*, p. 583.

23. Vermehren, *Reise*, p. 178.

24. Richardi, *SS-Geiseln*, p. 180.

25. Hassell, *Mother's War*, p. 175.

26. Hassell, *Mother's War*, p. 174.

27. Hassell, *Mother's War*, p. 174.

28. Hassell, *Mother's War*, p. 176.

29. James, *Moonless Night*, p. 179.

30. Churchill, *Spirit*, p. 208. It is possible that Churchill did not include the children or those who were technically servants, such as Visintainer and Wauer.

31. Smith, *Wings Day*, pp. 223–224.

32. "Franz Xaver Lechner statement," 24 September 1951, Judicial investigation of Stiller.

33. Payne Best, *Venlo*, p. 227.

15. Out of the Reich

1. The number of vehicles varies in different sources. Payne Best (*Venlo*, p. 227) believes there were five buses plus the truck in which he had traveled from Dachau, while Fey (Hassell, *Mother's War*, p. 179) counted "four immense buses brought down from Innsbruck." Jimmy James (*Moonless Night*, p. 181) recalls seven buses plus a supply truck for the SS guards.

2. Payne Best, *Venlo*, p. 227.

3. The chronology of this incident is unclear. James (*Moonless Night*, p. 181) implies that it occurred on the day of departure from Reichenau, whereas Smith (*Wings Day*, pp. 222–223) is vague, implying it occurred over two days—Bader's arrival one day and the hangings the next. Where Bader's men had been is not clear, but several Prominenten recall him and his men "reappearing."

4. James, *Moonless Night*, pp. 180–181.

5. Payne Best, *Venlo*, p. 226.

6. Smith, *Wings Day*, pp. 222–223.

7. Smith, *Wings Day*, p. 224; James, *Moonless Night*, p. 181.

8. Vermehren, *Reise*, p. 183.

9. Hassell, *Mother's War*, p. 178.

10. Churchill, *Spirit*, p. 210.

11. Churchill, *Spirit*, p. 210.

12. Schuschnigg, *Austrian Requiem*, p. 239.

13. Churchill, *Spirit*, p. 211; Hassell, *Mother's War*, p. 179; Payne Best, *Venlo*, p. 227.

14. Mogensen, *Die grosse Geiselnahme*, p. 43.

15. Smith, *Wings Day*, p. 225; Vermehren, *Reise*, p. 184.

16. Kunkel diary.

17. Hassell, *Mother's War*, p. 179.

18. Wachsmann, *KL*, p. 583; Berben, *Dachau*, p. 188.

19. Quoted in Wachsmann, *KL*, p. 3.

20. Smith, *Wings Day*, p. 225; Churchill, *Spirit*, p. 212.

21. Smith, *Wings Day*, p. 225.

22. Churchill, *Spirit*, p. 212.

23. Hassell, *Mother's War*, p. 180.

24. Richardi, *SS-Geiseln*, p. 188; Kunkel, diary.

25. Payne Best, *Venlo*, p. 227; Smith, *Wings Day*, p. 226.

26. Smith, *Wings Day*, pp. 225–226.

27. Smith, *Wings Day*, p. 226.

28. Smith, *Wings Day*, pp. 226–227.

16. The Sunrise Conspiracy

1. Doherty, *Victory in Italy*, p. 192ff.

2. Doherty, *Victory in Italy*, pp. 196–197.

3. Doherty, *Victory in Italy*, p. 197.

4. Black, *Kaltenbrunner*, p. 243, n. 45; Wolff, interrogation.

5. Dulles, "Secret Surrender," pp. 199, 246.

6. Dulles, "Secret Surrender," p. 125.

7. Dulles, "Secret Surrender."

8. Lingen, *Dulles*, p. 55.

9. Dulles, "Secret Surrender," p. 116.

10. Smith and Agarossi, *Operation Sunrise*, p. 132.

11. Smith and Agarossi, *Operation Sunrise*, p. 132.

12. Smith and Agarossi, *Operation Sunrise*, p. 140.

13. Dulles, "Secret Surrender," pp. 226–227.

17. Appointment with Death

1. James, *Moonless Night*, p. 182.

2. Hassell, *Mother's War*, p. 179.

3. Schuschnigg, *Austrian Requiem*, pp. 239–240.

4. Payne Best, *Venlo*, p. 227.

5. The location of this turning and halt is not identified in any of the source narratives. It is inferred from prisoner narratives stating that it was about a mile short of Niederdorf (e.g., Hassell, *Mother's War*, p. 180), plus the fact that the Pragser Wildsee was the ultimate intended destination.

6. Doherty, *Victory in Italy*, p. 201.

7. Day, notes, no. 23, pp. 15–16.

8. Vermehren, *Reise*, pp. 185–186.

9. Payne Best, *Venlo*, p. 228.

10. Payne Best, *Venlo*, p. 228.

11. Payne Best, *Venlo*, p. 228.

12. Schuschnigg, *Austrian Requiem*, p. 240.

13. Schuschnigg, *Austrian Requiem*, p. 240.

14. Richardi, *SS-Geiseln*, p. 196 n. 68.

15. Payne Best, *Venlo*, pp. 228–229. According to Stiller's account (14 September 1951, Judicial investigation of Stiller), Stiller himself telephoned Ducia at Bolzano; this might be a post hoc attempt to make his handling of the situation look more competent. The narrative here is constructed by combining elements of Stiller's account with Payne Best's.

16. Churchill, *Spirit*, p. 213.

17. Vermehren, *Reise*, p. 186.

18. Stiller, "Trial statement," 14 September 1951, Judicial investigation of Stiller.

19. In his later statement, Stiller claimed that he contacted Ducia, who was supposedly in Bolzano, by telephone (Stiller, "Trial statement"). This contradicts Payne Best's statement that Ducia was in Niederdorf and came out to the convoy (Payne Best, *Venlo*, pp. 228–229).

20. Churchill, *Spirit*, p. 213; Smith, *Wings Day*, p. 228; Day, notes, no. 23, p. 16; James, *Moonless Night*, pp. 182–183.

21. Churchill, *Spirit*, p. 213. Slightly different versions of this conversation are given in Day, notes, no. 23, p. 17; Smith, *Wings Day*, p. 228; and James, *Moonless Night*, pp. 182–183. The version given here is an amalgam of the four, with a preference for Churchill and Day, who give the only direct eyewitness accounts.

22. Churchill, *Spirit*, p. 214. Notably, Peter Churchill doesn't identify his namesake in his published account of the meeting in the railwayman's cottage.

23. Day, notes, no. 23, p. 17.

24. Day, notes, no. 23, p. 17.

25. Kunkel, diary.

26. Kunkel, diary.

27. Payne Best, *Venlo*, p. 229.

28. Kunkel, diary.

29. Churchill, *Spirit*, p. 214–215. Churchill gives no indication of which prisoners were involved in this.

18. Plan of Execution

1. Von Flügge statement, 4 June 1945.

2. Schuschnigg, *Austria Requiem*, p. 240. Schuschnigg's diary places this revelation two days later; however, his chronology of events at this point is problematic and may have been confused by later editing.

3. Payne Best, *Venlo*, p. 228.

4. Payne Best, *Venlo*, p. 228.

5. Hassell, *Mother's War*, p. 181; Churchill, *Spirit*, p. 215. The narrative that follows is based on slightly conflicting accounts given by Hassell and Payne Best (*Venlo*, p. 229), of which the latter is more reliable, the former containing some garbled hearsay.

6. Payne Best, *Venlo*, p. 229.

7. Day, notes, no. 23, p. 25.

8. Day, notes, no. 23, p. 25. Day was apparently unaware that Bonin had come into Niederdorf for the purpose of contacting Vietinghoff, and believed that the idea had come about solely because of the chance encounter in the Goldener Stern.

9. Day, notes, no. 23, p. 18.

10. Payne Best, *Venlo*, p. 229.

11. Richardi, *SS-Geiseln*, p. 197, n. 72.

12. Payne Best, *Venlo*, pp. 229–230.

13. Joos, *Leben*, p. 143.

14. Pünder, *Von Preussen*, p. 176.

15. Richardi, *SS-Geiseln*, p. 197.

16. Hassell, *Mother's War*, p. 183.

17. Payne Best, *Venlo*, p. 230.

18. Payne Best, *Venlo*, pp. 230–232.

19. Payne Best, *Venlo*, pp. 230–232.

20. James, *Moonless Night*, p. 186.

21. James, *Moonless Night*, p. 186.

22. James, *Moonless Night*, p. 186; Smith, *Wings Day*, p. 232.

23. Smith, *Wings Day*, p. 233.

24. Smith, *Wings Day*, p. 233.

25. Smith, *Wings Day*, pp. 233–234.

26. Churchill, *Spirit*, p. 218.

27. James, *Moonless Night*, p. 186.

28. James, *Moonless Night*, pp. 186–187.

29. Smith, *Wings Day*, p. 234.

30. Smith (*Wings Day*, p. 234) writes that they left from the Bachmann, but according to Jimmy James (*Moonless Night*, pp. 186–187) it was the town hall.

31. James, *Moonless Night*, p. 187.

32. Payne Best, *Venlo*, p. 232; Day, notes, no. 23, pp. 19–20. Payne Best never forgave Mad Jack Churchill. Replying to a 1968 letter from him, Payne Best wrote, "Had you stayed with us in April 1945 at the time when our party faced its greatest danger and when the services of a man of your calibre would have been invaluable, my present reaction to you and to your letter might be different" (Payne Best, letter to "Jack" Churchill, 25 March 1968, Payne Best papers).

33. Day, notes, no. 23, p. 20

34. Churchill, *Spirit*, p. 219.

35. Churchill, *Spirit*, pp. 219–220; Smith, *Wings Day*, p. 235.

36. Day, notes, no. 23, pp. 21–22.

37. Pünder, *Von Preussen*, p. 176.

19. The Fatal Day

1. Beevor, *Berlin*, pp. 342–343.

2. Beevor, *Berlin*, pp. 341–342.

3. Richardi, *SS-Geiseln*, p. 201, n. 86; Kunkel, diary.

4. Payne Best, *Venlo*, pp. 232–233.

5. Bonin, quoted in "Führer Häftlinge."

6. Bonin, quoted in "Führer Häftlinge." The account given in this brief newspaper article differs slightly from that given by Payne Best in *Venlo*, pp. 233–234. The latter version is favored here.

7. Payne Best, *Venlo*, pp. 232–233.

8. "Statement of Bogislaw von Bonin," 21 November 1951, Judicial investigation of Stiller.

9. Payne Best, *Venlo*, p. 233.

10. Payne Best, *Venlo*, p. 233. Payne Best claims that Bonin revealed at this meeting that he had already met the Wehrmacht officer appointed by Vietinghoff to liaise with the hostages and their SS guards. This must be an error of memory, because the officer did not arrive until late that evening (see Chapter 20).

11. Payne Best, *Venlo*, p. 233.

12. Payne Best, *Venlo*, pp. 233–234.

13. Payne Best (*Venlo*, p. 234) spells the name "Major Stavisky," an aural misspelling.

14. Payne Best, *Venlo*, p. 234.

15. Day, notes, no. 23, p. 21.

16. It isn't clear whether Garibaldi was simply reneging on his promise or making a judgment based on the inconclusive, seemingly unsuccessful outcome of Bonin's plan.

17. Day, notes, no. 23, p. 21.

18. Day, notes, no. 23, p. 22.

19. Day, notes, no. 23, p. 22.

20. Payne Best, *Venlo*, p. 234.

21. Payne Best, *Venlo*, p. 234.

22. Payne Best, *Venlo*, pp. 234–235. At this point Payne Best recalls that he, Bonin, and Liedig went to confer with the Wehrmacht officer appointed by Vietinghoff. However, this appears be a confused or oversimplified memory, conflating that day's events with a subsequent incident (see Chapter 20).

23. Payne Best, *Venlo*, pp. 235–236.

24. Kunkel, diary; Joos, *Leben*, p. 71.

25. Day, notes, no. 23, p. 25.

26. Ducia, *Tatsachenbericht*, cited in Richardi, *SS-Geiseln*, p. 203.

27. Ducia, *Tatsachenbericht*, cited in Richardi, *SS-Geiseln*, p. 203.

28. Ducia, *Tatsachenbericht*, cited in Richardi, *SS-Geiseln*, p. 203.

29. Emma Heiss-Hellenstainer, quoted in Richardi, *SS-Geiseln*, p. 203.

30. Ducia, *Tatsachenbericht*, cited in Richardi, *SS-Geiseln*, p. 204.

31. Payne Best, *Venlo*, p. 236; Ducia, *Tatsachenbericht*, cited in Richardi, *SS-Geiseln*, p. 204.

32. Payne Best, *Venlo*, p. 236.

33. Kunkel, diary.

34. Ducia, *Tatsachenbericht*, cited in Richardi, *SS-Geiseln*, p. 209.

20. Showdown with the SS

1. Richardi, *SS-Geiseln*, p. 215.

2. Richardi, *SS-Geiseln*, p. 212.

3. Richardi, *SS-Geiseln*, p. 213.

4. Richardi, *SS-Geiseln*, p. 213.

5. Richardi, *SS-Geiseln*, pp. 213–214.

6. Alvensleben, report, 10 November 1945, Payne Best papers; "Alvensleben statement," 19 December 1951, Judicial investigation of Stiller.

7. Alvensleben, report; "Alvensleben statement," Judicial investigation of Stiller.

8. Richardi, *SS-Geiseln*, p. 215.

9. "Alvensleben statement," Judicial investigation of Stiller.

10. "Alvensleben statement," Judicial investigation of Stiller.

11. "Alvensleben statement," Judicial investigation of Stiller.

12. Alvensleben, report.

13. Payne Best, *Venlo*, p. 238. According to Alvensleben, the cases of drink were arranged by him and did not arrive until later in the day (Alvensleben, report). Payne Best makes little mention of Alvensleben's intervention, focusing almost exclusively on his own role as leader and organizer. His chronology also differs from Alvensleben's. The narrative given here resolves the differences.

14. Alvensleben, report.

15. Payne Best (*Venlo*, p. 233) erroneously places this meeting nearly twenty-four hours earlier.

16. Alvensleben, report; "Alvensleben statement," Judicial investigation of Stiller.

17. Richardi, *SS-Geiseln*, p. 216.

18. Richardi, *SS-Geiseln*, p. 217; Alvensleben, report; "Alvensleben statement," Judicial investigation of Stiller.

19. Payne Best, *Venlo*, pp. 233, 235. According to Payne Best, this meeting took place the day before, on 29 April (see also Smith, *Wings Day*, p. 238), but Alvensleben's narrative places it on 30 April. The latter seems more likely.

20. Smith, *Wings Day*, p. 238; Payne Best, *Venlo*, p. 235.

21. Payne Best, *Venlo*, p. 235.

22. Smith, *Wings Day*, p. 238.

23. Smith, *Wings Day*, pp. 238–239.

21. Danger in Paradise

1. Payne Best, *Venlo*, p. 239.
2. Loeffel, *Family Punishment*, p. 128.
3. Loeffel, *Family Punishment*, pp. 104, 112.
4. Richardi, *SS-Geiseln*, p. 203.
5. Payne Best, *Venlo*, p. 239.
6. Richardi, *SS-Geiseln*, p. 224.
7. Smith, *Wings Day*, p. 239.
8. Smith, *Wings Day*, p. 239; Payne Best, *Venlo*, p. 239.
9. Richardi, *SS-Geiseln*, p. 224.
10. James, *Moonless Night*, p. 191.
11. Richardi, *SS-Geiseln*, p. 221.
12. James, *Moonless Night*, p. 191.
13. Hassell, *Mother's War*, p. 184.
14. Hassell, *Mother's War*, p. 184.
15. Payne Best, *Venlo*, p. 239.
16. Richardi, *SS-Geiseln*, p. 224.
17. Richardi, *SS-Geiseln*, p. 224.
18. Richardi, *SS-Geiseln*, p. 227.
19. Smith, *Wings Day*, p. 240.
20. Richardi, *SS-Geiseln*, p. 227.
21. Smith, *Wings Day*, p. 240.
22. Payne Best, *Venlo*, p. 240.
23. Payne Best, *Venlo*, p. 241.
24. Payne Best, *Venlo*, pp. 240–241; James, *Moonless Night*, p. 192.
25. Payne Best, *Venlo*, p. 242.
26. James, *Moonless Night*, p. 192.
27. Churchill, *Spirit*, p. 222.
28. Doherty, *Victory in Italy*, p. 201.
29. Smith, *Wings Day*, p. 243.
30. Richardi, *SS-Geiseln*, p. 243.
31. Smith, *Wings Day*, p. 242.
32. Smith, *Wings Day*, p. 242.
33. Churchill, *Spirit*, p. 222.

34. Smith, *Wings Day*, p. 243.

35. Richardi, *SS-Geiseln*, pp. 237–238.

36. Smith, *Wings Day*, p. 243. According to Payne Best (*Venlo*, p. 242) this occurred on 2 May, but Day's own notes (no. 23, pp. 25, 27) make clear that it was 1 May.

22. Running the Gauntlet

1. This account is based primarily on interviews given by Churchill in 1977 and 1979 to Earl Moorhouse.

2. Churchill does not specify this place, but his subsequent encounter with an American unit fixes the location as the Merano road northwest of Bolzano.

3. Brower, "Remount Blue," pp. 95–96.

4. Brower, "Remount Blue," p. 97.

5. James, *Moonless Night*, p. 192.

6. Day, notes, no. 23, p. 25; Payne Best, *Venlo*, p. 242.

7. Smith, *Wings Day*, p. 244.

8. Day, notes, no. 23, p. 27.

9. Smith, *Wings Day*, pp. 244–245.

10. Day, notes, no. 23, p. 27.

11. Smith, *Wings Day*, p. 245.

12. Day, notes, no. 23, p. 27; Smith, *Wings Day*, p. 245.

13. Day, notes, no. 23, pp. 27–28; Smith, *Wings Day*, p. 245.

14. Day, notes, no. 23, p. 28; Smith, *Wings Day*, p. 246.

15. Day, notes, no. 23, p. 28; Smith, *Wings Day*, p. 246.

16. Day, notes, no. 23, p. 28; Smith, *Wings Day*, p. 246.

17. Day, notes, no. 23, pp. 28–29; Smith, *Wings Day*, pp. 246–247.

18. Day, notes, no. 23, pp. 29–30; no. 2, p. 7.

19. Day, notes, no. 2, p. 7; no. 23, p. 30. After the war, Day apparently exchanged Christmas cards with the people he met on this quest, but although he recorded their home addresses in Trento he seems to have recalled little about their lives.

20. Day, notes, no. 23, p. 30.

21. Day, notes, no. 23, p. 30; no. 2, p. 7; Smith, *Wings Day*, pp. 247–248.

22. Day, notes, no. 23, p. 30.

23. Day, notes, no. 23, p. 31.

24. Day, notes, no. 23, p. 31.

25. Day, notes, no. 23, p. 31.

26. Day, notes, no. 23, p. 32.

27. The official cease-fire was ordered at 1840 hours on 2 May, but according to the regiment's war diary, "there was no elation at victory—the situation still remained too tense" and "remained thus strained" until the late afternoon of 4 May (351st Infantry Regiment, History for May 1945, pp. 2–3).

28. Day, notes, no. 23, p. 32.

29. 351st Infantry Regiment, History for May 1945, p. 3

30. Richardi, *SS-Geiseln*, pp. 237–238.

31. Richardi, *SS-Geiseln*, p. 76; Lingen, *Dulles*, p. 245; Wolff, letter to Alexander, 10 September 1947, Barr papers, Columbia University.

32. Wolff's final radio message, confirming his intention to surrender to the Allied troops when they arrived to liberate the hostages, does not appear to have been received until the early hours of 6 May, however, by which time his plan had been overtaken by events.

23. Dash for Deliverance

1. Payne Best, *Venlo*, p. 243.

2. Mogensen, *Die grosse Geiselnahme*, p. 52.

3. Hassell, *Mother's War*, p. 185.

4. Churchill, *Spirit*, p. 222.

5. Richards, *Clandestine Sea Lines*, pp. 589–590.

6. Churchill, *Spirit*, p. 223.

7. Churchill, *Spirit*, p. 223. It is more likely that the weapons were Walther P38s, which were the standard-issue German sidearm during World War II (although Lugers remained in limited use). The name "Luger" seems to have been used by Allied personnel for all German semiautomatic pistols, in the same way that "tommy gun" was used to denote all submachine guns and machine pistols, not just Thompson models.

8. Churchill (*Spirit*, pp. 223–224) doesn't identify the unit or even the village where he met them—only that it was "some ten miles" from Niederdorf. The only American formation in the area at that time was the 339th Infantry Regiment, which had been sent far ahead of the rest of the 85th Division. The encounter probably took place at either Sexten (on Highway 52), where the regimental command post was established on 3 May, or Carbonin (on Highway 51), where the regiment's battalions were located at that time (339th Infantry Regiment, Operations Report, pp. 3–4). Both are roughly ten miles from Niederdorf.

9. Churchill, *Spirit*, pp. 223–234; 339th Infantry Regiment, Operations Report, p. 4.

10. Richardi, *SS-Geiseln*, pp. 243–244.

11. Payne Best, *Venlo*, pp. 243–244

12. Müller, *Bis zur letzten Konsequenz*, pp. 275–276.

13. Koop, *In Hitlers Hand*, p. 189.

14. Payne Best, *Venlo*, p. 244.

15. Koop, *In Hitlers Hand*, p. 190.

16. Day was unable to recall the general's name afterward and thought, mistakenly, he might be called Greeley (notes, no. 23, p. 33).

17. Smith, *Wings Day*, pp. 250–251.

18. Dawn at San Candido was at 0417 hours and sunrise at 0451 hours on 4 May 1945 (calculation via suncalc.net/#/46.7323,12.2779,11/1945.05.04/10:15;).

19. 2nd Battalion, 339th Infantry Regiment, Operations Report, p. 2.

20. There is no record of the involvement of the regular company commanding officer, Captain John Atwell, in the mission planning. It has been said that he had been

injured a few days earlier or was on detachment (Heiser, personal communication to Sayer); however, he was present later in the day (Payne Best, *Venlo*, p. 246).

21. 339th Infantry Regiment, Operations Report, pp. 3–4.
22. 2nd Battalion, 339th Infantry Regiment, Operations Report, p. 2.
23. 2nd Battalion, 339th Infantry Regiment, Operations Report, p. 2.
24. Ferdinand, letter to Moorhouse, 22 January 1979, Sayer collection.
25. Doherty, *Victory in Italy*, p. 202.
26. Ferdinand, taped interview, 22 January 1979, Sayer collection.
27. Ferdinand, taped interview, 22 January 1979.
28. Ferdinand, taped interview, 22 January 1979.
29. Payne Best, *Venlo*, pp. 245–246.
30. James, *Moonless Night*, p. 194.
31. Vermehren, *Reise*, p. 205ff.
32. Hassell, *Mother's War*, p. 186.
33. Payne Best, *Venlo*, p. 246.
34. Payne Best, *Venlo*, p. 247.
35. Schuschnigg, *Austrian Requiem*, pp. 241–242.
36. Some German sources (e.g., Lingen, *Dulles*, p. 245) credit Wichard von Alvensleben with liberating the hostages. This is half true in the trivial sense that his arrival marked the end of their SS/SD custody, but the Prominenten remained in significant danger until the arrival of American forces.
37. Day, notes, no. 23, p. 33.
38. Richardi, *SS-Geiseln*, pp. 237–238.
39. Schuschnigg, *Austrian Requiem*, p. 243.
40. Day, notes, no. 23, p. 34.
41. James, *Moonless Night*, p. 197.

Epilogue

1. Counterintelligence Corps, Dossier XE-003166, Franz Liedig.
2. Payne Best, letter to Vera von Schuschnigg, Payne Best papers.

Bibliography

Unpublished and archive sources

2nd Battalion, 339th Infantry Regiment, US Army, Operations Report, May 1945: National Archives and Records Administration (NARA), Washington, DC.

339th Infantry Regiment, US Army, Operations Report, May 1945: NARA, Washington, DC.

351st Infantry Regiment, US Army, History for April–May 1945: NARA, Washington, DC.

Barr, Norbert, papers, NYCR89-A47: Rare Books and Manuscript Library, Columbia University, New York.

Brower, David R., "Remount Blue: The Combat Story of the 3d Battalion, 86th Mountain Infantry of the 10th Mountain Division," compiled 1948 for University of California Press: available online at archive.org/details/RemountBlue.

Churchill, Jack, interviews and notes, June 1977 and January 1979: Earl Moorhouse archive, now in the collection of Ian Sayer.

Counterintelligence Corps, US Army, Dossier XA-0244414, Richard Schmitz: NARA, Washington, DC.

Counterintelligence Corps, US Army, Dossier XE-123106, Karl Friedrich Bader: NARA, Washington, DC.

Counterintelligence Corps, US Army, Dossier XE-003166, Franz Liedig: NARA, Washington, DC.

Day, Harry M. A., unpublished memoir notes: Archive of RAF Museum, London.

Ferdinand, Arthur, letters and recollections concerning the rescue of hostages in May 1945: Earl Moorhouse archive, now in the collection of Ian Sayer.

Flügge, Wilhelm von, statement to Captain N. E. Middleton, DAPM, 78 Section, SIB, AFHQ at Capri, 4 June 1945, WO 328/4 June 1945: National Archives, Kew.

Heiser, John (339th Infantry Regiment historian), personal communications to Ian Sayer, July 2011.

Huppenkothen, Walter, Flossenbürg-Müller message, Bletchley decrypt: available online at cryptocellar.org/Flossenbuerg/Huppenkothen_msg.pdf.

Judicial investigation of Edgar Stiller for complicity in the murder of Georg Elser at Dachau in April 1945, Landgericht München II, Jg106/50: State Archives, Munich.

Kállay, Miklós, statement to Captain N. E. Middleton, SIB, Capri, 3 June 1945, WO 328/17 June 1945: National Archives, Kew.

Kunkel, Karl, diary 1945 and statement, Staatsanw. 34475/2: State Archives, Munich.

Landgericht Augsburg, judgement of the Landgericht Augsburg in the case of Walter Huppenkothen, 15 October 1955, ref. 1Ks21/50.

McGrath, John, letter to Sigismund Payne Best, 14 April 1945: Walter L. Leschander Collection, Hoover Institution, Stanford University.

Moorhouse, Earl, "Hitler's Hostages," unpublished manuscript: Earl Moorhouse archive, now in the collection of Ian Sayer.

"Müller Order," 5 April 1945: Walter L. Leschander Collection, Hoover Institution, Stanford University.

Payne Best, Sigismund, papers in the collection of the Imperial War Museum, London.

Wauer, Paul, statement to Capt. N. E. Middleton, SIB at Capri, 21 May 1945, WO 328/43 June 1945: National Archives, Kew.

Wolff, Karl, interrogation by Colonel H. A. Brundage, 31 August 1945: NARA, Washington, DC.

Wymeersch, Raymond van, statement of Flight Lieutenant Raymond Leon Narcisse van Wymeersch to 69 Section Special Investigation Branch, Resina, Naples, 14 May 1945: National Archives, Kew.

Published sources

Beevor, Antony. *Berlin: The Downfall: 1945*. London: Viking, 2002.

Berben, Paul. *Dachau 1933–1945: The Official History*. London: Norfolk Press, 1975.

Birnbaum, Pierre. *Léon Blum: Prime Minister, Socialist, Zionist*. New Haven: Yale University Press, 2015.

Black, Peter R. *Ernst Kaltenbrunner: Ideological Soldier of the Third Reich*. Princeton, NJ: Princeton University Press, 1984.

Brissaud, André. *The Nazi Secret Service*. New York: W. W. Norton, 1974.

Cesarani, David. *Final Solution: The Fate of the Jews 1933–49*. London: Macmillan, 2016.

Churchill, Peter. *The Spirit in the Cage*. London: Hodder and Stoughton, 1954.

Colton, Joel. *Léon Blum: Humanist in Politics*. Durham, NC: Duke University Press, 1987.

Davidson, Clarissa. *God's Man: The Story of Pastor Niemoeller*. Westport, CT: Greenwood, 1979.

Distel, Barbara. "Dachau Main Camp." In *Encyclopedia of Camps and Ghettos* Vol. 1A, edited by Geoffrey P. Megargee. Bloomington: Indiana University Press, 2009.

Doherty, Richard. *Victory in Italy: 15th Army Group's Final Campaign 1945*. Barnsley, UK: Pen & Sword, 2014.

Drooz, Daniel B. *American Prisoners of War in German Death, Concentration, and Slave Labor Camps*. Lewiston, NY: Edwin Mellen, 2004.

Dulles, Allen W. "The Secret Surrender." *Harper's*, July 1966.

Falconer, Hugh Mallory. *The Gestapo's Most Improbable Hostage*. Barnsley, UK: Pen & Sword, 2018.

Freeman, Roger A., Alan Crouchman, and Vic Maslen. *The Mighty Eighth War Diary*. Revised edition. London: Arms and Armour, 1990.

"Führer Häftlinge." *Der Spiegel*, 20 February 1967, pp. 54, 59.

Hackett, David A., ed. and trans. *The Buchenwald Report*. Oxford: Westview Press, 1995. Originally published as *Bericht über das Konzentrationslager Buchenwald bei Weimar*. Supreme Headquarters Allied Expeditionary Force, April–May 1945.

Hagen, Walter [Wilhelm Höttl]. *Unternehmen Bernhard*. Wels, Austria: Verlag Welsermühl, Wels und Starnberg, 1955.

Hassell, Fey von. *A Mother's War*. London: John Murray, 1990. Edited by David Forbes-Watt and published in US as *Hostage of the Third Reich* (New York: Scribner's, 1989).

Hoffmann, Peter. *The History of the German Resistance 1933–1945*. London: Macdonald and Jane's, 1977.

Höhne, Heinz. *Canaris: Hitler's Master Spy*. London: Secker and Warburg, 1979.

Huebner, Todd. "Flossenbürg Main Camp." In *Encyclopedia of Camps and Ghettos* Vol. 1A, edited by Geoffrey P. Megargee. Bloomington: Indiana University Press, 2009.

James, B. A. "Jimmy." *Moonless Night*. William Kimber, 1983.

Joos, Joseph. *Leben auf Widerruf, Begegnungen und Beobachtungen im KZ Dachau 1941–1945*. Trier, Germany: Paulinus Verlag, 1948.

Kállay, Miklós. *Hungarian Premier*. Westport, CT: Greenwood, 1970.

Koop, Volker. *In Hitlers Hand: Sonder- und Ehrenhäftlinge der SS*. Cologne: Bohlau Verlag, 2010.

Lang, Jochen von. *Top Nazi: SS General Karl Wolff*. New York: Enigma, 2013.

Lessner, Erwin. "Hitler's Final V Weapon." *Collier's Weekly*, 27 January 1945, p. 14.

Lingen, Kerstin von. *Allen Dulles, the OSS, and Nazi War Criminals*. Cambridge: Cambridge University Press, 2013.

Loeffel, Robert. *Family Punishment in Nazi Germany: Sippenhaft, Terror and Myth*. Basingstoke, UK: Palgrave Macmillan, 2012.

Marcuse, Harold. *Legacies of Dachau: The Uses and Abuses of a Concentration Camp, 1933–2001*. Cambridge: Cambridge University Press, 2001.

Marrus, Michael Robert, ed. *The Nazi Holocaust Part 5: Public Opinion and Relations to the Jews in Nazi Europe* Vol. 2. Munich: K G Saur Verlag, 1989.

Middlebrook, Martin, and Chris Everitt. *The Bomber Command War Diaries: An Operational Reference Book*. London: Viking, 1985.

Minott, Rodney G. *The Fortress that Never Was: The Myth of the Nazi Alpine Redoubt*. London: Longmans, 1965.

Mogensen, Jørgen. *Die grosse Geiselnahme: Letzter Akt 1945*. Copenhagen: Polnisch-Skandinavisches Forschungsinstitut, 1997.

Müller, Josef. *Bis zur letzten Konsequenz: Ein Leben für Frieden und Freiheit*. Munich: Süddeutscher Verlag, 1975.

Mulley, Clare. *The Women Who Flew for Hitler: The True Story of Hitler's Valkyries*. London: Macmillan, 2017.

Neveu, Cédric. *Le Gestapo en Moselle*. Strasbourg: Editions du Quotidien, 2015.

Nuremberg Tribunal. *Trial of the Major War Criminals before the International Military Tribunal, Nuremberg 14 November 1945–1 October 1946* Vol. IV. Nuremberg: International Military Tribunal, 1948.

Parrish, Michael. *Sacrifice of the Generals: Soviet Senior Officer Losses, 1939–1953*. Oxford: Scarecrow Press, 2004.

Payne Best, Sigismund. *The Venlo Incident: A True Story of Double-Dealing, Captivity, and a Murderous Nazi Plot*. London: Hutchinson, 1950.

Petropoulos, Jonathan. *Royals and the Reich: The Princes von Hessen in Nazi Germany*. Oxford: Oxford University Press, 2006.

Pünder, Hermann. *Von Preussen nach Europa*. Stuttgart: Deutsche Verlags-Anstalt, 1968.

Richardi, Hans-Günther. *SS-Geiseln in der Alpenfestung: Die Verschleppung prominenter KZ-Häftlinge aus Deutschland nach Südtirol*. Bozen, Italy: Edition Raetia, 2005.

Richards, Brooks. *Clandestine Sea Lines to France and French North Africa 1940–1944*. Vol. 2 of *Secret Flotillas*. London: HMSO, 1996.

Schacht, Hjalmar. *My First Seventy-Six Years*. London: Allan Wingate, 1955.

Schiff, Victor. "'Last Fortress' of the Nazis." *New York Times*, 11 February 1945, p. SM5.

Schlabrendorff, Fabian von. *The Secret War against Hitler*. London: Hodder and Stoughton, 1966.

Schuschnigg, Kurt von. *Austrian Requiem*. London: Gollancz, 1947.

Schwarz, Friedrich. "Rohde, Lothar." In *Neue Deutsche Biographie*. Historical Commission and Bavarian Academy of Sciences, 2003. www.deutsche-biographie.de/pnd139265996.html.

Smith, Bradley F., and Elena Agarossi. *Operation Sunrise: The Secret Surrender*. London: Andre Deutsch, 1979.

Smith, Marcus J. *Dachau: The Harrowing of Hell*. Albuquerque: University of New Mexico Press, 1972.

Smith, Stuart. *Otto Skorzeny: The Devil's Disciple*. Oxford: Osprey, 2018.

Smith, Sydney. *Wings Day: The Man Who Led the RAF's Epic Battle in German Captivity*. London: Collins, 1968.

Stafford, David. *Endgame 1945: Victory, Retribution, Liberation*. London: Little, Brown, 2007.

Stein, Harry. *Buchenwald Concentration Camp, 1937–1945*. Göttingen, Germany: Wallstein Verlag, 2004.

Stuhlpfarrer, Karl. *Die Operationszonen "Alpenvorland" und "Adriatisches Küstenland" 1943–1945*. Vienna: Verlag Bruder Hollineck, 1969.

Vermehren, Isa. *Reise durch den letzten Akt*. Hamburg: Christian Wegner Verlag, 1946.

Wachsmann, Nikolaus. *KL: A History of the Nazi Concentration Camps*. London: Little, Brown, 2015.

Waller, John A. "Reichsführer Himmler Pitches Washington." CIA Center for the Study of Intelligence, 14 April 2007. cia.gov/library/center-for-the-study-of-intelligence/csi-publications/csi-studies/studies/vol46no1/article04.html.

Young, Peter. *Commando*. New York: Ballantine, 1968.

Zegenhagen, Evelyn. "Innsbruck (SS-Sonderlager)" and "Innsbruck I." In *Encyclopedia of Camps and Ghettos* Vol. 1A, edited by Geoffrey P. Megargee. Bloomington: Indiana University Press, 2009.

Index